KU-308-004

WITHDRAWN

WP 2090743 5

INTRODUCTION TO EDUCATION
Series editor: Jonathan Solity

SUPPORT SERVICES

SUPPORT SERVICES

Issues for Education, Health
and Social Service Professionals

Edited by

Jonathan Solity

and

Graham Bickler

UNIVERSITY OF WOLVERHAMPTON
LIBRARY

2090743   CLASS
371.
CONTROL
0304327069   9·
DATE   SITE   Sup
-4. JUN 1997   WL

CASSELL

Cassell
Villiers House   387 Park Avenue South
41/47 Strand   New York,
London WC2N 5JE   NY 10016-8810

© The editors and contributors 1994

First published 1994

All rights reserved. No part of this publication may be
reproduced or transmitted in any form or by any means,
electronic or mechanical including photocopying, recording or
any information storage or retrieval system without prior
permission in writing from the publishers.

British Library Cataloguing-in-Publication Data
A catalogue record for this book is available from the British
Library.

ISBN 0-304-32706-9 (hardback)
      0-304-32704-2 (paperback)

Typeset by Colset Private Limited, Singapore
Printed and bound in Great Britain by
Redwood Books, Trowbridge, Wiltshire

CONTENTS

Notes on Contributors

Graham Bickler (Consultant in Public Health Medicine, South East London Health Authority, London)
Graham Bickler has worked in public health in London for nine years after training to be a general practitioner. His main interests are screening, immunization, primary care and women's services.

Paul Booton (Lecturer in General Practice, King's College School of Medicine and Dentistry, London)
Paul Booton is a GP at a large fund-holding practice in south-east London. He is a lecturer and curricular sub-dean at King's College School of Medicine, where he is responsible for coordinating and developing undergraduate medical education. He comes from a long line of schoolteachers. In his spare time he makes stained-glass windows.

Jonathan Dare (Consultant in Child Psychiatry, King's College Hospital, London)
Jonathan Dare has been a consultant for fourteen years with special interests in teaching, liaison work with hospital and community staff, and writing on the consultation process. He is a specialist family therapist involved nationally with accreditation as well as being a tutor and course consultant to different university Master's courses in family therapy.

Moira Dick (Consultant in Community Paediatrics, West Lambeth Community Care (NHS) Trust, London)
Moira Dick is responsible for community child health services in Lambeth, south-east London, and is medical director of the Mary Sheridan Child Development Centre and chair of the Child Development Team.

Frances Gardner (Lecturer in Education, University of Warwick)
Frances Gardner currently teaches and researches in child psychology. Formerly

she was Lecturer in Clinical Psychology at the Institute of Psychiatry and Senior Clinical Psychologist at the Bethlem Royal and Maudsley Hospitals, involved in training clinical psychologists and working with children with learning difficulties and behaviour problems. Her research interests and publications are in parent–child interactions and children's behaviour problems.

Ravi Kohli (Senior Lecturer in Social Work, Middlesex University)
Ravi Kohli's main teaching responsibilities and research interest focus on social work with children and families, within the framework of the Children Act 1989. Before this job he was, for a number of years, a generic social worker and a senior practitioner in social work with children and families in London.

Sue Morris (Senior Educational Psychologist: Tutor to Professional Training Course in Educational Psychology, University of Birmingham)
Sue Morris has worked as an educational psychologist in Birmingham, Coventry, and Hereford and Worcestershire local authority psychological services. Her major professional interests include developing skills in interviewing children and enabling schools to research and develop their policies and practices in meeting pupils' diverse individual needs.

Donal O'Sullivan (Consultant in Communicable Disease Control, South East London Health Authority, London)
Donal O'Sullivan has worked in the surveillance and control of communicable disease at both national and local level. Currently he fulfils these functions for an inner London population and is working together with education and school health services to improve communicable disease control in schools.

Jonathan Solity (Lecturer in Educational Psychology, University of Warwick)
Jonathan Solity taught primary-aged children in the north of England and worked as an educational psychologist in the West Midlands before his present appointment. He has published widely and researched into children with special needs, assessment, teaching reading, parental involvement in children's learning and the management of children's behaviour. He has written and co-authored numerous books: *Bridging the Curriculum Gap* (Open University Press); *Classroom Management: Principles to Practice* (Routledge); *A Teacher's Guide to Special Needs* (Open University Press); *Teachers in Control* (Routledge); and *Special Education* (Cassell).

Juliet Stone (Lecturer in Special Education, University of Birmingham)
Juliet Stone is a tutor to the teacher training courses in visual impairment. Previously she was the Senior Advisory Teacher for children with visual impairments in Gloucestershire.

Alec Webster (Director, Centre for Literacy Studies, University of Bristol)
Alec Webster worked as a teacher, educational psychologist and adviser before

his present appointment as a university teacher and researcher. His main writing and research interests lie in the field of deaf education, literacy and educational evaluation. His books include *Deafness, Development and Literacy* (Methuen); *Children with Hearing Difficulties* (Cassell); *Children with Speech and Language Difficulties* (Cassell); and *The Hearing-Impaired Child in the Ordinary School* (Croom Helm).

Jannet A. Wright (Joint Appointment at the National Hospitals' College of Speech Sciences and the Institute of Education, London)
Jannet Wright's research interests include collaboration between teachers and speech and language therapists and services for children with specific language difficulties.

FOREWORD

The 1980s and 1990s have witnessed unprecedented changes to the education system. These have had a dramatic impact, particularly in relation to:

- schools' relationships with parents and the community;
- the funding and management of schools;
- the curriculum;
- the assessment of children's learning.

It can be an extremely daunting task for student teachers to unravel the details and implications of these initiatives. This Introduction to Education series therefore offers a comprehensive analysis and evaluation of educational theory and practice in the light of recent developments.

The series examines topics and issues of concern to those entering the teaching profession. Major themes representing a spectrum of educational opinion are presented in a clear, balanced and analytic manner.

The authors in the series are authorities in their field. They emphasize the need to have a well-informed and critical teaching profession and present a positive and optimistic view of the teacher's role. They endorse the view that teachers have a significant influence over the extent to which any legislation or ideology is translated into effective classroom practice.

Each author addresses similar issues, which can be summarized as:

- presenting and debating theoretical perspectives within appropriate social, political, and educational contexts;
- identifying key arguments;
- identifying individuals who have made significant contributions to the field under review;
- discussing and evaluating key legislation;
- critically evaluating research and highlighting implications for classroom practice;

- providing an overview of the current state of debate within each field;
- describing the features of good practice.

The books are written primarily for student teachers. However, they will be of interest and value to all those involved in education.

Jonathan Solity
Series Editor

ACKNOWLEDGEMENTS

We would like to thank Oxford University Press for permission to reprint Table 4.2 in Chapter 4 from D. Fielding (1987) Working with children and young children. In J. Marzillier and J. Hall (eds), *What Is Clinical Psychology?*

Thanks also to Sue, Anna and Jack for their continued support, patience and the 'time out' to complete this book; and to Penny for her unfailing support at a pregnant point in her life.

ABBREVIATIONS

ACPC	Area Child Protection Committee	DSTM	District Speech Therapy Manager
BPS	British Psychological Society	ENT	Ear, Nose and Throat
BSL	British Sign Language	EP	Educational Psychologist
CAO	Child Assessment Order	EPO	Emergency Protection Order
CCDC	Consultant in Communicable Disease Control	ERA	Education Reform Act 1988
CCETSW	Central Council for Education and Training in Social Work	ESO	Emergency Supervision Order
		FHSA	Family Health Service Authority
CGC	Child Guidance Clinic	GMC	General Medical Council
CHC	Community Health Council	HIV	Human Immunodeficiency Virus
CMO	Clinical Medical Officer	HMI	Her Majesty's Inspectors; Her Majesty's Inspectorate
CO	Care Order		
CPR	Child Protection Register	ICO	Interim Care Order
CQSW	Certificate of Qualification in Social Work	IQ	Intelligence Quotient
		LA	Local Authority
DES	Department of Education and Science	LEA	Local Education Authority
		LMS	Local Management of Schools
DFE	Department for Education		
DHA	District Health Authority	MOEH	Medical Officer of Environmental Health
DHSS	Department of Health and Social Security		
		NC	National Curriculum
DipSW	Diploma in Social Work	NFCA	National Foster Care Association
DoH	Department of Health		
DPH	Director of Public Health	NHS	National Health Service

OFSTED	Office for Standards in Education	SEAC	School Examinations and Assessment Council
RHA	Regional Health Authority	SSD	Social Services Department
SAT	Standard Assessment Task	SW	Social Worker

PART 1

INTRODUCTION

This section explains the book's rationale and structure, the values and beliefs underpinning the book, the contexts in which services are currently working and the issues they are facing.

CHAPTER 1

Support services: setting the scene

Jonathan Solity and Graham Bickler

This chapter aims to:

- explain the rationale and structure of the book;
- make explicit the beliefs and values which underpin the book;
- provide an overview of the background and contexts in which educational, health and social service professionals function.

RATIONALE

This book forms part of Cassell's Introduction to Education series. The aim of the series is to present student teachers and teachers in the early stages of their careers with a critique of major topics and issues in the field of education. Authors contributing to the series subscribe to the view that it is essential to have a teaching profession that is well informed, critical and aware of the impact it can have on the lives of children.

Whilst this theme is central to the book, the content is broadened to encompass the contribution of other professional groups who also have an impact on children's development. Although many children have either minimal or no direct contact with many of the support services introduced in this book, the approaches adopted by these professionals mean that will probably have an indirect influence on children through their parents, families and teachers.

A second theme underpinning both the series and this book is the desire to give readers knowledge and frameworks through which to understand educational practice. This is done in the belief that possessing knowledge is enabling, empowering and an aid to decision making. Gaining insights into the role and functions of support services is as important for different professional groups as it is for parents, teachers and children. This is particularly so when set in the context of the current practice of the professionals represented in this book.

A third theme running through the book is the view that meeting children's needs is a collaborative process whose success depends on developing a series of successful partnerships. Central to these is the capacity of those involved to negotiate their perceptions of children and the nature of their physical, social and cognitive development.

STRUCTURE AND SCOPE

The book has been divided into five parts which reflect the nature of the difficulties and problems that are referred to different support services.

Part 1: Introduction

This explains the book's rationale and structure, the values and beliefs underpinning the book, the contexts in which services are currently working and the issues they are facing.

Part 2: Psychological and psychiatric services

There are strong historical and theoretical links between psychological and psychiatric services. At one time psychiatrists had a controlling influence on the practice of clinical and educational psychologists employed in the health and education services respectively. The chapters in this section reflect the dramatic changes that have occurred within the professions and the nature of the relationships existing between them. The old hierarchical order has been replaced with a partnership where different perspectives and expertise are shared in the interests of children. Whilst professional relationships have developed along more collaborative lines, the theoretical underpinnings of the professions have also broadened to provide a common starting point for all three professional groups.

One major implication of these changes is that the certainties of past practice have been superseded by greater ambiguity. Not only is the nature of referred problems wide-ranging but they can be interpreted in a variety of ways, so that it is not always easy to define who has the problem. The role of psychologists and psychiatrists requires them to understand children's difficulties from a variety of perspectives and to negotiate rather than impose interventions. There is now considerable overlap in their professional involvement with children. This can create tensions, but psychologists and psychiatrists frequently confront similar issues when working with families and schools.

Usually the crucial factor determining whether problems are dealt with by psychologists or psychiatrists is who makes the referral and that person's perceptions about what educational psychologists, clinical psychologists and child psychiatrists do. In general, if school- or home-based problems come to the attention of those working within the education department, the referral will be to educational psychologists. Problems coming to the attention to those employed in the health service are most likely to be referred to either clinical psychologists or child psychiatrists.

Part 3: Social work services

Social workers also have strong historical and professional links with psychiatrists and psychologists, and many of the points made in the previous section apply equally to social workers. However, their theoretical starting point has often been different and their work with children has always had a significant and demanding statutory component, which until recently was not an issue for psychologists. Ravi Kohli discusses in considerable detail the development of the social work profession and the factors that have shaped practice. This is the only chapter discussing professional issues which relate to social service departments, so it is considerably longer than the others. This is necessary in order to offer a thorough understanding of the role of social workers, influences on their professional development and the importance and impact of the 1989 Children Act.

Part 4: Health services

The three chapters in Part 4 relate to various aspects of doctors' work with children. Whilst all parents will be aware of their GPs and the ways in which they treat illness, they may be less sensitive to the current issues facing GPs which influence both their capacity to meet the health needs of the community and the ways in which they are trying to develop preventive approaches to health care. Similarly, whilst parent and professional groups will know of the regular medical check-ups which take place within schools, they are less likely to be familiar with the professional and organizational issues within the school health service and how it might develop in the future. In Chapter 9 Donal O'Sullivan discusses how health and local authority staff work together to control infection within schools. Many of the concerns about inter-professional relationships are similar to those explored in the rest of the book.

Part 5: Services for specific problems

This part concentrates on three support services that focus on particular difficulties experienced by children: hearing, vision, and speech and language. Whilst the scope of the problems discussed here is narrower than elsewhere in the book, similar themes emerge.

Although the structure of the chapters varies, all chapters cover the following issues:

- defining the nature of the service;
- the background to the development of the profession;
- the role of the service;
- the organization of the service, including the way children are referred;
- the theories that underpin practice;
- assessment and intervention;
- the social and political influences on practice;
- the impact of legislation on practice;
- issues and future developments.

The services included in the book have until recently been regarded as statutory support services provided by education, health and social service departments. Recent legislation (which is discussed later in this chapter) has influenced the relationship of these services within the public sector and it can no longer be assumed that they will continue to be funded or managed exclusively by the public sector.

It has to be acknowledged that the range of services covered in the book is not comprehensive. In particular, the numerous voluntary services have not been included. One reason for this is that currently they function outside the statutory sector. Nor are they readily grouped together in terms of theoretical basis or professional practice. Although voluntary agencies can be categorized according to their aims and methods of working, they frequently perform more than one function. Currently the voluntary agencies can be seen to engage in:

- fund-raising;
- awareness raising;
- offering advice and support;
- political lobbying;
- promoting the public profile of single issues.

The practices that are described and issues that are raised in this book apply to all support services, irrespective of their source of funding. The direct work undertaken with children and families by voluntary services sometimes overlaps with or complements that of education, health or social service departments. Furthermore, many voluntary agencies employ, on a full-time or part-time basis, some of the professional groups introduced here. So psychologists, psychiatrists, paediatricians and others are often employed by groups outside the statutory sector, but the professional issues raised here are pertinent to their role within the voluntary sector.

Another area that has not been covered is that of the various support services, such as special needs and specific learning difficulties, currently employed by local education authorities (LEAs). Their patterns of organization and methods of working are similar to the services which have been included. Many LEA support services work directly with specific children, offer advice to class teachers and organize in-service courses. They have not been included because they do not always have direct contact with parents, they cover a wide range of areas beyond the scope of this book, and many of the general issues and problems in these services are, in a way, already covered in the book.

We have not included services for pre-school handicapped children, which are often part of LEA provision. This is because the focus of this book, and of the Introduction to Education series generally, is on students intending to teach school-age children (4–19). However, several contributions do discuss the importance of early intervention when responding to children's difficulties. Sue Morris, Frances Gardner and Moira Dick summarize the involvement of educational psychologists, clinical psychologists and the community health services respectively in pre-school, multidisciplinary assessments.

To summarize: the aim of this book is to give readers knowledge, explanations and frameworks within which to examine the role of educational, health and social service support services. The methods of practice discussed and issues raised by different professional groups are equally relevant to those working for voluntary agencies, whose work invariably overlaps with and complements that of public sector professionals. The next section introduces the contexts in which support services now function.

CURRENT CONTEXTS: EDUCATION

Concepts of special education have undergone radical change as the conventional wisdoms informing practice have been challenged and reviewed. In part this has occurred as those working in educational contexts have addressed a broader range of issues in considering why some children have difficulties. When assessing the nature of children's educational difficulties it is not only a question of identifying the children's strengths and weaknesses. The attitudes, values and beliefs of those working with children are also central in determining how problems can be overcome. So, for example, to feel that children in wheelchairs require special school rather than mainstream placements is as much a reflection of our beliefs and views on segregated education as an indication of children's needs.

One of the most significant changes in special education has taken place in relation to the way children's difficulties are categorized and defined. The 1944 Education Act led to an increase in the number of recognized categories of handicap from seven to eleven, which resulted in a large increase in the number of special schools and of children being educated in them. By the 1960s special education was something that took place outside the mainstream sector, with the 'educationally subnormal – mild' population by far the largest category.

It was not until the mid- to late 1970s that increasing concern was expressed about the validity of offering differential provision for those seen to be experiencing difficulties. Arguments were advanced from a number of perspectives. First of all, many of those working within the field of educational assessment questioned the use of intelligence tests in special education. In particular, criticisms focused on their cultural bias and whether children's performance reflected the quality of teaching received and educational opportunities, rather than learning potential. Questions about the reliability of predicting future achievement were fuelled by research emerging from the United States, which suggested that when high-quality teaching was provided, children considered educationally disadvantaged made excellent progress, commensurate with that of their peers. The IQ test score came to be seen as less important than the educational provision available.

Educationalists concerned about creating equal educational opportunities also questioned the provision of segregated special education. This was not thought compatible with the aims of offering all children equal educational opportunities irrespective of gender, race, social class or perceived level of ability. The call was made to integrate those with difficulties with their peers in ordinary schools.

The Warnock Report (DES, 1978)

This report can be seen as representing the state of thinking about special education at the time it was published. It effectively shaped attitudes and practice for the 1980s. The report:

- suggested that the aims of education were the same for all children;
- recommended replacing notions of handicap with that of special educational needs;
- promoted the concept of integration.

Aspects of the Warnock philosophy emerged in the 1981 Education Act on special educational needs, which came into force in April 1983.

1981 Education Act

This Act (DES, 1981) offered a legal interpretation of special educational needs that was distinctly different from earlier legal epithets designed to define the nature of children's problems. Whereas previous legislation defined difficulties in terms of the characteristics of individual children and the nature of their handicap, the 1981 Act defined special needs in terms of the educational provision required to meet children's needs: 'A child has special educational needs if he has a learning difficulty which calls for special provision to be made for him.' Special educational needs are thus defined in terms of whether or not a child has a learning difficulty which requires special educational provision. It is the presence or absence of appropriate resources within a child's existing school environment that ultimately determines whether a child has special educational needs. It is not simply a matter of assessing the individual characteristics of a child in isolation, without reference to the contexts in which learning takes place.

Since the implementation of the 1981 Act numerous publications and HMI reports have reflected the emerging consensus that the nature of children's difficulties has to be seen in context. For example, the National Curriculum Council (1989a, 1989b) in its advice to schools on how to meet special educational needs stated that:

> Special educational needs are not just a reflection of pupils' inherent difficulties; they are often related to factors within schools which can prevent or exacerbate some problems. (1989a, p. 1)

> The interaction between the pupil and the school, including its curriculum, can also lead to learning difficulties. We need, therefore, to define the conditions in which children and young people can learn successfully and to ensure that the school curriculum enables these to be met. (1989b, p. 1)

These quotes are illustrative of the way HMI and government have recognized the interactive nature of children's learning.

The statutory assessment procedure

The 1981 Act introduced a new formal statutory assessment procedure for identifying children's special educational needs and the most appropriate provision to meet those needs. The procedure, which a number of authors in the book have referred to as *'statementing'*, can be initiated by anyone (parent, teacher, psychologist, health or social services professional) who has reasonable grounds for supposing that a child has special educational needs, although in reality it is most likely to be a parent, teacher or educational psychologist.

Parents are formally notified that an assessment period is about to start to ascertain their child's educational needs and that they can make their views known to representatives of the LEA. Once permission has been given, the director of education asks the relevant teachers, an educational psychologist and school medical officer for their opinions about the child. Each professional undertakes an assessment and then writes a report, known as the *advice*, in which they are required to comment on children's educational needs and the most appropriate provision to meet them.

The DES (1989) has emphasized that the statutory assessment procedure calls for close cooperation between parents and all the statutory services, and a thorough understanding by each of the participants of the part which they and others play in this process. Each professional is responsible for his or her own advice. The professional must feel confident that the opinions offered can be substantiated and give an accurate account of his or her understanding of a child's needs. Once all the advice has been received, the designated LEA officer, acting on behalf of the director of education, determines whether special educational provision is necessary. If the child is felt to have special educational needs a *statement* is issued detailing the nature of the child's needs and the provision to meet them.

1988 Education Reform Act

The 1988 Education Reform Act required all maintained schools, including special schools, to follow the National Curriculum. It forms the basis of what all children are to be taught, and was introduced in order to:

- ensure that all children follow a similar curriculum;
- raise standards;
- enable children to have their progress assessed at the ages of 7, 11, 14 and 16;
- provide the means by which parents and others can compare the effectiveness of schools.

At best the National Curriculum provides a general framework in which all teachers and schools (although not those in the private sector) now have to work. Whilst many educationalists recognized the value of a common curriculum in some form, concerns continue to be expressed about:

- the way it was introduced;
- the assumptions and ideology behind its introduction;
- the way it is being used to provide parents with crude outcome measures by which they can compare schools.

Local management of schools

Provision was made under the 1988 Education Reform Act for mainstream schools to take greater control over their own budgets. This is now being extended to special schools. Prior to the 1988 Act, funds came directly to LEAs, who determined priorities: they decided how money should be spent across the authority and who should provide services. The 1988 Act required LEAs to devise a formula by which schools would largely be funded directly and so could decide for themselves how best to deploy resources. Part of the formula, which had to receive government approval, included funding for children with special educational needs. However, LEAs retained money for essential services such as educational psychologists and were still responsible for maintaining educational provision for statemented children with special educational needs, whether in mainstream or special schools.

As more money is now going directly to schools, less is being retained centrally by LEAs for educational psychologists, special needs support services and specialist teaching staff. Nevertheless, education support services face an uncertain future as the full implications of local management of schools (LMS) are recognized. It is possible that they will be severely cut in future years or that schools will buy in their services on a more *ad hoc* basis. This would severely reduce the scope and potential of preventive work, which has been a marked feature of these services in recent years. For example, a recent Department for Education consultation paper (DFE, 1993) on LMS recommended that LEAs retain their school psychological services centrally because of their statutory assessment responsibilities under the 1981 Education Act. One consequence of this is that LEAs may limit the extent of any preventive and advisory work in favour of psychologists' legal duties to provide advice within the statementing process.

Russell (1992) endorses the view that LEA services face an uncertain future and envisages that the long-term impact of LMS will almost certainly be the fragmentation and disempowerment of the LEA as the coordinator and planner of services. She argues that similar changes in health and social services departments will necessitate new relationships with the private and voluntary sectors.

To summarize: the current context for educational support services is one of continuing change, concerns over future funding arrangements and the implications of this for services and children. Certainly many of the more impressive initiatives and developments in practice in recent years are threatened by inadequate resources.

CURRENT CONTEXTS: HEALTH

Although many people's experiences of the health service have been remarkably constant, there is no doubt that the service has undergone profound changes over the last few years. A variety of pressures and influences, ranging from consumerism and holistic approaches to politics and market pressures, have altered what health professionals do and how they do it. This section gives a brief overview of recent organizational changes in the National Health Service (NHS) and of some of these other developments. Many of them are also explored in Chapters 2, 7 and 8.

Pre-1974

There was little change in the organization of health services from the introduction of the NHS, in 1948, until the NHS and local government reforms of 1974. The health service was divided into three distinct parts:

- the hospital sector run by regional hospital boards;
- general practice administered by local family practitioner committees;
- the 'community health services'.

Whilst the first two were part of the NHS – although managed separately – the community health services, which included school health services, child health clinics and family planning clinics, were part of local government. The Medical Officer of Health, as the senior doctor in the local authority, was responsible for environmental health officers, district nurses, health visitors, clinical medical officers and others.

Hospital doctors were NHS employees, but GPs were independent contractors. Their obligations were to fulfil a rather vague contract with the local Family Practitioner Committee – the predecessor of today's Family Health Services Authority (FHSA). There were no managers to tell them what to do. In Chapter 8 Paul Booton explains how this rather curious state of affairs came about – and why it still exists. Its significance now is that whilst hospital doctors, including consultants, can in theory be instructed to work in particular ways and to particular priorities, GPs' work can only be influenced, not directed, by the FHSA.

During the early 1970s this three-way split in the service came to be seen as a problem. There was considerable dissatisfaction with the lack of coordination of services that inevitably arose when different organizations were involved, and with the weakness of local planning mechanisms. The reorganization that followed affected both the NHS and local government.

1974–91 and the Griffiths reforms

The main aims of the 1974 changes were to increase coordination between the community and hospital sectors, and to establish clearer lines of accountability. Community health services were removed from local authority control and made the responsibility of newly created district health authorities (DHAs). These organizations, which covered populations of around 250,000, were given the responsibility of running both hospital and community health services. This change, the government argued, would facilitate closer links between the hospital and the community, allowing care to be organized more efficiently and effectively. DHAs were made accountable to regional health authorities (RHAs), covering populations of about 3 million, and the accountability of RHAs to the Department of Health produced a mechanism which allowed integrated local planning, but within general priorities decided by the Department of Health.

11

GPs' relationships with family practitioner committees were unaffected by all these changes.

Unfortunately, the desired coordination was not achieved. For one thing, GPs remained separate from DHAs, and there were several services which both GPs and community health services provided. The most relevant were child health and family planning services. So far as child health is concerned, developmental screening, immunization services and a range of minor problems may be dealt with in several different settings. Chapters 7 and 8 explore this issue further.

Secondly, the hoped-for integration of community and hospital services did not really materialize. The hospital and the community found themselves competing for the limited resources of the DHA. This was often compounded by the complex responsibilities of DHAs, which had to provide community-based services for local residents as well as hospital services for whoever needed them, irrespective of where they lived. The competition for resources was not simply between hospital and community, but between routine community services for local people and specialized hospital services for all-comers. Not surprisingly, the more glamorous hospital services tended to win.

Finally, despite the clear lines of responsibility between the Department of Health and DHAs, the approach to management within DHAs made it hard for them to implement change. This arrangement, known as 'consensus management', meant that the various professional groups in the DHA had to agree about any proposed changes. Since there was no one in charge, it was easy for anything to be blocked. This was exaggerated by the problem of professional and managerial conflict. Doctors are the classic example of a 'profession', and they are very hard to manage. Put more concretely, consultants do not often take kindly to being told what to do by non-medical colleagues. Until the mid-1980s the combination of consensus management and a powerful medical profession created an environment where what is now seen as effective management was impossible.

The Conservative government asked Roy Griffiths, the managing director of J. Sainsbury plc, to review the management function in the NHS, and his report (DHSS, 1985) led to some major changes. A formal management structure was introduced into health authorities and it was made clear that doctors were as much a part of that structure as others. This caused a clear shift of power away from doctors and towards non-medical managers. Many doctors opposed this change, but others realized that greater accountability was more likely to be in the public interest. After all, doctors' skills are in dealing with patients, not with managing organizations.

The 1991 NHS reforms

Whatever the effects of the Griffiths reforms, the problems caused by a general decline in public sector funding during the late 1980s created problems for the government. As Paul Booton explains in Chapter 8, opposition from the major professional bodies to the effects of what they saw as the underfunding of health care pushed the government into reviewing the NHS. Looking back, it is hardly surprising that the Thatcher government found a solution to the crisis by turning to the market, even though many health policy analysts had for many years argued that there were good reasons for keeping the market out of the health sector.

The key to understanding the 1991 NHS reforms and the 'internal market' lies in the distinction between 'purchasers' and 'providers'. DHAs had previously been funded to provide services, regardless of who the patients were or where they lived. Now they receive money from the Department of Health to purchase services for their residents from hospitals, community units or elsewhere.

Hospitals became 'providers', and their responsibilities are to provide services for the residents of those DHAs with whom they have contracts. Although some hospitals remain accountable to DHAs – and are called 'directly managed units' – most 'opt out' (of DHA control) and become NHS Trusts. These Trusts remain part of the NHS, but have far more freedom to function than they had when they were part of DHAs. The government argued that since markets improve efficiency in the private sector, so they would in the NHS. Hospitals would compete against each other for contracts with DHAs, whilst DHAs would assess the health care needs of their residents and determine which providers could best meet these needs within the available resources.

The second major change was the development of GP fund-holding practices. Such practices now receive extra money to purchase a limited range of health care for their patients from hospital or community providers, in much the same way as DHAs do for their residents.

It is still too early to understand the full effects of these changes. For the most part, health professionals continue to do the same work in the same way that they did before. It is possible that the increased explicitness about what money is being spent on will lead to clearer decisions being made about which services will, and which will not, receive funding. It may be that more marginal services and professional groups will suffer. This could happen either as a result of priorities decided by purchasers, or as a result of decisions made by providers. There is some evidence that patients of fund-holding practices are getting faster treatment than others, and it seems likely that this will continue. Such patients may also be able to obtain a wider range of services.

Other influences

Perhaps inevitably, changes and developments in the nature of health care and in professionals' understandings of their practice have paralleled wider changes in society. Major critiques of medicine, such as those written by Illich (1978) and Kennedy (1981), appeared at around the same time as the public was coming to expect more of professionals in general. Though doctors are still held in awe by many, more people question their role and status. Within general practice in particular, there is now a clear understanding of the centrality of patients' views, and of the importance of the whole person. Deterministic and biological accounts of illness are increasingly being replaced by models which include the psychological and social worlds.

Unlike the education and social services, these developments have not appeared in any legislative frameworks. Rather, they are increasingly being adopted as good practice through education, peer pressure, audit and the managerial process.

CURRENT CONTEXTS: SOCIAL SERVICES

The roles and responsibilities of social workers (and their professional pre-decessors) have always been closely linked to legislation. The 1989 Children Act is now the major influence on social workers, and it provides the framework under which they work. In Chapter 6 Ravi Kohli discusses the Act in detail and explores its many implications for social workers. As well as providing the context in which social workers practise, it has ramifications for a wide range of professional groups. Russell (1992) sees it as an Act for *all* support services, and as being based on five principles:

- the welfare of children;
- partnership with parents;
- the importance of families and of supporting them in their caring role;
- recognizing the views, wishes and feelings of children and parents;
- corporate responsibility, with services working collaboratively.

Pugh (1992) considers that the Act envisages three main roles for local authorities in relation to children under the age of 8:

- the duty to provide for children in need;
- the duty to register all day care provision for children under 8 (which is in operation for more than two hours per day);
- the duty to review the level, pattern and range of provision of childminding and day care, taking account of nursery and primary education, every three years. The review is to be carried out jointly with education services and must involve consultation with health authorities, voluntary agencies and others. The review must then be published.

The Act therefore outlines principles and responsibilities for both authorities and parents. However, as with any legislation, it can be interpreted in numerous ways, so there is considerable scope for inconsistencies in practice across the country. The definition of 'children in need' within the Act is:

- those unlikely to achieve or maintain or have the opportunity for achieving or maintaining a reasonable standard of health or development without the provision of services;
- those whose health or development is likely to be significantly impaired or further impaired without the provision of such services;
- those who are disabled.

It will be left to social service departments to determine the parameters within which the Act is implemented, and which children are determined to be in need. Unlike the 1981 Education Act, the Children Act does not legislate for a formal statutory assessment procedure to determine which children are in need, and this is likely to lead to considerable variability between services.

Similarly, whilst it is admirable to encourage and legislate for collaborative working between different services it is notoriously difficult to achieve in reality. So for example the Department of Health's (1990) review of English local authorities' child care statements noted that:

> simply asserting the need for cooperation does not of course produce it (although it may well be a necessary stage in achieving it), and research inspections have repeatedly indicated that 'departmentalism' at the local level is a persistent obstacle to effective working with children and families. (1990, p. 31)

The work of social workers, more so than for any other professional group represented in this book, is determined to a great extent by legislation and the statutory duties it imposes. They have an unenviable task, especially given their prominent public profile and the frequent media attention attracted to their involvement in such issues as child abuse and child care.

What emerges from the discussion on the contexts in which education, health and social service professionals work is a number of concerns, common to all professional groups, which reflect the complex ways in which political, legislative and philosophical issues interrelate and influence practice. These areas are addressed in Chapter 2.

REFERENCES

DES (1944) *Education Act.* London: HMSO.

DES (1978) *Special Educational Needs, Report of the Committee of Enquiry into the Education of Handicapped Children and Young People* (The Warnock Report). London: HMSO.

DES (1981) *Education Act.* London: HMSO.

DES (1988) *Education Reform Act.* London: HMSO.

DES (1989) *Assessments and Statements of Special Educational Needs: Procedures within the Education, Health and Social Services* (Circular 22/91). London: HMSO.

DFE (1993) *Local Management of Schools.* Consultation paper. London: DFE.

DHSS (1985) *NHS Management Inquiry* (The Griffiths Report). London: HMSO.

DoH (1990) *Child Care Policy: Putting It in Writing. A Review of English Local Authorities' Child Care Policy Statement.* London: HMSO.

HMSO (1989) *The Children Act.* London: HMSO.

Illich, I. (1978) *Limits to Medicine.* London: Calder & Boyars.

Kennedy, I. (1981) *The Unmasking of Medicine.* London: George Allen & Unwin.

National Curriculum Council (1989a) *Implementing the National Curriculum: Participation by Pupils with Special Educational Needs* (Circular 5, May). York: NCC.

National Curriculum Council (1989b) *A Curriculum for All: Special Educational Needs in the National Curriculum.* York: NCC.

Pugh, G. (1992) A policy for early childhood services. In G. Pugh (ed.), *Contemporary Issues in the Early Years: Working Collaboratively for Children.* London: Paul Chapman.

Russell, P. (1992) Boundary issues: multidisciplinary working in new contexts – implications for educational psychology practice. In S. Wolfendale, T. Bryans, M. Fox, A. Labram and A. Sigston (eds), *The Profession and Practice of Educational Psychology*. London: Cassell.

FURTHER READING

Solity, J. E. (1992) *Special Education*. London: Cassell. This book, written primarily for parents, governors and teachers, introduces readers to issues, concerns and developments in the field of special education. It highlights the major implications of recent UK legislation for children with special needs, in the context of the more general changes within the education system.

CHAPTER 2

Support services: issues

Jonathan Solity and Graham Bickler

Several issues emerged from the discussion in Chapter 1 about current contexts which appear consistently in later chapters in this book. These are:

- developing partnerships: working with parents;
- developing partnerships: multidisciplinary work;
- the nature of children's difficulties;
- the focus of assessment and intervention;
- who is the client?
- resources and organization;
- professional issues.

The way different professional groups identify and frame these issues varies. This chapter:

- provides an overview of the issues and concerns facing those currently working within support services in education, health and social service departments;
- focuses on the impact of these influences on children's education as well as highlighting their influences on health and social service departments;
- explores the way support services function and the constraints they experience.

A common theoretical link between issues is the way in which explanations of children's difficulties have been extended to examine the contexts in which they occur.

DEVELOPING PARTNERSHIPS: WORKING WITH PARENTS

Parents have always been seen as crucial to their children's development, but it is only in recent legislation that their extensive involvement in school life has been sanctioned. These changes have increased parental choice of their children's schools, offered them greater participation on school governing bodies and, following the 1981 Education Act, given them greater rights with respect to children with special needs. The 1989 Children Act has also clarified and strengthened the role of parents in child protection, but within the health sector there has been an increasing understanding of how professionals can maximize their impact by working with parents outside specific legislative frameworks.

Wolfendale (1992), in charting the arrival and impact of parents in education, notes that in textbooks on the history of education, parents are conspicuously absent, except for references to their primary legal duty to send children to school. The 1970s, however, saw a dramatic increase in the level of parental involvement in children's learning. Numerous projects were initiated by schools to formalize and systematize parental contributions to the learning process. Parental involvement became a fertile area for research and demonstrated the effectiveness of parents as educators in a variety of areas.

Recent legislation highlights the changing relationships between parents and schools. In Chapter 6 Ravi Kohli suggests that the 1988 Education Reform Act and the 1989 Children Act are pulling in different directions in relation to their impact on relationships with parents. In the past, education was often viewed as a series of partnerships. Central government worked in tandem with local government, which in turn was in partnership with its schools, which in turn forged links with, and involved, parents in their children's education. Within the new legislation, the balance of power has shifted away from local authorities towards central government and schools. The change in control brings a very different philosophy on how education is to be conducted.

In the past, central and local government planned as best they could to provide a system of education that attempted to be egalitarian in nature. The aim was to provide equality of opportunity, and government determined how best to allocate resources to achieve this. LEAs had flexibility over how they funded the education service and could offer support to schools that experienced difficulties in meeting children's needs. In principle at least, LEAs could assist schools in making the best possible provision for the children under their care.

The concept of partnership and planning is now replaced with that of the 'market-place'. Parents rather than children have become the consumers of the education services. It is envisaged that parents will shop around, looking for a best buy amongst the schools within their locality. Parents will be helped in their decision making by the publication in the national and local press of the results of the Key Stage Assessments, which use Standard Assessment Tasks and take place when children are 7, 11, 14 and 16. These are based on children's progress in the three core subjects of the National Curriculum. Schools also have to report to parents annually on their children's progress. These reports are derived from teachers' classroom assessments of children's progress, and potentially can be highly informative.

Ravi Kohli's chapter highlights concerns within the social work profession that published league tables may increase the resolve of schools to do little to adapt to the needs of children who do not achieve acceptable levels. One consequence of having disenchanted children is that it increases the likelihood that they may become truants from school. Kohli draws attention to research demonstrating a connection between children's absence from school and their coming to the attention of social services. Educational legislation requiring schools to publish the results of children's assessments can be seen to undermine the notion of parent–teacher partnerships. The 1989 Children Act emphasizes parental responsibilities and the obligations on parents and social workers (and other agencies) to work in partnership to provide or enable primary care to take place.

Practice within the health service is also being underpinned by the philosophy of the market-place, with the result that aspects of relationships between GPs and parents can be seen in some ways to be developing along comparable lines to those in education. In Chapter 8 Paul Booton observes that GPs must now prepare leaflets informing patients of existing services, although there are no available outcome measures or league tables to allow patients to draw conclusions about the quality of care offered. Although outcome measures are being developed, they remain unrefined and have a number of serious limitations.

The quality of work with parents depends on the attitudes and values of those who have most frequent contact with them. When children experience difficulties, parents are understandably at their most vulnerable and are sensitive to suggestions that they are at fault. Professionals need to be receptive to the ways in which good relationships can be established.

Relationships have typically been underpinned by a recognition of the need to involve parents in aspects of their children's education, health and social care. However, the concept of *parental involvement* often failed to recognize parents' expertise, knowledge and rights. As a result, professional relationships based on parental involvement have been developed to embrace the concept of parental *partnerships*.

Wolfendale (1992) draws attention to the critical differences between forging collaborative *partnerships* with parents and merely *involving* them in children's learning. She identifies four key principles that professionals working with parents are in general committed to, and that are central to developing positive *partnerships*, but which are not necessarily features of parental *involvement*:

Rights

Parents have fundamental rights to take part in decision making on their children's education. Wolfendale argues that it is important that parents not only know their rights, but are aware of how to express them.

Equality

Parents have equal status with the professional with whom they have contact. Whatever understanding and insight professionals gain following their assessments of children's needs, this is but one piece in a complex jigsaw, to be set alongside the views of parents.

Reciprocity

All those working with children can benefit from a productive discourse on children's needs. Reciprocal involvement rests on the premise that each person contributing to a dialogue is sharing information and expertise, but also accepting responsibility for decisions and their outcomes.

Empowerment

The aim of parental initiatives is to empower parents; that is to give them information so that they are in a better position to understand the various ways in which education, health and social service departments function, as well as the professionals employed by them, so that they are more capable of exerting their own rights.

In addition to embracing the above principles, Cunningham and Davis (1985) believe that effective work with parents is determined, in part, by the feelings and attitudes held by professionals about the parents with whom they work. Solity and Raybould (1988) highlight three fundamental aspects of developing effective partnerships:

- conveying respect;
- conveying empathy;
- being genuine.

The assumptions and principles on which partnerships with parents develop within educational contexts are similar for all professionals working with parents.

DEVELOPING PARTNERSHIPS: MULTIDISCIPLINARY WORK

The principles underpinning effective partnerships with parents are equally valid when working within collaborative, multidisciplinary contexts. As discussed in Chapter 1, in the past relationships between certain professional groups were conducted within a hierarchical framework. Although they can no longer be formally characterized in such a way, the qualifications and social status of different professions can effectively undermine truly collaborative partnerships.

Pugh (1992) sees barriers to effective partnerships as arising from historical factors and the professional jealousies of providers, rather than from the needs of children and their families. She argues that the basis for positive collaboration lies in professionals developing policies that specify aims and objectives and the mechanisms for planning, delivering and managing services in a coordinated way, drawing on the skills and expertise of parents as well as those of different professional groups.

The 1989 Children Act urges coordination of services, a process which may be undermined by the government's desire, under the 1988 Education Reform Act, to give schools greater responsibility for their own budgets via LMS and financial delegation. Tomlinson (1993) describes the ways in which school governors have taken over many of the tasks of LEAs, with the result that it may be more difficult for services to take an overview of needs within an entire authority if they are required to provide a service only to some schools. Other schools might buy in alternative, non-LEA services to meet their children's needs.

Russell (1992) believes that the concept of joint working with children with special needs has been an important feature of education, health and social services. However, as stated earlier, admirable intentions alone are not sufficient to translate principles into practice, as indicated by the Department of Health (1990), which commented that merely asserting the need for cooperation does necessarily produce it and that research and inspections have repeatedly indicated that departmentalism at the local level is a persistent obstacle to effective collaboration. Similarly the House of Commons Select Committee's report on the education for the under-fives (House of Commons, 1989) lamented the absence of evidence on a national scale of the cooperation necessary to achieve the best use of existing resources.

Barriers to effective professional collaboration are discussed by Powell and Solity (1990). They consider the social, interactive processes that are necessary for working with colleagues, and highlight negotiation skills as being crucial in promoting partnerships with parents and other professionals. They explore the dynamics of successful negotiations, indicate why these are not readily achieved and suggest ways in which problems can be overcome. Unless the interactive skills involved in negotiating are acknowledged and addressed, commitment and legislative imperatives alone are unlikely to lead to successful collaborative outcomes.

THE NATURE OF CHILDREN'S DIFFICULTIES

The current contexts in which the professional groups described in this book function reflect the changing explanations of children's difficulties. Examining the contexts in which difficulties occur and exploring the perceptions of those involved raises a number of issues. Parents and teachers are unlikely to welcome any suggestion that they may be part of the problem, and may be hostile to the idea that their perceptions and behaviour need to be considered in any overall analysis of children's difficulties. Historically, diagnosis and treatment have taken place in a neutral environment. In recent times increased understanding of the importance of context has made it more likely that interventions will be initiated in the settings in which problems occur. This may lead to increased visits to the school and home from educational psychologists, clinical psychologists, child psychiatrists, speech and language therapists and others. However, resource constraints may temper the extent of such professional practice.

Many support services advise others on how to manage problems rather than deal with them directly themselves. So psychiatrists may work with other health workers whilst educational psychologists, speech and language therapists and advisory teachers all organize in-service courses for teachers. This is an effective use of time and a more efficient way of dealing with problems. For example, one hour spent on an in-service course with thirty teachers can have an impact on the learning experiences of a large number of children, and certainly more than if a member of a support service saw teachers or children individually. Giving teachers skills in this way enables them to become more effective at preventing problems. HMI (DES, 1989), in its survey of support services for special educational needs, commented that 'the new pattern of provision evolving within most services was a reduction in the amount of time devoted to teaching pupils, in favour of more time spent advising and training teachers' (para. 18). Child psychiatrists now spend up to 30 per cent of their time in consultative work with teachers and other professionals who have more direct contact with children.

FOCUS OF ASSESSMENT AND INTERVENTION

The contributions to this book reflect a general trend in the focus of assessment and intervention around children's educational, health and social needs. This has developed from the recognition that problems can arise from the way in which children interact with their environments. The contexts in which problems emerge then become the focus of the intervention, not just the child. Many psychologists, psychiatrists and social workers see the starting point in their investigation as the referring agent, and not the child. The initial focus is on understanding why the child is seen to have a problem, and for this it is necessary to appreciate the perceptions and motives of the person who identifies the problem in the first place. The intervention which follows may then involve the whole family or teachers in exploring the nature of their interactions with children on a broader basis than the specific child with the problem.

Within education there has been a gradual shift in the focus of assessments and interventions through the following sequence:

- *the child*, and finding out what is 'wrong' with the child;
- *the task*, and finding out whether it is too hard or easy, sufficiently interesting, providing opportunities to use and apply different teaching methods and offering a wide range of learning opportunities;
- *the broader classroom learning environment* and the way this is organized to meet children's needs, the way the child is taught and the nature of children's interactions with their teachers and peers;
- *the wider educational environment*, which includes LEA policy making and the way that support services liaise and work together.

These developments have been mirrored in health and social services departments, where the focus of intervention has moved from individual children to their interactions with their families and peers.

Within health, this change in understanding can be seen to mirror the critiques of the 'medical model' (Mechanic, 1978) and a shift towards holistic concepts of health. In the medical model the account of illness is very deterministic and biological, with interventions involving medicines or surgery. Holistic approaches emphasize the psychological and the social worlds, see patients as people and have a much broader understanding of what interventions may be possible. They are also empowering and recognize the importance of negotiation and professional–client relationships.

A further dimension to the focus of intervention, which is prominent in education, health and social service departments, is the commitment to preventive approaches to meeting children's needs. These have become an important aspect of the work of support services but in some areas are under threat, given recent legislative changes. At a time of increased accountability and the transfer of responsibilities from local education and health authorities to central government, schools, NHS Trusts and fund-holding GPs, there will be pressures to demonstrate effectiveness through crude indicators reflecting the efficacy of services rather than the less tangible and quantifiable effects of preventive strategies. This may happen despite an increased professional commitment to broadly preventive approaches.

WHO IS THE CLIENT?

Exploring issues surrounding the nature of children's difficulties raises the inevitable question: 'Who is the client?' Whilst this may appear to be a relatively easy question to answer, it is becoming increasingly difficult to resolve in the light of recent legislation and developments in professional practice. As members of support services have questioned their role within education, health and social service departments, and have developed preventive approaches, it has become more difficult to establish the identity of the client.

Although children have usually been the reason for initial referrals to support services, the focus of intervention (as discussed earlier), for numerous reasons, has often been parents or teachers. For example, social work with children, child psychiatry and child psychology are to some extent different from other branches of these disciplines. In the adult fields, it is usually (though not always) adults who recognize that they have problems in their lives and seek professional help to address them. In social work with children, child psychiatry and child psychology, although children are seen to have the problem, they do not refer themselves. The problems they present are invariably identified and articulated by someone else, usually parents or teachers. They see that the child has a problem and expect the professional to effect a cure.

As special education developed, the nature of difficulties was increasingly located within the contexts in which they occurred and so those interacting with children became another factor in considering how problems could be overcome. A similar process has occurred in other areas such as speech and language therapy and hearing impairment. As explanations to account for children's difficulties have encompassed an increasing range of factors, so the answer to the question 'Who is the client?' has become less clear. It has also exposed serious conflicts of interest between professionals, children and whoever referred them.

Given the changing nature of partnerships in education, health and social services and the way problems are being construed, the client is now more likely to be defined as the source of the referral; that is, the person who feels there is a problem (parent, family, teacher, school, LEA), rather than the child. However, as notions of the 'market-place' underpin practice within education, health and social services, it is possible that the new consumers, whether they be parents or schools, will be prepared to engage only those support services that accept *their view* of a problem. In relation to education services this is likely to be in terms of 'within-child' variables, as this is a less threatening position than the alternative, environmental perspective discussed in the earlier section, 'The nature of children's difficulties'. This scenario potentially creates an area of conflict between professionals and parents and their respective views of who is the client.

The potential extent of the conflict in relation to schools was highlighted by Croll and Moses (1985). They examined teachers' views on the causes of pupils' difficulties and indicated that there was a clear reluctance to attribute problems to factors lying within the school. The main reason for children being either 'slow learners' or 'poor readers' was attributed to the children's 'IQ/ability', or 'other within-child factors' or 'home/parent'. In fewer than 3 per cent of cases were difficulties related to school/teacher factors. On the basis of this research teachers appeared reluctant to identify factors within the school or classroom environments as responsible for a child's difficulty in learning. If these findings are generalizable, it raises the question of whether support services will feel compelled to respond to difficulties within the terms of reference in which they are referred, that is to try to 'cure' children with problems, rather than to contextualize children's difficulties.

Another element to the question, 'Who is the client?', depends on whether members of support services see themselves first and foremost as *professionals*, accountable to their professional bodies, or *employees* of education, health or social service departments. Seeing their role in *professional* terms implies that potential clients are either the source or subject of the referral. In these circumstances the client could then be the employer, schools, parents or children, depending on the nature of the problem. However, where members of support services regard their role primarily as authority *employees*, clients may still be schools, teachers, parents and children, *but not the employing authority*. Within this scenario the client is most likely to be seen in traditional terms as the child.

The nature of the relationship between the support service professionals and their clients is potentially complex and unclear and depends on how children's problems are interpreted and whether the 'professional' or 'employee' hat is being worn. Inevitably there will be tensions and conflicts between these issues, with implications for how interventions take place and how channels of professional accountability are developed.

Accountability

Parents and teachers have also expressed concern about their relationships with support services, not because of any underlying assumptions about the nature of children's difficulties but because they had real concerns about the impartiality of a service employee with whom they worked. For example, do educational psychologists offer an independent professional view, or might they be swayed by the LEA and only recommend provision that the LEA can afford, or that is currently available? The reports by the Audit Commission and HMI (1992a, b) and research by Rodgers (1986) indicate that such fears are not without substance. Similar issues appear in social work and the health sectors, where professionals are managed within organizations that have particular priorities and often a lack of resources. The managerial message reaching the professional may conflict with his or her professional opinion.

Parents may resolve the conflict by seeking advice from professionals who endorse their view of a problem but are independent of an LEA. Russell (1992) has suggested that there is anecdotal evidence for such moves amongst parents. She believes that within the new culture of individuality, parents feel that they have more control of services that are employed privately and are independent of LEAs. Russell senses that parents regard private assessments as more honest than LEA ones. But advising parents about children's needs and provision in a private capacity carries no responsibility to provide recommended resources and in no way takes account of the level of funding within authorities or the competing demands for those funds. The independent adviser can be seen as writing a blank cheque for parents, but without any knowledge of how much money is in the bank.

RESOURCES AND ORGANIZATION

The availability of resources and that of service organizations are closely related areas. One of the recurring themes in this book is the way in which resources influence the quality of service offered. Yet, it could be argued that all successful management is about getting the most from existing resources, and few would disagree with this approach. What seems to happen is that professional and organizational boundaries obstruct this generally acceptable view of the relationship between resources and outcomes.

Nevertheless, Juliet Stone in Chapter 12 highlights the limitations imposed on services for the visually impaired with only one or two qualified staff compared to what can be accomplished within a larger service, particularly where services have similar school-aged and pre-school populations. It is not just a question of the availability of greater expertise and experience within a larger team, but the benefits which accrue from being able to work collaboratively with colleagues and having appropriate peer support. Ravi Kohli in Chapter 6 and Jonathan Dare in Chapter 5 both suggest that one of the consequences of resource problems is that professional groups retreat into narrow definitions of their territory, or even, as is the case with social work, to the statutory minimum. So again it is the crucial inter-sectoral and multidisciplinary aspects of work that suffer; yet it is primarily these which are often central to solving complex problems.

The 1981 Education Act linked the assessment of children's special educational needs to the available resources and the way they are being used. Special education is a resource issue. Education professionals contributing to the statutory assessment procedure are required by the legislation to make recommendations about children's needs and suitable provision, irrespective of what is currently available within an LEA. However, LEAs frequently pressurize their employees to recommend what is available, even if it is not quite appropriate to children's needs.

So support services have been placed in an unenviable position: not only are their working conditions, assessment and intervention approaches determined in part by resources, but their professional opinion may be compromised by their relationship with their employer.

PROFESSIONAL ISSUES

The quality of provision received should not be determined by geographical location. Yet the contributors to this book have stated on many occasions that provision varies enormously across the UK both within and between various support services. On the one hand, this can be viewed positively as recognizing that requirements in one part of the country are different from those in another. As a result, differential resources and provision reflect varying needs. On the other hand, there is cause for concern if children are not receiving the same support as their peers elsewhere. The authors have commented that it has not always been easy to illustrate the full range of practice adopted by their colleagues on a national scale.

Authors refer frequently to the expectations of them as professionals and 'experts' within their fields. To be seen as an expert carries expectations which professionals have not always found comfortable, given the changing ways In which children's difficulties are now seen. As interventions have moved away from the assumptions of the medical model towards broader interpretations and preventive approaches, the aim has been to negotiate the nature of problems with the referrer, explore the ways they can be overcome and ultimately help clients to help themselves, rather than to expect the problems to be resolved by an expert.

A recurring theme in this chapter has been the complex professional dynamics that exist in work within education, health and social services. Tensions and conflicts surround the contradictory position of being a member of a professional group but employed within the public sector, where the expectations and needs of the employer may have to assume priority over those of clients. How these conflicts are resolved is a matter, initially, for services themselves. What emerges from the literature on support services is the importance of colleagues working collaboratively to negotiate a realistic and practical policy for meeting children's needs.

The following chapters develop the issues raised here and explain their relevance to the contributors' own professional contexts.

REFERENCES

Audit Commission and HMI (1992a) *Getting In on the Act: Provision for Pupils with Special Educational Needs: The National Picture*. London: HMSO.

Audit Commission and HMI (1992b) *Getting In on the Act: Provision for Pupils with Special Educational Needs: A Management Handbook for Schools and Local Education Authorities*. London: HMSO.

Croll, P. and Moses, D. (1985) *One in Five: The Assessment and Incidence of Special Educational Needs*. London: Routledge & Kegan Paul.

Cunningham, C. and Davis, H. (1985) *Working with Parents: Frameworks for Collaboration*. Milton Keynes: Open University Press.

DES (1978) *Special Educational Needs, Report of the Committee of Inquiry into the Education of Handicapped Children and Young People* (The Warnock Report). London: HMSO.

DES (1981) *Education Act*. London: HMSO.

DES (1988) *Education Reform Act*. London: HMSO.

DES (1989) *A Survey of Support Services for Special Educational Needs*. London: DES.

DoH (1989) *The Children Act*. London: HMSO.

DoH (1990) *Child Care Policy: Putting It in Writing. A Review of English Local Authorities' Child Care Policy Statement*. London: SSI/HMSO.

House of Commons (1989) *Educational Provision for the Under Fives*, Education, Science and Arts Committee, Session 1988–9, First Report. London: HMSO.

Mechanic, D. (1978) *Medical Sociology*. New York: Free Press.

Powell, M. and Solity, J. E. (1990) *Teachers in Control: Cracking the Code*. London: Routledge.

Pugh, G. (1992) A policy for early childhood services. In G. Pugh (ed.), *Contemporary Issues in Early Years: Working Collaboratively for Children*. London: Paul Chapman.

Rodgers, R. (1986) *Guiding the Professional: A Survey of LEA Guidelines for Professionals of the 1981 Education Act*. London: Spastics Society.

Russell, P. (1992) Boundary issues: multidisciplinary working in new contexts – implications for educational psychology practices. In S. Wolfendale, T. Bryans, M. Fox, A. Labram and A. Sigston (eds), *The Profession and Practice of Educational Psychology*. London: Cassell.

Solity, J. E. and Raybould, E. C. (1988) *A Teacher's Guide to Special Needs: A Positive Response to the 1981 Education Act*. Milton Keynes: Open University Press.

Tomlinson, J. (1993) *The Control of Education*. London: Cassell.

Wolfendale, S. (1992) *Empowering Parents and Teachers: Working for Children*. London: Cassell.

FURTHER READING

David, T. (ed.) (1994) *Working Together for Young Children*. London: Routledge. This is a book of edited papers written by various professionals involved in work with young children. Authors describe their roles, the ways they support families and the way they relate to other services.

Wolfendale, S. (1992) *Empowering Parents and Teachers: Working for Children*. London: Cassell. The book looks at the the increasing representation of parents in education and their contribution to the school process.

PART 2

PSYCHOLOGICAL AND PSYCHIATRIC SERVICES

INTRODUCTION

There are strong historical and theoretical links between these services. At one time psychiatrists had a controlling influence on the practice of clinical and educational psychologists employed in the health and education services respectively. The chapters in Part 2 reflect the dramatic changes that have occurred within the professions and the nature of the relationships between them. The old hierarchical order has been replaced with a partnership where different perspectives and expertise are shared in the interests of children. Whilst professional relationships have developed along more collaborative lines, the theoretical underpinnings of the professions have also broadened to provide a common starting point for all three professional groups.

One major implication of these changes is that the certainties of past practice have been superseded by ambiguity. Not only is the nature of referred problems wide-ranging but they can be interpreted in a variety of ways, so that it is not always easy to define who has the problem. The role of psychologists and psychiatrists requires them to understand children's difficulties from a variety of perspectives and to negotiate rather than impose potential interventions. There is now considerable overlap in their professional involvement with children. This can create tensions, but psychologists and psychiatrists frequently confront similar issues when working with families and schools.

Usually the crucial factor determining whether problems are dealt with by psychologists or psychiatrists is who makes the referral and that person's perceptions of what educational psychologists, clinical psychologists and child psychiatrists do. In general, if *school-* or *home*-based problems come to the attention of those working within the education department, the referral will be to educational psychologists. Problems coming to the attention of those employed in the health service are most likely to be referred to either clinical psychologists or child psychiatrists.

CHAPTER 3

Educational psychology

Sue Morris

Educational psychology is a relatively young profession, dating from 1913, when Cyril Burt was appointed as the first school psychologist to the London County Council. Educational psychologists comprise a small professional group (approximately 1500 members) who are, in the main, employees of LEAs. A small but growing number work in the private sector whilst others are employed by charities such as the Spastics Society and Barnardo's.

There is considerable variability in the practice both of individual educational psychologists and of different LEA psychological services. However, there is, as with any profession, a substantial area of common ground in terms of training, knowledge, skills and professional accountability, which to some extent unites members of the profession and differentiates them from other professional groups.

This chapter focuses on LEA psychologists – the majority of qualified practitioners – and presents:

- the background to the development of the profession;
- an overview of the organization and professional remit of educational psychology services in England and Wales;
- a summary of the training of educational psychologists which reflects the roles and tasks they undertake;
- a focus on key aspects of the theoretical rationale which underpins their work;
- a review of current practice and the ways the profession may be expected to develop in the future.

BACKGROUND TO THE DEVELOPMENT OF THE PROFESSION OF EDUCATIONAL PSYCHOLOGY

This section describes two parallel forces which shaped the early development of the profession. The first, and arguably more powerful, was the development of policies and practices governing the education of children with special educational needs. The second was the development of child guidance services to address growing concerns about socially deviant and delinquent behaviour in children and young people. The section concludes by reviewing the pressures from within the profession to adopt a broader remit and to apply a wider range of psychologically based interventions than was traditionally the case up until the mid-1970s.

Assessment of special educational needs

The 1899 Elementary Education (Defective and Epileptic Children) Act required school boards (the LEA counterparts of the day) to cater for a newly created category of pupils. 'Defective' children were defined as 'those who by reason of mental or physical defect are incapable of receiving proper benefit from the ordinary school, but are not incapable by reason of such defect of receiving instruction in special classes or schools'. So the school boards were faced with the need to differentiate three groups: those whose needs could be met in the ordinary schools; those whose needs could be best met in special schools or classes; and those who were deemed to be so severely disabled as to be ineducable, even with special provision. This discriminatory legislative policy was the basis from which psychologists developed their formative contribution to public education.

Initially the selection and certification of defectives fell to doctors, but the validity of their methods and conclusions was increasingly criticized by teachers, parents and education officials. With the development of psychometric assessment techniques (structured methods designed to test and measure abilities with reasonable reliability) at the turn of the century, and – perhaps more significantly – the development of intelligence or IQ testing, academic psychology was seen as being capable of providing an objective basis for discriminating between normal children, educable mental defectives and ineducable mental defectives.

Cyril Burt allocated half of his time to assessing individual children and half to research when appointed to the London County Council. He subsequently played a major role in legitimizing the use of IQ testing in making decisions about whether children with learning difficulties should be taught in special schools. His work was influential in leading teachers and administrators to look to personnel with expertise in psychology, psychological techniques and education to take a central role in the identification and assessment of pupils' special needs.

Over the years until the publication of the Summerfield Report (DES, 1968), educational psychologists' professional skills were based largely upon the administration and interpretation of psychometric tests. They combined their dual assessment role of:

- assessing children's needs for special educational treatment; and
- assessing personality, particularly with reference to the needs of maladjusted or delinquent children.

To this day educational psychologists continue to play a role in discriminating between children through determining which children can realistically have their needs met in mainstream settings and which require additional support, either in the ordinary school or, in some cases, within special classes or units. The additional task of differentiating between educable and ineducable children was removed relatively recently by the implementation of the 1970 Education (Handicapped Children) Act in 1971, which gave all children, including those with severe learning difficulties, the right to receive education rather than only training and/or care.

The emergence of child guidance clinics

The second major force shaping the role of early psychological services in the UK was the development of child guidance clinics (CGCs). The first CGC was established in America in 1921, to be followed in 1929 by the Child Guidance Training Centre in London, and in 1932 by the first British local authority child guidance clinic. Educational psychologists were employed as members of the growing number of child guidance teams and school psychological services until the late 1960s.

Child guidance clinics evolved largely to combat political embarrassment at the economic and human waste caused by the growing problems of juvenile delinquency. As with special needs, testing played a significant role in shaping the public view that psychology had a relevant and valid contribution to make in the assessment and treatment of young offenders. This time it was the personality inventory, derived from newly developed statistical techniques known as factor analysis, which gave psychologists a relevant professional tool. This enabled them to address the essentially economically and politically driven task of illuminating and treating young people's socially non-conforming, criminal and maladjusted behaviour.

The reconstructing movement

The Summerfield Report (DES, 1968) endorsed the view that the central contribution of educational psychologists lay in the identification, diagnosis and treatment of individual children with learning and/or adjustment problems. Research, which had been a central component of Burt's work, was almost completely overlooked as having a relevant professional role, as were the wider potential applications of psychology to the task of supporting the learning and development of *all* children in mainstream and special schools, not only those seen to be experiencing difficulties.

Although the Summerfield Report was not instrumental in galvanizing change within the profession, a dissatisfaction emerged with the status quo among practising educational psychologists at around this time. The total complement of 326 educational psychologists working in England and Wales in 1968 clearly had their work cut out if intensive individual casework was to be their staple diet. Long waiting lists became the norm as demand exceeded supply. Although children with problems formed the majority of those on educational psychologists' waiting lists, they were often the least likely to benefit from the educational psychologists' intervention.

It became increasingly apparent that assessments based on the medical model, which had dominated professional practice since the turn of the century, were disappointingly ineffective. Explanations of school failure which took account of the environmental determinants of behaviour instead of individual pathology came to be seen as more realistic and valid. In addition, they provided a practical base from which children's progress could be promoted. In contrast, the simple role of tester appeared sterile, as did the reactive and crisis intervention nature of much of the work.

All these factors led to a phenomenon known as the 'reconstructing movement' (Gillham, 1978) in the late 1960s and early to mid-1970s. It developed as a number of relatively creative and influential educational psychologists sought to redefine their role. The goal of this movement was to apply a wider range of relevant psychological skills and knowledge to a far larger population of children than the small minority with the most severe and intransigent difficulties.

The reconstructing movement advocated three principal directions for change:

- a decreased emphasis on direct work with individually referred children;
- an increased emphasis on indirect methods. These approaches are based upon an appreciation of the value of consultation and research, and adopt systems methodology to influence organizational change, for example through affecting school policy, or the attitudes and behaviour of adults towards children;
- an increased emphasis on preventive work, especially through advisory work and courses for parents, teachers and other direct workers.

The mission of the reconstructing movement is by no means accomplished. A number of unresolved tensions continue to compete with the professional values and beliefs of educational psychologists. For example, in practical terms, no psychological service in England or Wales has yet achieved the staffing ratio of one educational psychologist per 5000 children aged 0–19 years recommended by the Warnock Report (DES, 1978). The majority of educational psychologists are constrained by the effects of competing demands for inadequate resources, and waiting lists are by no means a thing of the past.

Secondly, there is a gap between the role and methods which educational psychologists themselves believe to be productive, and the expectations of many teachers, parents and LEA administrators. The belief that the primary value and contribution of educational psychologists lies in the assessment and (direct or indirect) treatment of individual children with learning difficulties and social adjustment problems, remains prevalent, even among those who have *prima facie* evidence of the value of wider applications of psychology in more broadbased advisory or preventive work.

Thirdly, it would appear that the test-orientated background of educational psychologists, particularly the ubiquitous intelligence test and the pervasive, if spurious, notions of IQ and mental age, have been instrumental in supporting the belief amongst service users that children's difficulties are largely attributable to within-child deficits, such as low ability or relatively fixed (and measurable) personality traits. Where such views are held the rationale for environmentally based interventions, such as family therapy or developing classroom management skills, is less likely to be appreciated.

Finally, the 1981 Education Act created conservative expectations about the role of educational psychologists. In many services the resulting level of statutory individual casework is taking up such a substantial proportion of psychologists' time as to render tokenistic more constructive, complementary preventive initiatives.

Overall, the picture of what educational psychologists actually do some twenty or so years after the dawn of the reconstructing movement is still one with a high proportion of individual casework with children referred as having learning, developmental and/or behavioural difficulties. The extent to which psychometric tests are used as a key component of educational psychologists' assessment role varies considerably. The most recent review of practice by HMI (DES, 1990) suggests that the preventive, systemic and developmental work advocated by the movement is a feature of contemporary service delivery, albeit neither on the scale nor with the degree of priority that many educational psychologists would wish.

Training of educational psychologists

The training of educational psychologists is lengthy and wide-ranging and enables them to fulfil the broad spectrum of research, preventive, developmental and reactive casework functions advocated by the profession since the mid-1970s.

The regulatory body for psychology is the British Psychological Society (BPS). All who seek to use the descriptor 'psychologist', and be registered as such, must satisfy the BPS that they are eligible for registration as chartered psychologists. For educational psychologists in England, Wales and Northern Ireland eligibility for the status of chartered educational psychologist is conferred by satisfactory completion of the following:

- a good honours degree in psychology or its equivalent recognized by the BPS. The psychology degree forms a major learning resource for educational psychologists. It provides a range of theoretical models through which to interpret human behaviour, and skills in problem formulation and research;
- a teaching qualification and a minimum of at least two years' teaching experience. This component of training is something of a mixed blessing. Arguably it is their training and experience as teachers which confers some degree of credibility upon psychologists' advice about classroom management, assessment, instructional design and curricular adaptations, in the eyes of some teachers. On the other hand, this component of professional training has obvious practical difficulties for psychology graduates, who may find difficulty gaining places on a PGCE course when they have no degree-level grounding in a National Curriculum core or foundation subject. Additionally, a professional training route rendered so lengthy and disjointed by this detour into a career in teaching is likely to be unattractive to many psychology graduates when compared with the more straightforward routes into other careers in applied psychology;
- postgraduate training in educational psychology followed by a year's supervised practice. There are at present thirteen professional training courses in

England, Wales and Northern Ireland, usually of one year's duration, all of which lead to a master's degree. These courses all follow a common core curriculum constructed and closely monitored by the BPS to ensure that entrants to the profession gain appropriate knowledge and practical experience.

(The system in Scotland is slightly different in that a teaching qualification and experience are not required, and the postgraduate training course is of two years' duration. Similarly, there is no requirement for a teaching qualification and experience for educational psychologists – or their counterparts – in other countries within the European Community.)

The training process comprises a balance between university-based seminars, workshop sessions and fieldwork practice, which is jointly and rigorously supervised by university tutors and practising educational psychologists. The substantial time allocation to practice in the field provides scope for trainees to gain supervised practice in direct work with children (0–19 years) with a wide range of abilities and disabilities. Moreover, it ensures that trainees work in a variety of school and community settings and complement their direct work with children with experience of using consultative, advisory, research and training modes within these settings.

DESCRIPTION OF SERVICES

Having looked at the history of the profession and the training of its members, this section gives an overview of what LEA services now look like.

What do educational psychologists do?

Our clients are children and young people aged from 0–19 years, particularly those whose development, learning or behaviour are a cause of significant concern to parents, teachers, other professionals with responsibility for them, or to the young people themselves. . . .

The mission of the Service is to have a positive impact on the quality of clients' social and educational experiences. . . .

Service users are likely to be teachers and schools, the LEA, parents and children and other professionals. (Principal, West Midlands Educational Psychology Service, Regional Professional Development Review Meeting, University of Birmingham, 1991)

Such a view of the key *raison d'être* of an LEA psychological service is unlikely to arouse controversy within the profession, although there are individual and regional differences in emphasis. The nature of the work undertaken by educational psychologists usually falls into one of three categories:

- casework;
- in-service and advisory work;
- research and development projects.

These three functions are complementary mechanisms through which educational psychologists seek to improve children's social and educational experiences. However, as explained earlier, LEAs and teachers often have a narrower view of the role and utility of educational psychology services. LEAs concerned to fulfil their statutory responsibility laid down in the 1981 and 1993 Education Acts, to identify, assess and make appropriate provision for pupils' special needs, typically emphasize the educational psychologists' role in the assessment process. Nevertheless, surveys implemented in a number of LEAs demonstrate that headteachers value the preventive, developmental work undertaken by educational psychologists, except at times of austerity, when emergency casework becomes the top priority.

Typically, educational psychologists' work is directed toward assessing or researching the child-focused problems referred to them by teachers, parents, LEA officers and professionals from health and social services departments. Educational psychologists aim to apply psychologically based knowledge and skills to illuminate the nature of those difficulties and to provide information, advice or direct action leading to their resolution and/or effective management. The majority of problems referred to educational psychologists relate to concerns about the performance and development of individual children and come from two major sources:

- teachers requesting psychological assessment of children's school-based social and learning difficulties;
- the LEA, in fulfilling the responsibility conferred upon it by the 1981 and 1993 Education Acts. Educational psychologists advise LEAs on the nature and degree of children's difficulties and the type of provision that would effectively accommodate their assessed needs.

As noted earlier, work from these two sources leads to an emphasis on casework. Educational psychologists usually seek to balance such casework with advisory work and in-service training. The aim is to pass on relevant psychologically based skills to parents and to professional groups working with children. This work is seen by educational psychologists as an important adjunct to casework. They believe that a wide range of applications of psychology in settings such as families, schools and children's homes, appropriately implemented by direct contact workers such as teachers, parents and carers, can exert a significant positive influence on children's development.

Kerr and Casteel (1988) note the enthusiasm of many educational psychologists for developing their work beyond the traditional 'special needs', child-focused aspects of their role, and HMI (DES, 1990) reports that educational psychologists are legitimately engaged in a wide range of activities as part of their contribution to the work of the LEA. In the area of in-service training examples are noted such as counselling support teachers concerned with emotional and behavioural difficulties, training and supporting pre-school Portage workers, organizing stress management workshops and counselling for teachers.

HMI also comments that in addition to the advisory work conducted with parents and LEA employees (for example teachers and parents), educational psychologists

regularly provide advice to a wide range of professionals working outside the LEA, including medical consultants, physiotherapists, speech and language therapists and social workers, and are frequently expected by LEAs to facilitate professional links with other services. This provides educational psychologists with a unique and valuable overview of the field of disability. (DES, 1990)

As stated earlier, most of the work undertaken by educational psychologists occurs within the LEA. However, in several authorities educational psychologists provide a service to social services departments to:

- give advice to field and residential social workers and service managers;
- prepare reports for the court in cases of contested residence or parental access, cases where children are victims of abuse, or where children and young people have committed offences;
- offer training and advisory services along similar lines to those described for working within the education service.

Finally, educational psychologists also seek to fulfil a research and development role within LEAs, schools, colleges and children's homes. Research and evaluation techniques can clarify not only patterns of need within systems and organizations, but also aspects of current practice which are effective in meeting those needs. Areas and directions which are most likely to enhance practice are highlighted and targeted for future intervention.

There is a major conflict for many psychological services: that of discharging their (only) statutory requirement (to assess, and provide advice to LEAs about the special educational needs of children referred under the 1981 Education Act), whilst complementing this necessary but limiting aspect of work with the wider professional remit of the service.

THE ORGANIZATION OF EDUCATIONAL PSYCHOLOGY SERVICES

There is typically one educational psychology service in each LEA, managed by a principal educational psychologist (PEP) who is professionally accountable to a senior education officer. Services vary considerably in size and composition: some include other professional groups such as social workers and advisory teachers, whilst others comprise exclusively educational psychologists. Additionally there may be posts for senior psychologists either to manage generic, geographically based teams of main-grade EPs, or to develop professional specialisms relating to particular age groups and/or areas of work, such as early years, post-16, child protection, juvenile justice, disruption in schools, bullying, family psychology and accommodating children with exceptional needs within the mainstream setting.

In some LEAs the domain of the psychological service is not restricted to education. For example, it is not uncommon for educational psychologists to hold contractual obligations to the social services department to assist in child-focused work, particularly in the areas of child protection and juvenile justice.

Access to educational psychology services

Psychological services exist to help children with difficulties, by:

- direct work with children;
- providing advice, training or other forms of support to their carers or educators;
- contributing to the development of the systems created to care for or educate them.

There is increasing support for the view that it is more productive to refer tasks, issues or problems, rather than individual children, to psychological services. For example, schools may refer problems of low staff morale, poor reading standards, or discipline problems with a particular class. In some cases the problem will be seen to relate to the development of individual pupils, where parents or teachers have significant concerns about aspects of children's behaviour or academic progress. Such children will be referred so that their particular educational needs can be assessed.

Many (but not all) services make regular time allocations to schools, institutions and organizations which cater for children (e.g. local authority children's homes, day nurseries, hospital-based pre-school child assessment units, colleges of further education). The educational psychologist's role involves identifying the priority needs of that establishment through consultation and then negotiating which needs can be addressed by the psychological service within an agreed period of time. Towards the end of this period progress is reviewed, needs reassessed, priorities redefined, and targets identified for the future.

The system of allocating time to particular tasks and establishments is designed to ensure that psychologists' time is directed towards priority needs on an equitable basis. Such arrangements are not intended to create a protective barrier to insulate psychologists from the depth of unmet needs which may exist in the communities they serve, nor are they designed to make psychologists inaccessible to concerned parents or children.

All parents (including those whose children are privately educated) have the right to contact psychological services, either directly or via the child's school or general practitioner. How services respond to such parental referrals depends on local circumstances, and in particular the competing demands on psychologists' time.

The one certainty is that referrals cannot be accepted without the consent of children's parents or legal guardians. An exception to this rule exists in the rare cases when LEAs choose to proceed with an assessment of a child's educational needs under the 1981 Education Act despite parental opposition. Even in these circumstances, educational psychologists will usually contact the parent(s) and attempt to build a positive working relationship in the best interests of the child. A further exception lies in cases where educational psychologists may be required by the courts to work with and provide advice or evidence about children, without parental involvement.

Self-referrals initiated by children and young people themselves are uncommon. It is relatively rare for such referrals to be accepted without parental knowledge and support. In practice most self-referrals are mediated by a familiar adult such as a parent, teacher or social worker, whom the child approaches in the first instance.

Interdisciplinary collaboration

Psychological services rarely, if ever, work in isolation. Whether or not arrangements and structures exist for formal collaborative work, all services are aware of the local network of related support services and strive to build positive relationships so that their combined resources can be harnessed to meet children's needs.

In the majority of LEAs interdisciplinary liaison is very effective in identifying and assessing pre-school children with special educational needs. The 1981 Education Act requires district health authorities and social services departments to notify LEAs of children under 5 whom they have identified as having a disability or developmental delay which may lead to their having special educational needs when they reach school age.

Usually educational psychologists, other representatives from the education service, health visitors, community medical officers, paediatricians, other health professionals and representatives from the Social Services Department meet routinely to review the progress of all identified pre-school children to plan for the future. Often multidisciplinary assessments and interventions are coordinated within a Health-Authority-based pre-school assessment unit. Educational psychologists typically play a major role, not only in their contribution to the assessment process, but also in supporting the child's transition from pre-school settings to school.

Whilst the 1981 Act requires the multidisciplinary assessment of school-aged children, this process is often conducted in parallel rather than by active collaboration of various agencies (Goacher et al., 1988). Educational psychologists almost invariably work closely with teachers but it would not be unusual for them to conduct assessments without directly contacting the relevant medical officer, for example.

The 1989 Children Act and the 1991 NHS and Community Care Act lend further weight to the principle of inter-agency collaboration in child-focused work and have prompted the further developments of EPs' active liaison with other agencies.

HMI (DES, 1990) felt that overall there is a picture of positive, if variable, task-focused liaison and collaboration with other agencies:

> Principal psychologists generally reported good working relationships with the medical and para-medical professions. Less regular contact was made with SSDs but when this occurred relationships were considered to be very good. Very little contact was made with the probation services. Within the LEA, sound working relationships are frequently encountered with special needs support and advisory teachers, although it is important that respective roles are clarified so that duplication of effort is avoided. Links with the Education Welfare Officer (EWO) service were considered to be important in most authorities. . . . Some psychologists worked with specialist careers officers but the contact was not frequent. Psychologists' involvement with voluntary bodies was varied. (DES, 1990, para. 34)

ASSESSMENT AND INTERVENTION: THEORETICAL AND METHODOLOGICAL CONSIDERATIONS

This chapter has described what educational psychologists do, why they do it and the theoretical background to their work. It now turns to a review of the different theoretical approaches that shape the work of educational psychologists.

Environmental explanations of behaviour

Previous sections of this chapter have emphasized educational psychologists' commitment to research, advisory work, in-service training and organizational developments, in addition to their assessment and intervention work with individually referred children. This commitment reflects the view that no matter what type or degree of disability, no matter what disadvantaging circumstances children experience, the quality of care and instruction they subsequently receive can make a considerable difference to their social, emotional and cognitive development (see Bee, 1989; Shaffer, 1989 for summaries of current understandings of the relative weightings of nature vs. nurture in shaping children's social, emotional and intellectual characteristics). A guiding principle for many educational psychologists is that the most productive applications of psychology in work with children lie in adapting key elements of their environment such as expectations, relationships, demands, support and feedback to enhance their developmental progress. Whilst this principle relates to individual casework, it is clearly more cost-effective to make environmental adaptations (such as changes in classroom organization, assessment arrangements and curricular initiatives) which potentially benefit many children.

Increasingly, educational psychologists have stressed that problems should be seen in terms of the context in which they occur and in relation to the interactions taking place between individuals, systems and organizations. In this contextually orientated work theoretical models such as applied behavioural analysis (see for example Leach and Raybould, 1977 or Bull and Solity 1987) have considerable practical utility to educational psychologists.

Equally relevant are the variously termed 'ecological' (Thomas, 1992) and 'ecosystemic' approaches (Upton and Cooper, 1990) which seek explanations of 'dysfunction' in the interactions of the various systems in which individuals are required to operate (for example family, classroom, school, peer group) rather than only in terms of within-child variables.

Utilizing an action research paradigm

Environmental explanations of behaviour have lent themselves to assessment and intervention approaches based on a problem-solving framework. The psychologist hypothesizes about the nature of children's difficulties, intervenes to overcome problems and evaluates outcomes. One example of problem solving is the action research paradigm.

Action research has been described as planned intervention leading to change. Its major elements include:

- an explicit statement of the experimental intervention (e.g. a language programme, a course of individual counselling, a study skills package, an individual reading and spelling programme);
- an explicit statement of the goals of the intervention (e.g. to improve oral English comprehension skills in a group of pupils);
- the determination of whether or not these goals were achieved (Goldman, 1978).

Action research allows for a flexible programme design within which data gathered through the process of monitoring the earlier phases of intervention have a formative value in fine-tuning future interventions. It is closely allied to the problem-solving paradigms which are again applicable to a wide range of problems from the individual to the organizational level. Sigston (1992) notes that although problem-solving frameworks vary in details and sophistication they all comprise three basic stages:

- *Clarifying* the referred problem by selectively gathering data, to test and refine initial hypotheses.
- *Intervening* through constructing and implementing an action plan informed by an understanding of the problem achieved during the previous stage.
- *Evaluating* intervention outcomes so that the fit between problem and solution can be checked out, the intervention revised and the problem reformulated in the light of new data.

Service users typically want action and change rather than explanations of unchanging problems. The dynamic, interventionist practice models briefly outlined above have considerable pragmatic appeal to practising educational psychologists. Moreover, they are flexible and can accommodate the necessarily eclectic nature of educational psychologists' work.

Process skills in collaborative and consultative work

According to Reason (1988), a collaborative approach to action research breaks down existing distinctions between researchers and subjects. Both work together to negotiate the details of planned interventions. The approach allows subjects to retain control of research objectives and to share responsibility for research outcomes; it also enables the educational psychologist to become a co-researcher rather than an independent expert.

During the 1970s and 1980s notions of collaborative enquiry became central to all aspects of educational psychologists' work, as both academic and applied psychology have drawn attention to the complexities inherent in any process of change, whether this relates to individuals, groups or organizations. At an ethical and philosophical level, the profession has increasingly sought to empower clients, be they children, parents, teachers or other professionals, by helping them to understand the nature of problems, so that they can assume greater control over available solutions. The process of collaborative research usually involves educational psychologists in probing, eliciting and reviewing clients' phenomenological interpretations of the realities reported by themselves and others.

In common with the action research and problem-solving approaches outlined above, taking account of the theories and subjective realities of clients and adopting the role of collaborative co-researcher to enable clients to find and implement viable, relevant solutions is as applicable to educational psychologists' individual casework as to their wider research, developmental and advisory roles.

Theory into practice

The principles associated with action research can be illustrated in the steps educational psychologists may take in responding to referrals where children are seen to have school-based learning difficulties. During the clarification phase discussion with the referrer aims to establish what information and advice is sought. Thereafter, the intervention is based on an analysis of the skills possessed by children, their own understanding of their difficulties and an analysis of the various contextual variables which may promote children's progress.

In some instances it may be relevant to compare children with their peers along some educational or developmental scale by using norm-referenced tests of ability, attitudes or attainment. In almost every case assessments also evaluate contextual variables such as family dynamics, how parents manage and relate to their children, and how problems relate to the functioning of the school, particularly in relation to curriculum delivery, approaches to classroom management and children's relationships with peers.

Time spent working individually with children constitutes only one component of the assessment process and is placed alongside additional sources of information such as:

- discussion with children's teachers, parents, carers or other professionals;
- direct observation of children in the home, school or nursery setting;
- monitoring children's learning and development over time in the light of the steps taken to overcome their difficulties.

Such interventions are a long way from the one-off assessments that prevailed only a decade or so ago which invariably resulted in a sterile classification of children's difficulties and failed to provide contextually relevant guidelines for meeting children's needs.

THE WAY FORWARD: TOWARDS A PUBLIC SERVICE ORIENTATION

The impact of the 1988 Education Reform Act is far-reaching and is felt at all levels throughout the education system. In this section only aspects of LMS and financial delegation are discussed as they are likely to have the most significant effect on the future deployment of educational psychologists.

It is not clear how educational psychologists will be managed in the future under LMS. This uncertainty is undermining the morale of the profession. Whilst the 1981 Education Act remains in force, LEAs will need to retain at least some educational psychologists centrally to meet the LEAs' responsibilities under the Act. This will be an extremely unattractive proposition to many educational psychologists if it represents the entirety of their responsibilities.

An alternative or complementary arrangement is financial delegation to schools. Under this system that portion of the LEA budget which currently funds its psychological service would be devolved to schools, which would then be in a position to determine whether they spent that devolved sum on the services of educational psychologists or alternative sources of support. Financial delegation has a number of implications for educational psychologists:

- The nature of their relationship with schools may change. Schools as pay-masters may well pay only for a particular type of service and so will be effectively dictating to EPs the nature of their assessments. Psychometrically based assessments may be preferred to the more time-consuming, and potentially more expensive, curriculum-based approaches.
- The role of educational psychologists may become narrower and focus on assessments of individual children rather than in-service training or research.
- There is a risk of conflict between the needs and rights of individual children and the interests of schools as they become more concerned with the needs of the majority than those of the minority, and with projecting a successful image in the financially orientated education market-place.

At present it is not clear how the future will unfold. It is critical that whatever the eventual shape of psychological services in the future and the sources of their funding, accessibility to the real client, the child, must be assured. To delegate budgets to schools clearly ignores the needs of pre-school children, families experiencing non-school-based concerns about their children's development, and many other aspects of educational psychologists' current contribution to community resources as a whole.

Uncertainties about the future of their profession have proved healthy for educational psychologists, denting complacency and prompting a sharply critical review of current practices. Educational psychologists have emerged from this process of critical reappraisal confident in the utility and relevance of their professional psychologically based skills to three core consumer groups:

- organizers of the education service (the officers and members of the LEA or whatever management groups emerge in the future);
- direct consumers of education services (the public, and in particular children and adult learners);
- providers of the education service, who fall into two groups:
  - those working within the education service (schools, colleges, etc.);
  - groups working outside the formal education service who are also concerned with children's development and learning (voluntary organizations, Social Service Department establishments, etc.).

Kerr and Casteel (1988) argue that educational psychologists offer knowledge, skills and experiences that enable these groups to become more effective in solving their own problems. However, in the past educational psychologists have singularly failed to inform consumers in any systematic way about their achievements or even about the services on offer. For example, the conflicting expectations of service delivery by educational psychologists and service users discussed earlier reflect this lack of information. For too long educational psychologists have rehearsed arguments justifying their practice only with one another, and have shared their successes more or less exclusively through conference presentations or academic articles. At last educational psychologists have acknowledged that it is their own responsibility if their customers seem to carry outdated and limiting expectations of their role.

Over the past two years a public service orientation has grown within which educational psychologists have systematically sought to inform customers of the range of services on offer, to ascertain customers' needs and wishes, to offer a high-quality service, to review its outcomes and then to feed back to the customer what has been achieved. Provided that these principles of responsiveness and accountability continue to be developed in practice, and that services resist the temptation to be jacks of all trades and to over-diversify, there are grounds for optimism. The broad spectrum of professional activity envisaged by the reconstructing movement (that is, the application of a wide range of psychological skills and knowledge to the task of supporting children's education and development through casework, balanced by a range of preventive and developmental functions) will continue to characterize educational psychologists' work throughout the 1990s.

REFERENCES

Bee, H. (1989) *The Developing Child*, 5th edition. New York: Harper & Row.

Bull, S. and Solity, J. (1987) *Classroom Management: Principles to Practice*. London: Croom Helm.

DES (1968) *Psychologists in Education* (The Summerfield Report). London: HMSO.

DES (1978) *Special Educational Needs* (The Warnock Report). London: HMSO.

DES (1990) *Educational Psychology Services in England: A Report by Her Majesty's Inspectorate*. London: DES.

Gillham, B. (ed.) (1978) *Reconstructing Educational Psychology*. London: Croom Helm.

Goacher, B., Evans, J., Welton, J. and Weddell, K. (1988) *Policy and Provision for Special Educational Needs: Implementing the 1981 Education Act*. London: Cassell.

Goldman, L. (ed.) (1978) *Research Methods for Counsellors: Practical Approaches in Field Settings*. New York: Wiley.

Kerr, T. and Casteel, V. (1988) The integrated advisory service. In N. Jones and J. Sayer (eds), *Management and the Psychology of Schooling*. Lewes: Falmer Press.

Leach, D.J. and Raybould, E.C. (1977) *Learning and Behavioural Difficulties in School*. London: Open Books.

Reason, P. (ed.) (1988) *Human Inquiry in Action: Developments in New Paradigm Research*. London: Sage.

Shaffer, D. (1989) *Developmental Psychology: Childhood and Adolescence*. 2nd edition. Monterey, CA: Brooks/Cole.

Sigston, A. (1992) Making a difference for children: the educational psychologist as empowerer of problem-solving alliances. In S. Wolfendale, T. Bryans, M. Fox, A. Labram and A. Sigston (eds), *The Profession and Practice of Educational Psychology*. London: Cassell.

Thomas, G. (1992) Ecological interventions. In S. Wolfendale, *et al. ibid.*

Upton, G. and Cooper, P. (1990) An ecosystemic approach to emotional and behavioural difficulties in schools. *Educational Psychology*, Vol. 10, No. 4.

FURTHER READING

The following books are highly recommended to those interested in reading in greater detail about professional educational psychology.

Gillham, B. (ed.) (1978) *Reconstructing Educational Psychology*. London: Croom Helm.

Jones, N. and Frederickson, N. (eds) (1990) *Refocusing Educational Psychology*. Lewes: Falmer Press.

Wolfendale, S., Bryans, T., Fox, M., Labram, A. and Sigston A. (eds) (1992) *The Profession and Practice of Educational Psychology*. London: Cassell.

The journal *Educational Psychology in Practice* provides a useful overview of issues relevant to the professional practice of EPs.

CHAPTER 4

Clinical psychology

Frances Gardner

INTRODUCTION

Clinical psychologists study psychology (often defined as the science of human behaviour, thought and development) at degree level, before studying its clinical applications at postgraduate level. This training is generic, allowing them to work with a range of child and adult psychological problems; but most specialize later and work mainly with a specific client group, such as people with learning disabilities, adults or children with emotional and behavioural disorders, or drug misusers.

This chapter explores the role of clinical psychologists through describing and discussing:

- the background to the profession;
- training and organization of the professional practice;
- theories underpinning practice;
- approaches to assessment and intervention;
- future directions.

It begins with issues that are common to the whole profession and later narrows its focus to clinical psychology services for children.

WHAT IS CLINICAL PSYCHOLOGY?

Clinical psychology is the application of psychological theory and research to helping people with emotional, behavioural and learning problems. These problems range from severe psychiatric disorders such as schizophrenia or anorexia nervosa to milder but nevertheless very distressing problems such as pre-school behaviour difficulties, marital discord or minor depression. Clinical psychologists also help people to cope with chronic medical or disabling conditions, such as diabetes, asthma or spinal injury. Most clinical psychologists are employed by the National Health Service (NHS).

Clinical psychologists frequently work in the places where their clients' problems occur such as in their own homes, residential homes for the elderly or the mentally ill, or schools and day nurseries. The main activities of clinical psychologists involve assessing clients' problems, intervening to help clients solve their problems, and evaluating the effects of interventions. Many clinicians also carry out research into the efficacy of particular types of intervention, and the assessment and intervention techniques used by clinical psychologists rely heavily on basic and applied research in psychology.

Apart from direct work with clients and their carers, clinical psychologists also advise and teach other professionals about how to use psychological techniques to help their clients. So health visitors may be trained to help parents manage their children's sleeping difficulties, and nursery staff may be helped with designing structured teaching programmes for children with learning difficulties. It is an important part of the clinical psychologist's role to disseminate applications of psychology to those who spend most time with clients, and who are therefore in a particularly good position to help them. Psychological techniques may be used in this way to prevent problems occurring in the first place, as well as to deal with them once they have arisen.

The role of psychologists (both clinical and educational) and psychiatrists is often confused, and although there is overlap in the functions of clinical psychologists and psychiatrists there are important differences in their skills. The unique contribution of clinical psychologists is the specialized knowledge they bring of psychological theory, research, assessment and measurement. These help inform, develop and evaluate the therapies they use. Differences between these professions are also explored in Chapters 2 and 5.

DEVELOPMENT OF THE PROFESSION

There has been a major change in the work clinical psychologists have done over the last fifty years. In the early days of the NHS, clinical psychologists worked as laboratory scientists, carrying out psychological tests to aid psychiatrists in the assessment of mental illnesses and handicaps. In the late 1950s and 1960s there were major developments in psychological research which led to clinical psychologists becoming much more involved in therapy. First, new ways were discovered of teaching people with severe learning difficulties using structured behavioural techniques (Clarke and Clarke, 1974). This contributed to a radical shift in social attitudes, emphasizing the rights and capabilities of people with learning difficulties. A central part of this shift was the idea that people should learn the skills for independent living in the community, rather than live in large impersonal mental handicap hospitals.

In the late 1960s, techniques were developed for helping parents and teachers to manage children's behaviour problems (Patterson, 1969). At the same time, research was carried out into effective ways of reducing fear and anxiety states using behaviour therapies. Clinical psychologists have been at the forefront of research and applications of these techniques with three major client groups: adult mental health, child mental health and mental handicap (now termed 'learning disabilities'). Compared with the behind-the-scene testers of the 1950s all this has created a very different role for the profession since the 1970s.

The Trethowan Report by the DHSS (1977) strengthened this new role by recognizing the independent professional status of clinical psychologists. It recommended that they should broaden their work beyond the three traditional client groups. Clinical psychologists now work in newer areas such as primary care (with general practitioners), the elderly, neurology, general medicine and surgery, physical and sensory handicap, drug abuse and forensic services. Instead of being directed by psychiatrists they now work collaboratively with a range of medical and other professionals.

TRAINING AND ORGANIZATION OF CLINICAL PSYCHOLOGISTS

Clinical psychologists are required to have a good honours degree in psychology, followed by a two- or three-year postgraduate clinical training. This is usually university based, leading to a master's degree, though some are trained in NHS-based schemes which last three years and lead to a professional diploma examined by the British Psychological Society (BPS). The BPS is also responsible for accrediting all university-based training.

Training, by whichever route, consists of academic study, long periods of supervised clinical practice in a range of settings, and an applied research project. In total, qualification takes a mininum of five to seven years to complete, but most clinical psychologists take even longer to train as they are encouraged to undertake doctoral research, or work as nursing, teaching or psychological assistants prior to starting a training course. After training, clinical psychologists register under the Royal Charter of the BPS and assume the title of Chartered Clinical Psychologist. This register is available to members of the public who may wish to check the credentials of a clinical psychologist. It also ensures access to a professional complaints and disciplinary procedure for members of the public, though there is usually also a procedure via the clinical psychologist's employing organization.

After training, a few clinical psychologists work in social services, and in the voluntary, industrial and private health sectors. However, most work in the NHS, and since access to clinical psychologists in relation to educational services is usually via the NHS the chapter concentrates on this sector.

Before the 1991 NHS reforms clinical psychologists were organized into health authority departments of psychology. Each department had a district head and a number of heads of different specialities so that psychologists were employed by, and accountable to, district health authorities. The aim of the psychology service was to service the health needs of the local population as well as the patients referred to a given hospital. Thus psychology departments had some autonomy in planning services and in deciding the setting in which they could be of most use. The NHS reforms would appear to reduce the autonomy of

Table 4.1 Childhood problems often referred to clinical psychologists

aggression	separation anxiety
fighting	obsessions
tantrums	coping with epilepsy
non-compliance	fears, phobias and worries
stealing	neurological problems, e.g. head injury
poor peer relations	poor school progress
delinquency	school refusal
overactivity	bullying
poor concentration	delayed language/development
bedwetting and soiling	autism
sleeping problems	bereavement
eating problems	distress following trauma
nervous habits	child abuse
depression, misery	learning disabilities
problems coping with	clumsiness
illness/disability, e.g. teasing,	
misery, anxiety and pain around	
medical procedures, preparation for	
surgery	

psychology departments by making them providers. In common with other professional groups their job is to provide the service for which the purchasing health authority is paying. Another effect of the reforms is that clinical psychologists may be employed by NHS trusts, as a result of some hospitals opting out of health authority control. It is not clear what these changes will mean for clinical psychologists, though many will continue to provide the sort of service they offered before.

CLINICAL PSYCHOLOGY SERVICES FOR CHILDREN

Referral

There are approximately 300 clinical psychologists specializing in work with children in the NHS in England. With parental permission, children can be referred to NHS psychology departments by a range of professionals from health, education and social services such as GPs, psychiatrists, paediatricians, health visitors, headteachers, educational psychologists and social workers. Parents can request a referral through their GP or other professional.

Problems referred to clinical psychologists

Most clinical psychologists spend a good deal of their time seeing children with emotional and behavioural problems referred to outpatient clinics. Since the late 1970s they have begun to expand both the settings they work in and the range of problems they deal with. These include more training and preventive work in community settings, as well as work with children who have chronic illnesses in home and hospital contexts. Table 4.1 lists some of the childhood problems dealt with by clinical psychologists.

Settings

In the past most clinical psychologists worked as part of hospital-based child psychiatric teams (see Chapter 5). Such teams were normally led by a consultant child psychiatrist, and comprised social workers, clinical psychologists and sometimes other health professionals. Children with a range of emotional and behavioural problems, and their families, were seen in hospital outpatient clinics for assessment by members of the team, before receiving regular therapy sessions. But the role of the clinical psychologist is changing. Although some still spend part of their time working in these hospital-based teams, they have recently begun to develop a wider community-based role. This has occurred for several reasons.

It makes sense to work with children and their carers in their own homes, nurseries and schools, rather than in the relatively artificial environment of the clinic. For example, by observing families at home, as well as asking parents and children about their perception of the problem, it is possible to develop a richer understanding of the many factors which influence children's problem behaviour. It allows psychologists to see how family members deal with difficult behaviour, to see how they interact on a normal day, and to see what resources are available for intervention, such as the amount of space and toys. Equally important, home visiting allows psychologists to support parents directly in carrying out difficult interventions, and to monitor their success. This is something that in a clinic can be done only 'second-hand' from parental reports. Any observations of parent–child interactions made in the clinic may not be representative of what happens at home.

Many families, especially those most in need, may find it difficult to attend clinics regularly, and so appreciate interventions being offered in their own homes, or in the child's school. Many young children at risk attend social services family centres and nurseries, or are in care, and it makes good sense to help parents or staff to work with children in these settings.

Passing on skills to staff such as nurses and teachers is an efficient use of scarce time. This may best be carried out by a psychologist who is familiar with the school or nursery, rather than one who works in the clinic. This kind of work is often seen as preventive, in that psychological skills are passed on which may benefit the way staff work with all the children in their care. This is a rather different approach to that of simply dealing reactively with problems as they occur and has potential for helping greater numbers of children than is possible with the more traditional model of designing individual programmes for each referred child. These changes parallel those taking place in the role of educational psychologists which are discussed in Chapter 3.

The change in role of clinical psychologists (see Table 4.2) is due in part to an increased awareness of the way psychological factors influence physical illness. Many clinical psychologists now work in hospital paediatric services, in both community and ward settings, using specific psychological techniques to help children with chronic illness or disability to control their anxiety and pain, to teach them to manage their own illness (e.g. asthma and diabetes), to prepare them for surgery, to help their families to manage the special care of the child and to counsel staff and parents about dying and bereavement.

Table 4.2 **Settings in which child clinical psychologists work and examples of their work**

Setting	Example
(a) Health	
(i) Community	Liaison/consultation with health visitors
Child welfare clinics	Parents' groups for behavioural, sleeping,
Health centres	feeding problems of under-5s
GP practices	
(ii) Hospital	
Antenatal clinics	Counselling of mothers with suspected handicapped child
	Counselling of adolescents deciding about termination of pregnancy
Intensive care neonatal units	Counselling for staff and parents
Paediatric assessment clinics	Assessment and remediation of development delays
Paediatric hospital wards	Preparation of parents/children for hospitalization
	Counselling of parents/staff dealing with terminally ill children
Casualty wards	Crisis counselling for adolescents who have taken overdoses
Psychiatric inpatient and outpatient units	Assessment and treatment with families of children showing emotional and behavioural problems
	Consultation/training of psychiatric child care staff (in psychological procedures)
(b) Social services	
(i) Local authority nurseries	Advice to nursery nurses concerning problems of child abuse
	Assessment of development delays
(ii) Community homes	Consultation with staff concerning management of difficult behaviour problems
	Counselling foster parents
(c) Voluntary organizations	Drop-in clinics for adolescents with drug-taking or alcohol problems (e.g. Samaritans, Adoption Societies, Brook Advisory Centres, Grapevine, etc.)

From Fielding (1987)

Paediatric assessment teams

Many clinical and educational psychologists (see Chapter 3) work in paediatric assessment teams. The role of these teams is to assess and help children, especially those of pre-school age, with a range of physical, developmental and learning difficulties. This requires the carefully coordinated efforts of a team consisting of speech and language therapist, physiotherapist, paediatrician and psychologist. Frequently there are also social workers, specialist teachers and occupational therapists in the team. Clinical psychologists are involved in assessing children's developmental progress and learning needs, counselling parents about the implications of their children's disability, and advising parents and professionals about managing behavioural and emotional difficulties. Giving such advice is a particularly important part of the psychologist's work because children with developmental and educational difficulties are more likely to have concomitant behavioural problems (Rutter *et al.*, 1970; Richman *et al.*, 1982). Clinical psychologists often play a strong part in team management and policy making; for example, developing new ways of involving parents in the way services are run, and in the help given to children.

Portage

Along with home teachers, members of the paediatric assessment team frequently form a 'Portage'-style home teaching service (Sturmey and Crisp, 1986). Portage, named after a town in Wisconsin, consists of a package of teaching materials, which the home visitor uses to design an individual teaching programme for child and parent. The aim of the system is to involve parents of pre-school children with developmental difficulties in the education of their children. Normally the Portage team is managed by an educational or clinical psychologist.

Many of the children who attend paediatric assessment centres may turn out to have special educational needs when they reach school age. Health service professionals have a statutory duty under the 1981 Education Act to inform an LEA of any children they believe to be likely to have special educational needs. If parents wish, children can then be assessed early by the LEA with the help of the paediatric assessment team. This may facilitate earlier entry into school, with special help, or allow arrangements such as mainstream support to be in place when children reach school age. The clinical psychologist or other members of the team may be involved in helping support children when they first start school, using their knowledge of children's needs.

Working with school-aged children with special educational needs requires collaboration with educational psychologists. By planning their work jointly, and keeping each other closely informed, clinical and educational psychologists can ensure that their work is complementary rather than overlapping.

Finally, some clinical psychologists are involved in developing preventive approaches to health care. For example, this has involved working with GPs to target high-risk groups in primary health care settings. Some clinical psychologists have been involved in health education interventions in schools which aim to prevent drug misuse and enhance child protection through social skills training (e.g. Health Education Authority, 1989).

THEORETICAL MODELS UNDERLYING CLINICAL PSYCHOLOGY INTERVENTIONS

The main model guiding assessment, intervention and research in clinical child psychology is social learning theory (Bandura, 1977; Herbert, 1991; Patterson, 1982). Some clinical psychologists incorporate other models such as psychodynamic and family systems theory, or use a mixture of approaches, depending on the needs of the child and family. After briefly describing the latter two models, the sections on assessment and intervention concentrate on social learning theory approaches, as these are most commonly used and are relatively accessible to other professionals. Interventions are strongly based on:

- research about normal child development and behaviour;
- systematic research into their effectiveness in changing children's behaviour (Yule, 1983; Kazdin, 1988; Watts, 1990).

Family systems approaches

Some clinical psychologists use a family systems approach to solving problems. An important assumption behind this approach is that each family member is affected by the behaviour and emotions of other members, in a reciprocal system of influence. Thus, discord in the marital couple would be assumed to affect other parts of the system, such as the behaviour of individual children, the mood of the parents, and the functioning of the whole family as a unit. Behavioural and emotional difficulties displayed by children are normally defined as problems in the whole family system, involving every member. Another important assumption is that the family is dynamic and constantly changing, as a function of the stage of its life cycle. Significant events such as the birth of a child, the onset of adolescence, or children leaving home are seen as stressful phases in this life cycle which require the family to adapt by changing roles and responsibilities.

Both assessment and intervention take place in the clinic, through a family interview with all members present. Assessment may involve the therapist directly observing family communication patterns through a one-way screen. Inferences are made about the patterns of family roles, conflicts and relationships which may be maintaining the child's apparent problem. Intervention aims to alter patterns of communication, decision making and problem solving through modelling and directives by the therapist. These may be carried out in the clinic and during homework tasks which the family work on.

Psychodynamic approaches

More rarely, clinical psychologists use psychodynamic approaches derived from Freudian and neo-Freudian theories. These usually involve individual clinic-based work with children, often through the medium of play. This has the drawback of involving others, such as parents, siblings and teachers, to a much lesser extent than other therapies. Traditional psychodynamic psychotherapy is a long-term enterprise, often taking one or more years of at least weekly sessions, and in this form is unsuited to the limited resources of the NHS. Both psycho-dynamic and family systems approaches also suffer from having little controlled research on their efficacy. Moreover it may be difficult for the therapist to assess whether changes in communication and behaviour achieved in the clinic generalize to changes in child or family behaviour at home.

Social learning theory approaches

Sometimes social learning theory approaches in psychology are termed 'cognitive-behavioural' because they encompass learning and problem solving through helping children to change both their behaviour and their thinking patterns (Hughes, 1988). The major assumptions underlying this approach are as follows:

- Much behaviour is learned through children's interactions with the social environment.
- Behaviour and learning are influenced by social contexts.
- Both normal and 'problem' behaviour are learned through similar mechanisms.
- As well as the social environment shaping the child's behaviour, children are also seen as active in influencing their own behaviour and that of others.
- Children's behaviour results from a complex mixture of current and past influences.
- Social learning takes place within a developmental context.

These assumptions are now briefly considered.

To a considerable extent children's behaviour is learned through their interactions with the social environment, including those in the family, peer group, classroom and neighbourhood. There are a number of mechanisms through which this social learning can take place, including observing others, experiencing or anticipating the consequences of one's actions (reinforcement), and through being taught rules, principles and strategies which guide social behaviour (induction) (Herbert, 1991).

Behaviour and learning are influenced by social contexts, so it is important for professionals to assess, understand and intervene in the appropriate context. Psychologists emphasize observing children's behaviour and that of significant others in the home, nursery, classroom or playground, in order to formulate hypotheses about the influences on their behaviour. Behaviour is assumed to be at least partly situation specific: we would not necessarily expect children's behaviour, or reactions of a parent in the clinic, to be the same as those at home. Similarly, if children are taught a new skill with a therapist to help overcome a problem, we would not necessarily expect this to generalize to complex real-life situations. For example, shy children may be taught social skills in small groups in order to help them join in games with peers but it should not be assumed that these skills transfer naturally to other contexts without the need for further planning and practice.

Both normal and 'problem' behaviour are learned through similar mechanisms. Problem behaviour is seen as quantitatively, rather than qualitatively, different from normal. For example, most 5-year-olds have tantrums, and show aggression and defiance from time to time. Only when these normal behaviours are excessively frequent, or distressing to others, or interfere markedly with children's schooling would they begin to be seen as a problem.

As well as the social environment shaping the child's behaviour, children are seen as active in influencing their own behaviour and that of others. Individual characteristics, such as temperament, abilities, thinking styles, self-esteem, motivation and physical health, can influence how children behave in a given situation, and will influence the reactions elicited from others. This is especially important when assessing factors which contribute to problem behaviour. The young child is not seen as a *tabula rasa* (blank slate) upon which parental attitudes and behaviour are written. Rather, parental behaviour towards children is led at least partly by the child's temperament, such as how noisy and wilful they are in the early months. This may then influence parental disciplinary practices and, in turn, children's behaviour, in a circular pattern which Bandura (1977) terms 'reciprocal determinism'.

Children's behaviour results from a complex mixture of current and past influences, and it is important that professionals do not jump to the simple conclusion that parents' behaviour is to blame, since this is rarely the whole story, and is potentially unhelpful to already distressed parents. In part, the aim of intervention is to help parents to understand how problems arise and that although they are in a strong position to help children to change, this does not mean that they are to blame for the problems. The approach emphasizes that individual differences between children are of great importance, and directly influence the behaviour of adults. Of course parental effects on children are also powerful, but it is important to recognize that these are not the only source of influence on children's behaviour.

Social learning clearly takes place within a developmental context. Society places very different expectations on children of different ages, and children's capacity for thinking, reasoning and problem solving about their own behaviour changes a great deal with age. This has implications for psychologists and others who deal with children's behavioural and emotional problems. First, assessing the significance of problems relies on knowing what is normal at different ages. Frequent bedwetting and tantrums at the age of 2 are not seen as unusual, whereas at 7 they would cause much greater concern. Secondly, when considering which strategies to use to help children overcome problems, the clinical psychologist takes into account children's verbal ability and general maturity in deciding to what extent they will involve children in monitoring and helping to change their own behaviour. With younger children, interventions may be managed by parents and therapists, with children largely 'passengers' in the process.

The rapid development of children means that many problems may resolve themselves without any professional involvement. This has helped to create a common myth, frequently communicated to worried parents, that pre-school children will simply grow out of behaviour problems. In fact, careful epidemiological studies, such as that of Richman *et al.* (1982), have shown that this is not the case, as over half the children in their sample who had behaviour problems at the age of 3 and 4 were still showing similar problems at the age of 8. Findings from large-scale research studies have indicated which problems are more likely to persist and which are transient.

ASSESSMENT AND INTERVENTION

After receiving a referral from a doctor, parent or other professional, clinical psychologists normally contact the child's parents and offer them, their child or the whole family an appointment. This often takes place in the clinical psychologist's office, though many clinical psychologists prefer to start with a home visit, especially if the problem is one that manifests itself mainly in the home. Sometimes children are seen initially with other professionals in a school, nursery or clinic, but only with the parents' full permission. Preferably parents should be present so that collaboration with the family is facilitated from the start.

Assessment

Psychological assessment has moved on a long way from the early days of the profession when formal testing in the clinic was the main technique available. Assessment now involves a range of methods, for example direct observation in home and school, parent and child interviews, completion of formal rating scales and sometimes formal testing, and often takes place in several settings. It follows from a social learning viewpoint that the aims of assessment are to establish:

- an understanding of children's behaviour in its natural settings, including possible triggers and consequences of behaviour;
- how behaviour is currently managed;
- baseline measures for children's behaviour, for example frequency and duration;
- a consensus about the exact nature of the problem, about what are the most important things to change and the degree of improvement aimed for;
- a detailed history of the presenting problem from parent interviews and their views on the current factors influencing their child's behaviour;
- the child's perspective on the problem;
- the resources, skills and social supports available to children and families to help them to combat problems.

The information gathered from the various informants and techniques is then put together into a *formulation* of the problem, which is effectively a set of hypotheses about the nature of the problem and the factors influencing the way it is caused and maintained.

Intervention

Intervention follows logically from a formulation of the problem and aims to change the salient causal factors. In so doing it constitutes a test of the validity of the formulation. The clinical psychologist aims to be flexible, being prepared to adjust the formulation and hence the intervention if later assessments show the problem is not improving as expected.

It is difficult to generalize about the form clinical psychology interventions take, as this depends very much on the circumstances of the case, the preferences of the family and the resources available to the psychologist. However, it will be based on theoretical principles, which for many clinical psychologists are social learning theory, and on research evidence about the kind of intervention that is most likely to be effective (Kazdin, 1988; Watts, 1990; Herbert, 1991). Some factors that appear to be clinically important are now discussed.

Negotiation

It is important that interventions are negotiated with, rather than imposed upon, families and children. Negotiation has to be genuine and carried out sensitively, as it is all too easy to gain the agreement of parents to carry out an intervention without gaining their true commitment. This is often the result of the psychologist's not spending enough time coming to an understanding of the family's view of problems and of the resources available to carry out a successful intervention. The same applies to interventions with staff in other settings.

The effectiveness of parents

It is highly likely that for home-based problems, parents will be asked to carry out the intervention, especially with pre-adolescent children, and that this will involve some kind of 'homework' tasks, outside the sessions with the clinical psychologist. This might involve recording or keeping a diary of their own and their children's behaviour, as well as carrying out a management plan as agreed (and often practised) in the sessions. At least some, if not all, of the sessions are likely to take place in the home, especially if parents are involved.

Common problems experienced at home include defiance, aggression to parents and siblings, and swearing and shouting to a level where parents feel stressed and that they have lost control of their children. Assessment shows what the main problems are and how parents currently handle them. Areas where parental management skills frequently need to be improved include:

- setting clearer rules for children;
- monitoring their behaviour more closely (Patterson, 1982);
- appreciating and joining in children's play and other activities (Gardner, 1987);
- responding more consistently to children's difficult behaviour, providing mild sanctions where necessary.

Clinical psychologists negotiate with parents about which skills are appropriate and which ones need to be changed. Parents then work on practising these in the home as problems arise.

Parents are expected to carry on this work for at least a part of each day, in between the psychologist's visits. Both parents' records and the psychologist's observations are used to monitor the success of interventions. A number of research studies have demonstrated the positive effects on children's behaviour of teaching these kinds of management skills to parents (Forehand and McMahon, 1981; Horne and Sayger, 1990; Patterson, 1982). Assessment may also show that the parents' difficulties are compounded by other problems such as depression or marital discord and psychologists may have to tackle these as well if a child management programme is to be effective.

The time scale of interventions

The time scale of interventions also varies a great deal. One or two sessions of basic advice may be offered. For more formal interventions, half a dozen or more sessions, at weekly or fortnightly intervals, may take place. These often need to be followed up and supported at less frequent intervals, beyond the inital intensive period, as complex and chronic behavioural problems can be difficult to resolve, especially in families who suffer from many different stresses (Patterson, 1982).

Interventions in organizations and with groups

So far, interventions have been discussed in relation to individual children and families. Another level of the clinical psychologist's work involves working to change the way that organizations or specific groups operate to help prevent or solve problems. For example, the clinical psychologist may work with ward staff to help introduce new routines for preparing children for surgery, based on methods shown to be most effective from research. The advantages of working with those directly involved with children are that:

- it is an efficient use of psychologists' limited time;
- staff have more time than clinical psychologists to spend with children;
- staff are able to apply new skills and knowledge to a potentially wider population than children referred to clinical psychologists;
- intervening in organizations and groups can help to prevent problems occurring in the future.

FUTURE DIRECTIONS AND CONCLUSIONS

This chapter has described some of the ways in which clinical psychologists work with children and their families, and the assumptions underlying their practice. It has focused on newer ways of working, with the emphasis on preventive work, through providing training and consultation to those who have most contact with children. Another important issue is that of providing a service which is more responsive to clients, for example by recognizing the individuality of family needs and values and negotiating interventions which take these into account. This is especially important when there are cultural and class differences between professionals and clients.

Currently there is a great deal of debate about the future directions the profession should take. A recent report commissioned by the Department of Health and carried out by independent consultants (MAS, 1989) recommended greater expansion of the clinical psychologist's role into areas of preventive and general medicine, and primary health care, which could be achieved through increases in the number of posts and training posts for clinical psychologists. The report affirmed the importance of psychologists' unique skills in applying psychological theory, assessment and research to health care delivery at the level of service management, staff consultation and the individual client. Working at all these levels would appear to provide the best chance of helping the greatest numbers of children, given the scarce resources available.

REFERENCES

Bandura, A. (1977) *Social Learning Theory*. Englewood Cliffs, NJ: Prentice-Hall.

Clarke, A. and Clarke, A. (1974) *Mental Deficiency: The Changing Outlook*. 3rd edition. London: Methuen.

DHSS (1977) *The Role of Psychologists in the Health Services* (the Trethowan Report). London: HMSO.

Fielding, D. (1987) Working with children and young people. In J. Marzillier and J. Hall (eds), *What Is Clinical Psychology?* Oxford: Oxford University Press.

Forehand, R. and McMahon, R. (1981) *Helping the Noncompliant Child*. New York: Guilford.

Gardner, F.E.M. (1987) Positive interaction between mothers and children with conduct problems: is there training for harmony as well as fighting? *Journal of Abnormal Child Psychology*, Vol. 15: 283–93.

Health Education Authority (1989) *Health for Life*. Walton-on-Thames: Nelson.

Herbert, M. (1991) *Clinical Child Psychology*. Chichester: Wiley.

Horne, A. and Sayger, T. (1990) *Treating Conduct and Oppositional Defiant Disorders in Children*. New York: Pergamon.

Hughes, J. (1988) *Cognitive Behavior Therapy with Children in Schools*. New York: Pergamon.

Kazdin, A.E. (1988) *Child Psychotherapy: Developing and Identifying Effective Treatments*. Oxford: Pergamon.

Management Advisory Service to the NHS (MAS) (1989) *Review of Clinical Psychology Services*. Cheltenham: MAS.

Patterson, G.R. (1969) Behavioral techniques based upon social learning: an additional base for developing behavior modification technologies. In C. Franks (ed.), *Behavior Therapy: Appraisal and Status*. New York: McGraw-Hill.

Patterson, G.R. (1982) *Coercive Family Process*. Eugene, OR: Castalia.

Richman, N., Stevenson, J. and Graham, P. (1982) *Preschool to School*. London: Academic Press.

Rutter, M., Tizard, J. and Whitmore, K. (1970) *Education, Health and Behaviour*. London: Longman.

Sturmey, P. and Crisp, A.G. (1986) Portage: a review of research. *Educational Psychology*, Vol. 6: 139–57.

Watts, F.N. (1990) *The Efficacy of Clinical Applications of Psychology: An Overview of Research*. Management Advisory Service to the NHS: Appendix to *Review of Clinical Psychology Services*. Cheltenham: MAS.

Yule, W. (1983) Child health. In A. Liddell (ed.), *The Practice of Clinical Psychology in Great Britain*. Chichester: Wiley.

FURTHER READING

Herbert, M. (1991) *Clinical Child Psychology*. Chichester: Wiley. This provides a comprehensive overview of assessment, intervention and research in the field.

Marzillier, J and Hall, J. (eds) (1992) *What Is Clinical Psychology?* 2nd edition. Oxford: Oxford University Press. An overview of the role of the clinical psychologist in a range of settings.

Kazdin, A.E. (1988) *Child Psychotherapy: Developing and Identifying Effective Treatments.* Oxford: Pergamon. This is a more advanced text, critically examining research into the effectiveness of interventions with children.

Forehand, R. and McMahon, R. (1981) *Helping the Noncompliant Child.* New York: Guilford.

Horne, A. and Sayger, T. (1990) *Treating Conduct and Oppositional Defiant Disorders in Children.* New York: Pergamon.

Hughes, J. (1988) *Cognitive Behavior Therapy with Children in Schools.* New York: Pergamon.

The last three of these books are more detailed guides to specific areas of psychological intervention.

CHAPTER 5

Child psychiatry

Jonathan Dare

There is often confusion about the nature, role and function of child psychiatrists. Child and Adolescent Psychiatrists, to give them their full name, are medical consultants employed by the National Health Service. After general medical training they specialize and gain higher qualifications in psychiatry before eventually becoming fully qualified in this (sub)specialism. There are between 300 and 400 consultant child psychiatrists in the UK.

The position and role of child psychiatrists cannot be understood in isolation from professionals of other disciplines with whom they work and jointly provide the child psychiatry service. In particular the distinction from psychologists (clinical or educational) is sometimes unclear. Psychiatrists' origin is within medicine and the study of physical and mental illness. The psychiatrist is able to recognize and treat, if necessary with medication, formal psychiatric illness and diagnose/detect physical illness. Psychologists, on the other hand, have no medical training and their origin is from the non-medical study of the functioning, nature and organization of non-pathological brain processes. However, in working with children there can often be considerable overlap between psychology and psychiatry and in practice they employ similar assessment procedures as well as using the same sort of therapeutic interventions.

Although I have emphasized the medical training of child psychiatrists, it is important to clarify that nowadays they do not use the classical 'medical model' (also see Chapter 1) in their understanding, assessment and management of children with emotional and behavioural difficulties. The classical medical model involves making a diagnosis based on taking a history, physical examination and laboratory investigation. It contains a focus on 'disease' – often without definition of cause. Child psychiatrists, in conjunction with other professionals with whom they work, follow a 'holistic' approach to understanding children's difficulties in which the problems are defined simultaneously in terms of their physical, psychological, social and family components. Great attention is now given to the meaning attached to the problem by the families and child involved.

This chapter examines the history of child psychiatry services in the UK, describes their role and identifies the current major issues within the profession and the service. It ends by speculating that its multidisciplinary and multi-agency nature places it in a position of strength in a period of social, legal and political change.

WHAT SORT OF PROBLEMS?

The vast majority of childhood problems referred to the child psychiatry service fall into two categories. The first is *conduct disorders* characterized by defiance, disobedience, aggression, antisocial and generally difficult behaviour. Such problems are often associated with truancy, stealing, and reading difficulties. When such problems lead the young person to contravene the law this becomes overt delinquency. The second type of problem is *emotional disorder* when children are unhappy, fearful, anxious, sad or depressed. These disorders may be associated with sleeping and eating disorders. Children who refuse to go to school and stay at home fall into this category – in contrast to the truant who acts in conjunction with peers and gets involved in the conduct disorder type of problems.

There can, of course, be overlap between these two broad groupings. Some children who exhibit conduct disorders will show evidence of emotional distress and upset. Similarly, some children who have emotional problems may get involved in conduct disorder activities. Nonetheless the distinction is important, particularly in relation to planning appropriate interventions.

In adolescence problems of a more adult type such as psychoses, depressive illness and anorexia nervosa are seen. Child psychiatrists also see young people who exhibit self-harm such as taking overdoses.

Michael Rutter's epidemiological surveys in the 1960s and 1970s found a prevalence (frequency) of psychiatric disorders in 10- and 11-year-olds in the Isle of Wight of 6.8 per cent. Of these 6.5 per cent were conduct and emotional disorders. The remaining 0.3 per cent were the exceptional minority with a more clearly recognizable formal psychiatric disorder. These included conditions such as infantile autism and the hyperkinetic syndrome presenting in earlier childhood. In Inner London, the frequency was double that on the Isle of Wight.

BACKGROUND TO THE DEVELOPMENT OF CHILD PSYCHIATRY

Although adult psychiatry became well established as a profession in the nineteenth century, child psychiatry is of much more recent origin. Breuer and Freud (1895) noted in their paper on hysteria that there was 'no adult neurosis without an infantile neurosis', but there was no systematic study of childhood psychiatric disorders until William Healy organized the first study of children's behaviour problems in Chicago in 1909. This was primarily to investigate the causes of juvenile delinquency. The first child guidance clinic anywhere in the world was opened in Boston, Massachusetts, in 1921.

The first clinic in the UK was established in 1926. These clinics functioned to meet the concerns of parents, schools and courts and in the early years were run under the aegis of a variety of voluntary agencies, local authorities and hospitals. The 1944 National Health Service Act led to greater integration of hospital-based child psychiatry departments and other hospital services. Child guidance clinics continued to be run jointly between local authority social service and education departments with medical input from the health service.

In addition to management and organizational changes, there have been some major shifts in the theoretical basis of child psychiatry. Until the 1960s, the major influence on treatment in child psychiatry came from various psycho-analytic schools. In their respective areas Anna Freud and Melanie Klein were, and remain, powerful influences. Greater understanding of child development and knowledge about emotional disturbance in children and possible treatment options came from the work of Winnicott and Bowlby. Both contributed greatly to the understanding of the development of personality characteristics. Bowlby's identification of the importance of attachment to parent figures was seminal, particularly his understanding of the damage caused to children subjected to multiple attachments. If in their upbringing children are exposed to more than a very small number of changes in parent caretakers, they become significantly emotionally damaged. They are impaired in their ability to form meaningful relationships as children, adolescents and finally in adulthood.

Lee Robins (1966) published a study of children referred to child guidance clinics in the USA in the 1920s who were followed up for thirty years. This gave a powerful impetus to academic research in child psychiatry. She found that children seen in such clinics for delinquent behaviour had a greatly increased risk of a variety of problems in adulthood such as marital difficulties, poor occupational achievement, psychiatric disorder, alcohol misuse and personality disorder.

Over the past twenty-five years Michael Rutter has made child psychiatry a respected and academically sound subject. His research in epidemiology (the study of the distribution of diseases and their causes) has enabled child psychiatry and its practitioners to become more effective and influential. Rutter has also established the appropriateness of child psychiatry as a preventive service in adult mental health. Thus by clarifying the relationship between childhood and adult problems treatment has become more appropriately focused. Furthermore, more precise knowledge has been gained about the prevalence of problems and the effectiveness of treatment and other interventions. Finally, Rutter's research has included specific educational issues such as children with reading difficulties and looking at how school can create the most effective environment for learning and behaviour.

These theoretical developments have occurred alongside a great increase in the variety and breadth of treatment in child psychiatry departments. This has enabled children and families with different problems to receive more specific treatments than in the past. Having reviewed the development of the service, this chapter now examines its current state.

DESCRIPTION OF THE SERVICE

The child psychiatry service is one of the few involving medical specialists to be run on truly multidisciplinary and multi-agency lines. Child psychiatrists work alongside NHS-employed clinical psychologists and child psychotherapists. In addition, most clinics have social workers who are employed by the local authority social services department. Clinics vary and may include other health service workers, such as psychiatric nurses, health visitors and family therapists. Other units may have remedial teachers from the local education department. In some services there are very close links with, and involvement of, educational psychologists.

Child psychiatry departments operate in two main settings. They are found in general hospitals and very occasionally in psychiatric hospitals. Such departments often have a specific link with local paediatric services. The other setting is child guidance units (synonymous with child guidance clinics), which are not sited within hospitals but are usually on health service premises, such as health clinics. Sometimes the premises are owned by the education authority or social services department.

Whatever the base of child psychiatry departments, all have a specific orientation towards the community, and liaise closely with local education and social services.

Training

Members of all the different professions comprising the child psychiatry service receive their basic training in their speciality. This is augmented by specialist postgraduate training in dealing with children who have emotional and behavioural problems. Child psychiatrists qualify as doctors and after doing various jobs in medical specialties there is a minimum period of three years as a registrar in which they gain a psychiatric qualification. This is followed by a further minimum period of four years as a senior registrar. This is the penultimate medical grade in which definitive and specialized experience is gained before consultant status is achieved. Most child psychiatrists have been medically qualified for some ten years before getting an appointment as a consultant.

Referral

As a result of the longstanding multidisciplinary and interagency nature of the child psychiatry service there is a long tradition of referrals being accepted from any professional or agency involved with children. Self-referrals have often been readily accepted. This contrasts with much health service provision, where referral from a doctor is required. However, the recent NHS reforms may affect this aspect of child psychiatry services as they could lead to demands that more referrals have a medical origin. Most departments encourage professionals to discuss the appropriateness (or otherwise) of planned referrals with them and telephone contact is often the preferred, quickest and most effective way of doing so. Some clinics encourage parents either to telephone or to call in if they wish to self-refer. If that facility is not available the appropriate step for parents is to consult their general practitioner.

In the past, child psychiatry services have tended to be unaffected by catchment area restrictions. That is, they have not been restricted to seeing only patients who live in the area of the local health authority – in stark contrast to adult psychiatric services. The health service reforms may affect this, leading child psychiatry departments to restrict access to children living in health authorities with which they have contracts. However, as most services are orientated to the local district, in most cases the local service is likely to be the most informed and appropriate to help children and families.

It is only in unusual circumstances that it is sensible for educationalists to seek contact with child psychiatrists outside their own locality. Child psychiatrists develop knowledge and expertise about the resources in a particular area and so seeking help beyond this may be non-productive. If referral to a more specialist centre is thought to be desirable, that should be discussed and clarified with the local child psychiatry service.

The vast majority of child guidance units and child psychiatry departments only run outpatient services. Practice in such departments varies but most try to avoid waiting lists of any significant length and they generally offer appointments within a few weeks of referral.

Day-patient and inpatient units are highly specialized and provide services on a regional health authority basis for more severely affected children whose problems are impairing their life functioning to a greater degree than could be managed on an outpatient basis.

Day treatment means that children do not need to be removed from their family but can attend a unit on a daily basis. Children normally go five days a week from 9 a.m. to 5 p.m. and there is usually some involvement with other family members during that period. There also needs to be careful coordination with education and social services.

Inpatient treatment is reserved for the most severely disturbed children. Very often this is for adolescents who are suffering from an overt psychiatric problem of a depressive or psychotic nature. Children are seldom admitted before being seen in an outpatient department. There are only a small number of such units in any one region.

RANGE OF SERVICES OFFERED TO CHILDREN WITH PROBLEMS, THEIR FAMILIES AND INVOLVED PROFESSIONALS

It is fundamental in child psychiatry to engage with all aspects of children's lives, so before treatment begins there needs to be an understanding of, and involvement with, those providing for a child's care (often the family) and education (often the school). This allows interventions which integrate the management provided by various professionals with the treatment offered by the child psychiatry services. Child psychiatry is always concerned to liaise and support those who have most contact with children to avoid undermining the involvement of those with more direct contact. Here the multidisciplinary nature of child psychiatry services provides an important mechanism for working with different professionals.

Assessment

Children referred to the child psychiatry services are usually assessed after careful contact and coordination with other professionals already involved with that child, such as educational, social and other health workers. As a result children are not often seen by the child psychiatrist until a liaison meeting or discussion has taken place between staff in the child psychiatry department and other concerned professionals. This consultation often obviates the need for direct intervention by the child psychiatry service, since such meetings can help those already working with children to use their skills to resolve the presenting difficulties.

When it has been agreed that there should be direct involvement, an appointment is offered. This usually takes place in the child psychiatry department, though if there are special logistic or other problems, special arrangements may be made for it to take place at school or home. The first interview usually involves the whole family in meeting the child psychiatrist. The purpose of such an interview is to understand the child, the child's position within the whole family and how the family relationships may contribute to the child's difficulties. It also helps to determine the best approach to treatment. Sometimes the first interview may be a joint one between the child psychiatrist, other involved professionals and the child or family. Such meetings aim to facilitate the work of those already involved with the child.

Interventions

There are a variety of different treatment approaches that can be used by child psychiatry if an assessment interview leads to direct work. This section briefly explores the major options. The decision about which type of therapy is most appropriate for which child is often based on the particular expertise of the therapist working with that child and family. There is not a specific type of treatment that is always used for a specific problem; the choice results from the interrelationship of the therapist's expertise and the child/family's views. However, there is a common thread that runs through all different approaches and interventions by child psychiatrists. Their way of understanding emotional, behavioural and psychiatric difficulties is to see them as arising from a variety of internal psychological, social, family and other influences on children's lives. Any treatment made by the child psychiatrist must be carefully integrated and coordinated with all other influences on that child and this requires that all the involved professionals have a carefully coordinated approach.

It is important to emphasize that the aim of all child psychiatric interventions is to help children live a more normal life individually and within the family so that they can grow up to be more secure and settled as older children and as adults. This will avoid the cycle of disadvantage whereby disturbed children grow up to be disturbed adults who themselves end up having disturbed children.

Individual therapy with children

Where it is decided that the best way of helping children is to work directly on an individual basis, parallel work will almost always be done with the parentally responsible adults. This casework (discussion with parent(s) about their understanding of the child's difficulties and how they may contribute to helping that child) is often undertaken by a psychiatric social worker. Subsequent intervention with the child may be undertaken by a child psychiatrist, clinical psychologist or child psychotherapist. The nature of such work varies considerably and can take a number of forms.

Psychodynamic approaches Often the intervention is psychotherapeutic in nature and is aimed at resolving underlying psychoneurotic conflicts arising from the child's earlier and current experiences of being parented. For younger children in whom play is their main way of expressing themselves, play and play materials are often used as the most appropriate form of communication. Through the medium of play children are often able to learn about and discuss their worries. Indeed play around worrying/anxiety-making topics can help the child feel less anxious by gaining greater understanding. Such work is usually done on a weekly basis for several months, on sessions lasting for around 45 minutes. As this work often involves the children in addressing painful psychological issues there can be a paradoxical increase in distress and upset during the early stages. Careful coordination and liaison with other professionals is of crucial importance, and casework with the parents also addresses such issues. It is important that children can rely on a high degree of confidentiality about their sessions with the therapist as without it they would not fully trust the therapist. This type of treatment is more commonly used with children who have emotional disorder type problems and is particularly helpful with children who have excessive fears, anxiety or depression.

Psychotherapy (the treatment of emotional and personality difficulties by psychological means) may take place up to four or five times a week in a process more akin to adult psychoanalysis. This approach is rare outside highly specialized centres. In psychotherapy there is often a re-creation between the child and therapist of a relationship akin to the parent–child relationship. This is called the 'transference relationship'. In this the patient transfers on to the therapist feelings and attitudes which have their roots in an earlier crucial relationship, usually with a parent or sibling.

In psychodynamic or psychotherapeutic approaches, the theoretical basis of the work is to help children's psychological world become more structured and stable. For those working with children, be they other family members or professionals, it is most important that they provide stability and security for them. The child's external reality must be as stable and secure as possible whilst his or her internal psychological world is going through the difficult process of self-understanding and change.

Behavioural approaches Individual therapy with children may also be of a behavioural type. Here the principles are to reward desired behaviour and ignore undesired behaviour. Looking at the precise context and antecedents of the problematic behaviours is also important. Behavioural interventions are used for a variety of problems, but especially in children with animal phobias. It is also used with star charts for problems such as bedwetting and soiling. When a behavioural approach is being used it is important that the management of the child is consistent. If the child gets different responses to and messages about his or her behaviour in different settings, this will be confusing and anti-therapeutic. The essence of this approach is that the consequences of a particular type of behaviour or action by the child are the same in all areas of the child's life, so close cooperation and involvement with parents in such work is essential.

Family therapy

Family therapy is one of the most widely used forms of treatment in child psychiatry. The underlying principle is that children's problems with emotions or behaviour arise as a result of dysfunctional family relationships. The therapy does *not* see the parents as at fault and causing the problem. The therapist sees the whole family's circular interrelationships working in a way that is no longer functional for the individuals within the family system.

The therapist works with the family, meeting on a fortnightly basis over a small number of months in sessions lasting from 60 to 90 minutes and involving all or most of the family members together. In two-parent families the involvement of both parents is frequently a crucial issue. In family therapy the therapists help families to come to their own solutions by facilitating their communication and the establishment of clear roles and boundaries between the generations and an appropriate hierarchy of authority and responsibility. The therapist does *not* tell families how they should behave, but helps them find a more functional way of interrelating. This type of approach is used with all types of family groupings including single-parent families, reconstituted families, separating families, foster and adoptive families.

In this approach great effort is directed towards promoting the competence of family members, and everyone involved should support the family as the resource to resolve the child's problems.

Group therapy

Group work can be used for children who have similar emotional and behavioural problems to each other. In this type of therapy children are encouraged to share their experiences, views and solutions but are guided by an adult therapist. It must, of course, be undertaken with children of comparable ages, and there are often logistic difficulties in establishing groups. Getting together children of a similar age with similar problems at the same time can often be very difficult.

It is often (and effectively) used for children who have been sexually abused, as it helps the child to feel that his or her experience is one shared by other children. Most importantly, sharing feelings helps reduce the inevitable feelings of guilt.

Drug therapy

The use of medication in child psychiatry in the UK is very limited. As with all other child psychiatric treatments it is used as only part of the overall management of the child. Medication on its own is never an appropriate way of treating psychiatric difficulties. The conditions in which drug treatment has an important part include the hyperkinetic syndrome, severe depression, severe tic problems and major psychoses such as schizophrenia.

Drug therapy is sometimes used in general practice for the treatment of enuresis (bedwetting). It is, however, of limited value because there is a very high rate of recurrence on withdrawal of the treatment. Behavioural techniques are widely used and are very effective for enuresis.

Consultation

The scale of child psychiatric disorder, with a prevalence of 7–14 per cent, and the small number (300–400) of child psychiatrists, means that child psychiatrists can be directly involved in the treatment of only a small proportion of children. Around 10 per cent of children with psychiatric disorders are seen in child psychiatry departments. To respond to the 90 per cent of children who might benefit from being seen by a child psychiatrist there has been a major development in consultation, and many psychiatrists spend up to 30 per cent of their time on consultative exercises. In consultation a child psychiatrist meets the professionals directly working with the child to facilitate their expertise in helping and managing the children for whom they are responsible. The child psychiatrist may help give insight and understanding to the origin of the problem and the management of such children. Most importantly, the child psychiatrist can help directly involved workers more clearly establish their roles for the benefit of the children for whom they care. The essence of such an approach is not for the child psychiatrist to act as an expert and tell other professionals how they should manage a child, but to provide a different but parallel perspective on the children and their difficulties.

There are many facilities such as schools for children with special needs and residential establishments where the child psychiatrist may be involved in this more general consultative fashion. The child psychiatrist may discuss individual children but more commonly will work with the staff to facilitate their ongoing work with children for whom they are caring. A typical pattern would be for the child psychiatrist to attend such an establishment on a weekly or fortnightly basis, often including staff group meetings.

The role of the child psychiatrist in such institutions may also be important in teaching and training for professional development. Indeed, this *teaching and training role* is an important part of the work of child psychiatrists with any establishment that deals with children on a regular basis.

ISSUES IN SERVICE PROVISION

Who is the client?

In child psychiatry the children are the clients but only rarely are they the ones who are complaining or asking for help. Most commonly the parents, teachers or social workers are the people who want children to behave differently. In child psychiatry this issue is crucial, as no matter what particular therapeutic intervention is made, it can be successful only if the family is motivated to be involved with treatment. If families are not motivated to attend or be involved in therapy, the chance of a successful intervention is virtually zero. In some ways this contrasts with the position for other agencies such as social services, where there may be a legal obligation for them to be involved and to make changes. With education, the law, of course, requires school attendance.

Conflicts and communication

The combination of the family's voluntary attendance at child psychiatry departments and the need for them to be motivated to change commonly causes problems for children where difficulties primarily present at school. Educationalists may have concerns about the children's emotional or behavioural status which form the basis of a referral to child psychiatry. The family, however, may view the problems at school as being entirely related to the school environment. They may see no logic or reason for working with a child psychiatry department towards family-based change because they do not experience problems or difficulties in the home environment. Alternatively, the family may view the need for change as residing only within the school setting. In these circumstances it is clear that there is virtually no motivation for the family to work with the child psychiatry department in any form of treatment. This can be a source of friction between school and child psychiatry, with educationalists sometimes perceiving the clinic's non-involvement as indicating that the child psychiatrist believes that there is no real problem. The reality is, of course, that the family may either have refused to attend or have come to a child psychiatry department and made it clear that they are not going to do any meaningful work. This situation particularly arises when teachers perceive that there are problems at home but the family either do not experience them, deny them or blame the school as the cause of the problems at home.

There can often be a schism between educationalists and child psychiatrists resulting from different ways of working and a lack of mutual understanding of the nature of others' involvement with the child. An example of this may lie in the experiences of educationalists in which they achieve successful outcomes when they teach people who are willing to learn new information and skills. Child psychiatrists, in contrast, normally work with families where giving information or teaching skills has failed to produce any significant change. The child psychiatrist has to work in a more indirect fashion than teachers usually do, and this difference in approach can cause confusion and misunderstanding.

These differences in attitude call for good liaison and communication. If a child psychiatrist fails to liaise properly with other agencies, there will be a failure to understand the nature and purpose of the psychiatrist's work. To compound this there is often an expectation by referring agencies that child psychiatric involvement will produce rapid changes. The reality is that change is slow, taking place over months rather than weeks.

Families can, on occasions, get caught between child psychiatry and one of the other groups of professionals involved in a child's life. A triangular relationship can occur in which the family and the child get caught up in unresolved issues between different agencies to the detriment of the child's well-being. An example of this would be when a child psychiatry department therapist agreed with a family that a child's problems resulted, in part, from the way they were being managed at school. The therapist would then fail to work effectively with the family because there would be some belief that change was needed in the school rather than the family. The solution would be a meeting between the school staff and child psychiatry professionals with or without the child and family. Such a meeting would clarify the differing issues and attitudes. Such problems are especially seen when there is not good and effective inter-agency communication. The family then may be the only medium by which child psychiatry communicates with other agencies.

A particular conflict of interest can arise between schools and child psychiatrists concerning areas of responsibility. The clinic is working primarily for the well-being of the child and family referred to them. The school, of course, wishes to do the best for any individual child but has, at the same time, to take into account the well-being of all members of a class or, indeed, all pupils in a school. Inevitably, on occasions what is best for the individual may not be best for a whole class or school. This can cause friction. In a similar fashion, child psychiatrists may wish the children to be treated in certain ways which are not consistent with the normal functioning of a school or its resources.

The need for good communication has been emphasized repeatedly. Great care must be taken in the patterns of such communication, inasmuch as it is essential that the right person is involved in discussions. It is entirely appropriate for a child psychiatrist to talk to the class teacher about the individual child and his or her behaviour. When wider issues that might affect others in the school and that demand different resources are under discussion, they need to be discussed at a higher level. The difference between the medical hierarchy and other professions' hierarchies may be important here. A medical consultant is at the highest level of professional authority in the medical world, but may be working with other professionals who have a lower position in their own hierarchy.

The multidisciplinary nature of child psychiatry teams has already been stressed. Their strength lies in bringing together professionals with different training and expertise. This enables children's difficulties to be reviewed and helped from a broad perspective. There is, however, a disadvantage which can create problems: the potential for disputes concerning power and authority within such teams. There are often unresolved issues about accountability between different professional groupings which may have an adverse effect on providing a good, well-coordinated and effective service.

Resources

Inevitably there are resource problems which limit the speed of response and numbers of children that can be seen in any one department. Deficiencies in resources can cause a number of problems for the child psychiatry service. This can lead to very great variations, with some clinics having waiting lists of several months whilst others close by may have no waiting list at all.

Whilst these problems have affected child psychiatry, like other parts of the health service, there is a particular problem for child psychiatry because of its inter-agency nature. At a time of resource problems there is inevitably a move for each agency and discipline to pull back within its own confines. A multidisciplinary inter-agency specialism such as child psychiatry may find the core principle of its work threatened, and there may be an unfortunate tendency towards less cooperation and openness and a greater degree of insularity and secretiveness.

One potentially worrying development is the widespread use of medication in countries such as the United States for children with psychiatric disorders. This is a consequence of services being totally driven by financial pressure; drugs prescribed by doctors can be much cheaper than the use of expensive therapists.

The importance of the interrelationship with social services departments has already been stated. With the unfortunate reduction in social service resources and an apparent increase in child abuse, social workers are becoming less able to make therapeutic interventions with children and families. This means that child psychiatry departments are under increasing pressure to work with children and families who would normally be seen as appropriate for a social services type of intervention. Similarly, there is pressure on child psychiatrists to be involved with more cases of abuse, even though these are best dealt with by social services under some form of statutory framework. Sometimes other agencies such as education can find themselves being unnecessarily directed back and forth between child psychiatry and social services.

Relationships with other professionals

One important area for child psychiatrists is their relationship with paediatricians; that is, the interrelationship of psychiatric and physical health. Children admitted to hospital for whatever reason suffer emotional consequences whilst at the same time emotional upset affects illnesses such as asthma and diabetes. It is important that there is close collaboration so that children and families are not presented with a false dilemma of identifying their child as having either a physical or a psychiatric illness. Nearly always there is an interplay of the two areas.

With child sexual abuse there has been considerable uncertainty about the role of child psychiatrists. In the last few years child sexual abuse has been recognized as much more widespread a phenomenon than was previously realized. Child psychiatrists had an important role in establishing the degree of such abuse. Their expertise in talking to young people meant they were often involved in the early disclosure interviews with children. This has led to some confusion about when child psychiatry should be involved in such cases and when social services should be involved. The situation is now more clear in that social services, with the police, is the agency that needs to investigate allegations and take on board the child protection role. After that, child psychiatry departments are more appropriately involved in treatment, either with individuals or with families, depending on the outcome of the investigatory work.

For education, especially in the larger conurbations, there is often a considerable degree of uncertainty as to where the school psychological services' role with children finishes and the child psychiatry department's starts. The more clearly the children's difficulties are seen as residing within the family context, the more clear it is that the child psychiatrist should be involved, although increasingly in recent years educational psychologists have worked extensively with families even when no problems have been experienced in schools. The educational psychologist is always the most appropriate person when the primary concern is the child's behaviour, or academic attainment, at school. In areas where health authorities and local authorities have the same geographical boundaries, this confusion is much less apparent.

The 1989 Children Act has profound implications for practice. It enshrines many of the good practices already described for child psychiatry such as multidisciplinary and inter-agency working, so in theory it should not have a profound effect upon the functioning of good child psychiatry departments. In reality there is likely to be a major resource problem. The Act requires that health services cooperate, when requested, with other agencies in the assessment of children and their families. The absence of extra resources for child psychiatry services may mean that there will be a shortfall. More assessments will mean less therapeutic intervention. This and other issues require that even more effort is put into communication between all those working with children, whatever authority or agency they come from.

FUTURE DEVELOPMENTS

The number of children who might benefit from child psychiatry departments is considerable but there is no significant likelihood of a meaningful increase in the numbers of child psychiatrists. This means that child psychiatrists should concentrate on developing the most effective use of their limited resources. In this respect, consultation has become an important part of their work and will continue to be so. In the future it is likely that child psychiatrists will wish to work with groups of professionals to ensure that there is a widespread and effective utilization of child psychiatric skills and expertise.

There is particular potential for developing child psychiatric expertise in professions allied to psychiatry. Community psychiatric nurses, clinical medical officers, health visitors and other community-based workers are increasingly having placements in child psychiatry departments. This further training, on top of their own professional skills, is another way of ensuring the wider availability of child psychiatric expertise.

Research in all areas pertaining to child psychiatry is widespread. There is particular interest in identifying the most effective form of treatment for different types of problems and difficult behaviours. This is closely allied to 'audit' – now an integral part of all health service working. A recent example of this has been in establishing that family therapy is the most effective form of treatment for teenagers suffering from anorexia nervosa.

There is a widespread consensus that as many children as possible, no matter what their disability, should be educated within the normal school system. Child psychiatrists increasingly need to work with children in ordinary schools who would have previously been placed in some form of special school education. Liaison between child psychiatrists and schoolteachers is crucial in establishing how and when a child psychiatrist should intervene with children exhibiting behavioural and emotional problems.

CONCLUSION

In recent years the 'family', with its potential for 'good' and 'bad' functioning and its influences on children, has been recognized as an important political issue. Child psychiatry, which has always concentrated on seeing children within the family setting, is potentially of central importance in thinking about families. For example, the investigations and reports into serious cases of child abuse over the past few years have emphasized the need for good and effective inter-agency cooperation. This has always been a central issue in the development of child psychiatry services in the UK. Child psychiatry can therefore be seen as being at the centre of the development of social policy.

Child psychiatrists have always prided themselves on their multidisciplinary and inter-agency skills, though this can lead to a considerable degree of role confusion and uncertainty by other agencies working with children. Although psychiatrists do not understand or see the children they work with as being 'mad' or 'bad', there is still widespread opprobrium attached to anyone seeing a psychiatrist. Both these factors reinforce the need for good communication and liaison between child psychiatrists and other professionals working with children. Families nonetheless are the greatest resource to help children to be emotionally stable and secure.

GLOSSARY

Autism
: A pervasive developmental disorder characterized by an impairment of social interaction; abnormality in communication and imaginative activity and ritualistic behaviour. The onset is usually before 36 months.

Hyperkinetic syndrome
: A condition characterized by short attention span, distractibility and 'disinhibited, poorly organized and poorly regulated extreme overt activity'. This is a specific condition to be differentiated from the term hyperactivity which is loosely used to define children who are overactive.

Tics   Sometimes known as habit spasms. These are repeated, sudden movements of muscles or groups of muscles, not under voluntary control, and are purposeless.

Schizophrenia   A mental illness. It is a psychotic disorder – one in which there is altered contact with reality. The individual may have belief systems and experience sensations which do not accord with objective reality. The condition is extremely rare before puberty. During adolescence its incidence gradually increases towards the 1 per cent found in the general adult population.

BIBLIOGRAPHY

Barker, P. (1988) *Basic Child Psychiatry*. 5th edition. Oxford: Blackwell Scientific.

Bowlby, J. (1971, 1975) *Attachment and Loss*, Vols I and II. London: Hogarth; New York: Basic Books.

Breuer, J. and Freud, S. (1895) *Studies in Hysteria*, Standard Edition, Vol. I. London: Hogarth Press.

Freud, A. (1980) *Normality and Pathology in Childhood*. London: Hogarth Press.

Glaser, D. and Frosh, S. (1988) *Child Sexual Abuse*. London: Macmillan Education.

Healy, W. (1915) *The Individual Delinquent – A Textbook of Diagnosis and Prognosis*. Boston: Little, Brown.

Hoffman, L. (1981) *Foundations of Family Therapy*. New York: Basic Books.

Klein, M. (1932) *The Psychoanalysis of Children*. London: Hogarth Press.

Minuchins, S. (1974) *Families and Family Therapy*. Cambridge, MA: Harvard University Press.

Robins, L. (1966) *Deviant Children Grown Up*. Baltimore: Williams & Wilkins.

Rutter, M. (1975) *Helping Troubled Children*. Harmondsworth, Middlesex: Penguin.

Rutter, M. and Hersov, L. (1985) *Child and Adolescent Psychiatry – Modern Approaches*. 2nd edition. Oxford: Blackwell.

Winnicott, D.W. (1965) *The Family and Individual Development*. London: Tavistock.

PART 3

SOCIAL WORK SERVICES

INTRODUCTION

Social workers have strong historical and professional links with psychiatrists and psychologists, and many of the points made in the previous section apply equally to social workers. However, their theoretical starting point has often been different and their work with children has always had a significant and demanding statutory component, which until recently was not an issue for psychologists. Ravi Kohli discusses in considerable detail the development of the social work profession and the factors that have shaped practice. This is the only chapter discussing professional issues which relate to social service departments, so it is considerably longer than the others. It offers a thorough understanding of the role of social workers, influences on their professional development and the importance and impact of the 1989 Children Act.

CHAPTER 6

Social work

Ravi Kohli

WHAT IS SOCIAL WORK?

Social work is a relatively new addition to the range of professions responsible for the provision of welfare in Britain. Partly because of its newness, definitions of what constitutes social work are hard to find (Jordan, 1984). It has been seen by some commentators as a profession concerned with social justice, fighting for the rights of the poor and needy who continue to be alienated by the social structures that surround them (Bailey and Brake, 1975). On the other hand some have suggested that social work must focus on individual work with clients, helping them to tolerate and accommodate to the circumstances in which they find themselves, often by using therapeutic interventions (Pearson et al., 1988). In this view the focus is on the subjective, internal world of the client as opposed to his or her external reality.

A third position focuses neither on the individual nor the client, but on their interaction. For example, Pincus and Minahan (1973) see social workers as aiming to enhance people's problem-solving and coping capacities, linking them to resources and services which they need, making sure that these services and resources work effectively on their clients' behalf, and contributing to social policy development.

This chapter takes a broad look at the history, underlying principles and current organization of social work. It starts by placing social work in a historical context. Here the ways in which philanthropists and state officials in the nineteenth century dealt with issues of morality, family life and poverty are examined. Consideration is given to the ways in which these continue to influence the formulation of statute, social policy and social work practice. The role of training in making connections between theory and practice is examined, followed by a description of the way services are currently organized within the statutory sector. Within this framework the type of work social workers do is discussed including the types of problems and difficulties they deal with in exercising their statutory responsibilities under the Children Act 1989. Attention is given to preventive work with families, investigative work in child protection and in the provision of substitute care for children.

The concluding section summarizes some important themes that emerge from social work with children and families, and the ways in which these may influence social work provision in the future.

BACKGROUND TO THE PROFESSION

Many of the complex issues facing contemporary social work in Britain have their roots in the Victorian era. A familiar question being asked today about the profession is whether social work is about caring for the deprived or controlling the depraved. The answer is never clear-cut because social work is and always has been about both care and control. It has always been difficult to strike a balance between providing care when resources are short and using legal sanctions carefully. Social work's struggle to find balances is, in part at least, a reflection of the broader relationship between the state and its most vulnerable citizens, where the carrot of state benefits has coexisted with the stick of means testing in providing a basic minimum of care for those struggling to make ends meet.

Social work in Victorian Britain

Throughout the nineteenth century social provision relied substantially on the family and the informal community. The formal systems of care comprised the state Poor Laws, the Church, and some employers' welfare provisions. These, combined with private benevolence and the rise of numerous friendly societies and charities, ensured that those experiencing extreme material hardship were cared for at a level of minimum subsistence.

The provisions were at best piecemeal, patchy and disorganized (Byrne and Padfield, 1978). To bring order into this state of affairs the Society for Organizing Charitable Relief and Repressing Mendacity was established in 1869. The title emphasized its functions in terms of care and control, and the Charity Organization Society (COS), which evolved from it, sought to maintain these dual aspects of help. For example Jordan (1984) notes that the COS sought to introduce a methodical way of working based on the thorough investigation of the habits and modes of life of applicants. Records of work with individuals and families were kept. These were discussed, progress was monitored and deductions were drawn about character, motivation, appropriate forms of help and other areas. Of those who came asking for help, about two-thirds were turned down (and judged to be undeserving) and only those who were considered to have been 'reduced to distress without fault or improvidence of their own' were helped (COS, 5th annual report, 1875, in Jordan, 1984, p. 40).

In order to be approved of as deserving help, the applicants needed to show that they agreed with the Society's objectives. These included 'the promotion of habits of providence and self-reliance, and of those social and sanitary principles, the observance of which is essential to the well-being of the poor and the community at large' and 'the repression of mendacity and imposture' (*ibid.*). In other words the limited help that was given meant that destitute families had to open their doors to allow officers from the COS to see how they lived, how they behaved, and whether they could become morally upright, responsible citizens as a consequence of the help provided.

There was an explicit trade-off between meeting the needs of society by reducing begging and petty crime, and meeting the needs of the poor by providing the barest minimum of food and shelter. In seeking to find a balance, the soft-policing role of social work's predecessors was emphatically established. Care and control became inimical aspects of the developing professional task.

Social work in the early twentieth century

At the beginning of this century there was a fundamental reconsideration of the reasons for the existence of social services, as well as how they were delivered. Crucially, there was a shift away from regarding these services as aspects of fitful state and voluntary benevolence, to seeing them as mainstream provision to which citizens of a civilized state had equal rights of access. Individualism gave way to collectivist provisions and the naked paternalism of the Victorian era was eroded. At a time when rapid industrialization and urbanization were taking place, poverty and homelessness were less easily attributed to personal failures or defective individual character, and more readily described as being products of the state's inadequate provision (Jordan, 1984).

During the early 1900s Parliament passed a number of important social policy laws (then known as 'the Liberal Reforms') which in effect formed the first phase of the Welfare State. The 1908 Children Act abolished imprisonment as a form of punishment for anyone under 14 years. The 1918 Maternity and Child Welfare Act encouraged all local authorities to provide services to safeguard the health of mothers and children, and the Education Acts of 1906 and 1907 provided for subsidized school meals and milk for children.

In the 1920s welfare services were established for those with physical disabilities and learning difficulties, through central government grants to local authorities and voluntary organizations. Social work developed in the probation service, in hospitals, and via voluntary organizations concerned with family welfare (including the moral welfare of unmarried mothers), youth activities and societies for handicapped children. For many workers within these organizations there was no formal training. Practice was informed by a wish to help, common sense and a working knowledge of legislation and procedures relevant to the organization.

The outbreak of the Second World War had a profound impact on the development of such services. The blitz, followed by the organized evacuation of children, led to long periods in which families coped with separation and loss. At that time, and as Richard Titmuss noted, social workers were needed

> because they knew about people and about distress, because they could help to bring the wide array of statutory and voluntary agencies to bear on the several needs of a particular individual at a particularly urgent appointed time, and because they were

qualified to report in practical terms on the ways in which one service reacted on another and on the people needing help. (Titmuss, *Problems of Social Policy*, 1950, quoted in Byrne and Padfield, 1978, p. 318)

The postwar consensus

The publication of the Beveridge Report in 1945 and the spate of social legislation in the 1940s, including the 1948 National Assistance Act, created the framework for the Welfare State as we know it today. Local authority children's departments were created following reviews of the care of children by the state. One review defined the roles of these newly created departments as being:

> to see that all deprived children have an upbringing likely to make them sound and happy citizens and that they have all the chances, educational and vocational, of making a good start in life that are open to children in normal homes. (Curtis Committee Report, 1946, para. 4.35, p. 143)

Other departments for other specialisms such as mental health and the care of the elderly were also established, and the 1950s and 1960s saw steady growth in social services. The expenditure of local authority welfare departments increased by 223 per cent in real terms between 1952 and 1968. With this increase the possibility of preventive work arose. It was argued that children could be supported in the community by their families, rather than be received into care with all the trauma and uncertainty that this involved. Until the 1970s, as Packman and Jordan (1991) note, the implicit basis of child care practice was that no fundamental conflict of interest existed between parents and children or between the state and parents. Statutory removal of children was viewed as exceptional, and good practice aimed at minimizing it.

This non-interventionist model of practice was maintained following the Seebohm Report (1968), the Local Authority Social Services Act 1970 and subsequent local authority reorganization. The main argument for service reorganization was that specialist departments were finding it increasingly difficult adequately to service families who experienced a multiplicity of problems. For example, families in which mental health and child care difficulties were simultaneously present were dealt with by different social workers from separate departments in disparate ways, depending on their specialism or departmental policies. A generalist approach was advocated, and workers from a variety of specialisms were placed within reorganized, larger social services departments (SSDs). These continue to carry lead responsibility for the provision of social work in Britain.

The consensus collapses

Another significant development in the 1970s was the death of Maria Colwell when she was 7 years old. She spent the early part of her life in the care of East Sussex Social Services Department, but following a court order she was returned home to the care of her mother and was killed by her stepfather (Hallett and Stevenson, 1980). The public inquiry into her death questioned the judgement of social workers and their superiors in meeting Maria's needs for safety and protection. Individual social workers as well as the organization in which they worked were blamed.

By the mid-1970s it was clear that the postwar consensus which saw social workers as playing a positive role in their work with children and families was under threat. Over the past twenty years, in the wake of further tragedies and scandals that have hit the media headlines, this consensus has almost entirely dissolved.

Jordan (1984) observed that the purpose of state intervention has been shifting over the past twenty years. It has become much more explicitly concerned with monitoring family life, and stepping in to protect vulnerable individuals from cruel or neglectful families, whilst the notion of support and supplementation of family care has been weakened. This has occurred as social services have come to be seen as expensive and a potential drain on national prosperity (1984, p. 98). So, as material deprivation has grown in the 1980s and 1990s (Oppenheim, 1990), social workers are in danger of reproducing a relationship with service users which would not be unfamiliar to their Victorian predecessors.

TRAINING

Training courses for social workers are run by universities and by some colleges of further and higher education. They vary from postgraduate courses, including some at master's degree level, through undergraduate to non-graduate diploma courses. They all last two years, and lead to a Diploma in Social Work (DipSW) – previously known as a Certificate of Qualification in Social Work (CQSW). All courses are validated by the Central Council for Education and Training in Social Work (CCETSW). Entrants are normally expected to have some prior work experience within a welfare setting as well as a grounding in the social sciences.

During training half the time is spent in a practice placement where trainees' work is closely supervised practice by teachers who themselves have received post-qualifying training in observing and evaluating the work of their students. With the heavy legal responsibilities carried by social workers, monitoring the quality of work is important, particularly given the possibility of the abuse of statutory powers (Prosser, 1992).

Reflecting the broad range of tasks social workers are expected to undertake, academic institutions provide a training based on a range of disciplines including applied psychology, sociology, welfare law and social policy. Trainees are expected to develop casework skills – that is, skills in interviewing, assessing and counselling individuals. Furthermore, skills in working with families and groups are taught. This basic training is generalist, but after qualifying social workers continue to receive training in a variety of specialisms such as working with children and families, working with people with learning difficulties, mental health, welfare benefits and in the use of the statutes which govern practice. All social workers currently working with children and families should have received further training in the application of the Children Act 1989.

Theory and practice

In pre-qualifying training, considerable emphasis is given to the relationship between theory and practice. The example below is of a theoretical framework particularly pertinent to developing an understanding of social work with children and families.

Bowlby's *attachment theory* (Bowlby, 1973, 1979, 1988) has had some influence on the social work profession. He explored the relationship between childhood experiences and their impact on people's capacity to make relationships in adulthood, and suggested that there was a link. If childhood experiences have been dominated by separation, lack of security or stability or if relationships have frequently been marked by violence or anger, the turbulence created by these forms of behaviour might lead to imbalances in other, later relationships. These may be marked by, for example, a lack of trust and difficulties in forming and sustaining intimate relationships. Individuals may carry an image of themselves as poor and undervalued, they may lack confidence and the power to be agents rather than objects of change. Conversely, good enough experiences of parenting, in which they have felt protected, safe and nurtured and have made secure attachments, would promote self-worth, the capacity to promote positive interactions and responses, the ability to express their own needs and to tolerate and meet the needs of others (Fahlberg, 1981).

In this theory there is a fundamental distinction between the care-giver who is able to provide a secure psychological base for children by setting limits to acceptable behaviour which are clear, consistent and adaptable over time and the care-giver who acts inconsistently, unpredictably and perhaps violently, becoming a saboteur of children's need for safety and care.

Polarities presented in this simple form are of limited use to the complex reality social workers face in assessing and working with parents and children. However, it is interesting to note the ways in which this theory complements the broader social work roles of providing limits to acceptable behaviour, of care-giving, and of acting in a way which is explicit and comprehensible to the client. In working with children the social worker is attempting to be 'a reasonable parent' to children in need of care and protection, when such experiences may ordinarily have been absent in children's lives.

In using attachment theory as a general framework for understanding their work, social workers may make connections between what they offer children in the present and how this compares with the children's experiences in the past. Some of the current guidelines for child protection practice reflect this theoretical base (DoH, 1988). The guidelines are used extensively by social workers to provide a consistent approach to the assessment of children who may need protection from harm.

There are, however, limits to the use of attachment theory. Because of its focus on the individual, some practitioners have looked for psychological explanations for behaviour and ignored material or structural ones. This has been roundly criticized in much social work literature (Preston-Shoot and Agass, 1990). Secondly, in developing a framework which takes into account racial and cultural differences between social workers and clients, the literature on attachment and loss has been produced and used in Western nations but its universal applicability has yet to be validated (Ahmad, 1990). Whilst acknowledging the limits of applicability, attachment theory continues to inform some important aspects of social work with children and families.

ORGANIZATION OF SERVICES

The majority of qualified social workers are employed by local authorities in their Social Service Departments (SSDs). The next biggest employers are the probation services, and some social workers also work in the voluntary and private sectors. Currently just under 30,000 social workers are employed in SSDs (DoH, 1992), an increase of some 10,000 in the past ten years.

Most staff in SSDs who are directly involved in face-to-face work are organized within teams. They either specialize in working with particular client groups such as children and families, mental health, older people, people with psychological disabilities and learning difficulties, or are generalist in nature, serving all client groups living in a particular geographical locality or patch. Each team has a leader who supervises team members, and there are two main components of this supervisory role: ensuring the workers' accountability to the agency and promoting the workers' professional development. Other aspects of supervision include maintaining acceptable standards of professional performance in carrying out duties, and ensuring that the client derives maximum benefit from the services (Parsloe, 1981; Blom-Cooper, 1985).

A hierarchy of managers separates the team leader from the Director of the SSD, and the work of the department is usually accountable to councillors via the Director. Legal responsibility for the provision of many services including day care, child protection work, initiating care proceedings, and the provision of substitute care with foster carers and in children's homes is largely retained by the SSD. In addition, specialist workers may be involved in recruiting, training, supporting and monitoring the quality of care provided by substitute carers.

Access to services

Before looking at what social services do, it is convenient initially to discuss how services are accessed. Under the Children Act local authorities are required to publish information about the services they provide or, where appropriate, those provided by other organizations. Some already do this via a directory of services, so when making a referral such information should ordinarily be available.

Referrals can come from a variety of sources depending on the nature of the work involved. Self-referrals for services are most common for day care, substitute care, and people seeking to become foster parents and voluntary helpers. Health visitors, GPs, police, staff at Department of Social Security offices, members of the clergy, Citizens' Advice Bureau staff, and neighbours, friends and relatives of clients may all be involved in the referral process.

The role of social workers

In this section, four different roles for social workers are described. These are not meant to be comprehensive or exclusive, but rather they provide a framework for understanding the later section on what social workers do. The first is as a service provider and the second is as a gatekeeper to further specialist help. In the third, a quality assurance role is seen as a necessary aspect of the job, and finally a broadly politicized role is identified.

The social worker as a service provider

Here the worker is seen to be working on an individual basis with clients in helping them to define the problems and difficulties they are experiencing as well as in identifying how they help themselves or who helps them in dealing with these. Practical and financial difficulties in relation to social disadvantage and deprivation, and relationship difficulties including isolation and lack of social support are often the focus of the work (Gibbons, 1991).

At a practical level, for example, parents requiring day care [Children Act 1989, ss. 71–9] or substitute care [s. 20 (1)] for their children are regularly referred to and seen by social workers. Similarly, financial help for those experiencing hardship may be assessed as necessary, especially for those caring for children in need [s. 17 (10)]. Whereas these aspects of the one-to-one relationship are straightforward in that it is reasonably clear who is asking for and giving what type of help to whom, dealing with relationship difficulties is more complex, especially the relationship difficulties that have led to the abuse of children. In a sense, the caring aspect of social work is transformed into one where social workers' legal responsibilities to protect children become paramount. This may be experienced as controlling. Acting to protect children from harm may in itself be experienced as abusive by the carers (Prosser, 1992).

The dilemma for practice that is discussed later in this chapter is how to work with parents and children in a way which is constructive for all, so that the rights of children and of those with parental responsibilities are balanced with the duties of the state to promote and protect 'children in need' or at risk of abuse.

The social worker as gatekeeper

In many instances, recognition of the limits of knowledge and competence within the profession has led many social workers to develop skills in using the various formal networks of help around them on behalf of their clients. For example, referring to and working alongside agencies such as Citizens' Advice Bureaux or law centres in helping clients manage money problems or legal issues is common practice for many social workers. Equally, seeking and using therapeutic resources such as child guidance clinics, where workers with substantial training can offer specialist help, can be a useful option when the client and the social worker agree that such help is necessary. For clients whose first language is not English, the services of translators and interpreters may be sought by the social worker in order to facilitate communication (Finlay and Reynolds, 1987).

Mediating between different resources and coordinating their activity in this way is not simply a peripheral aspect of good practice for social workers, but also a central one within the framework of child protection. For example, social services departments are obliged to convene child protection case conferences where a child has been deliberately hurt or neglected (DoH, 1991). In doing so social workers must seek the views of all parties, including carers and those with parental responsibility. Commonly, teachers, doctors, health visitors, police officers and other relevant professionals are invited to share their views via a child protection case conference. Should the child's name be placed on the Child Protection Register (CPR) – a list of all children living in the area who are considered to be at risk – the social workers have a number of tasks. Apart from seeing the child regularly, they must coordinate other people's involvement in monitoring the child's well-being and make sure that the child and carers receive the type of help that is necessary to provide effective care and protection. This may be through SSDs or other agencies.

The social worker and quality assurance

Much current practice involves working with people who are poor. Because poverty is so paralysing for those experiencing it (Mack and Lansley, 1992), a day-to-day task for social workers is making sure their clients have access to material and financial help provided by the state or by agencies such as charities. For the clients, negotiating with agencies which represent the state is never easy, as social workers know through criticisms that have been made of their own profession (Franklin and Parton, 1991). A complex web of bureaucracy surrounds the provision of some services, so they may appear overwhelming to those who already feel marginalized. Good practice may mean acting as an advocate to ensure that clients' rights are adhered to, that necessary services are made available and that existing appeals mechanisms are used to derive maximum benefits.

Social work and social policy

Given social work's concerns with the rights and entitlements of those at the margins of society, many practitioners make a natural connection between working with people on an individual basis and identifying collective needs which have to be met through policy enactment. Social workers have traditionally been concerned with linking the personal with the political, simultaneously focusing on the public solutions to the 'private ills' of individual experiences (Preston-Shoot and Agass, 1990). The task of making and sustaining such links has never been easy, as the temptation is always to individualize, and to some extent pathologize, those who ask for social work help as victims of their own feckless-ness. Nevertheless, a robust humanitarian streak in social work has challenged the increasingly threadbare nature of the safety net of welfare provision in Britain: for example, the questioning of the efficacy of the Social Fund in meeting claimant need by the British Association of Social Workers (BASW, 1987).

The profession has striven to maintain links with pressure groups such as Shelter and the Child Poverty Action Group in highlighting deficiencies in benefits and services to its client population. It has also supported single-issue causes such as the 'Children in Danger' campaign organized by the National Children's Home in 1985 (White, 1991). This emphasized the cost to children of parental unemployment, and made links between child abuse and the stresses and strains of material deprivation.

Considered together, these roles confirm social work as a profession which is uneasy with the process of compartmentalizing problems and their solutions. Connections are made between individuals, their immediate contacts and the broader political and social environment. Resolution is sought by way of direct service provision, negotiation, mediation, and where necessary by advocacy and the exertion of political pressure. A report by Barclay (1982), considering the roles and tasks of social workers, noted that:

> To translate this objective into action demands a rejection of the idea that one part of the person in need can be isolated from other parts, that the person can be separated from other people and treated in a vacuum, or that the material and structural aspects of the problem can be separated from the emotional. An attempt must be made [by social workers] to see people and their needs as a whole and to take account of their views about what services, if any, are to be provided. (Barclay, 1982, p. 35)

Balancing the needs of service users with the limited resources available is a difficult task. In the rest of this chapter this balancing act is considered in relation to social work with children and families, although the processes of finding balances and making connections are familiar to all social workers.

WHAT SOCIAL WORKERS DO

Much of current social work with children and families is linked to the 1989 Children Act, so in describing the duties, roles and responsibilities of social workers it is best to be clear about their connections with the legislation. In principle, the focus of work lies in four broad areas:

- responding to referrals;
- the prevention of family breakdown;
- the investigation of harm to children and the use of child protection procedures;
- the use of statutory measures to remove children from home, and provide substitute care with foster parents or in residential units.

In discussing these areas, the ways in which parents, teachers, social workers and others can work together are identified and the points at which consensus diminishes and conflict arises are highlighted.

Responding to referrals

It is likely that the referrer would initially see or speak to a duty social worker – that is, someone who is responsible on a daily basis for responding to all matters which are not yet allocated to a particular social worker. If the referral cannot be dealt with immediately, then it is taken to a weekly allocation meeting to determine the client's needs and the priority of the referral, and to nominate a social worker to undertake the work.

When a referral is made, social workers follow a generally established set of rules:

- Identify the client. As a general rule, families looking after children in need should expect that the children are identified as the clients.
- Establish that the referral has been discussed with the client before contacting the SSD. There are some instances when issues of confidentiality arise, particularly when a referral is made in relation to child protection issues. Anonymity of referrers can be preserved if protecting the child would be jeopardized if the source of referral became public knowledge.
- Obtain as full a picture as possible of the circumstances leading up to the referral. Again, when children are referred those with parental responsibility over them are contacted to gain their views. Other significant members of the client's networks, both formal and informal, have their views elicited by the social worker.
- Pool the information to identify any commonalities and differences that exist about the nature of the problems described and the abilities of those concerned to deal with them.
- Prioritize the problems and plan the work to establish who is dealing with what, within what time scale and in what manner.
- Keep the records about the referral and subsequent action accessible and comprehensible to clients. Facts are kept separate from opinions, and where information needs to be kept confidential this is to be made explicit to all parties.
- Review the work every three to six months, and involve all significant members of the formal and informal networks. Planning for future work is a joint endeavour.
- Be clear at all times about the appeal mechanisms available to the client and other people, should there be complaints about the work.
- When terminating services, ensure that all parties, especially clients and their carers, know for how long the records about the case are going to be kept.

Although the aim is to be clear and consistent, there are several reasons why the path from referral to closure may not be smooth. First, the pressure of work combined with a lack of resources means that many cases remain unallocated. Workers develop a siege mentality where only statutory cases are dealt with (Satyamurti, 1981). Indeed, some local authorities argue that it is even hard to meet all statutory requirements, especially in the allocation of child protection work (Glastonbury *et al.*, 1987). Secondly, when statutory action is taken and enforced entry is made into children's or families' lives, the rather sombre and rational steps of good practice described above may be blocked by all sorts of fears and worries. For example, when parents are present at child protection case conferences, participants often play down their concerns or remain silent about them because they fear that their own relationships with the parent or child will suffer as a consequence of their disclosures (Hallett and Stevenson, 1980). Thirdly, social workers, like other welfare professionals, may develop a way of dealing with referrals that labels clients. With 'the battered child' or 'the violent parent', the adjective becomes the defining feature of a case and the whole person or the context in which he or she exists is minimized (Satyamurti, 1981). Fourthly, social workers may not keep clear notes, share records or separate fact from opinion, even though all these are demonstrably in the clients' and professionals' best interests (Prosser, 1992). Finally, some local authorities are not clear about appeal mechanisms, confirming the general sense of powerlessness experienced by many social work clients (Øvretveit, 1986).

These difficulties are real. They are everyday experiences for clients and social workers (Preston-Shoot and Agass, 1990), and they are a threat to good practice.

Preventive services

Robinson sees the tasks of the adults involved in bringing up children as being about socializing children: enabling 'the development of the person as a social being and participant in society' (1978, p. 13). Children's learning (in its broadest sense) takes place primarily within the family, secondly within the school, and thirdly, if the family or school cannot meet the child's needs, via social work. All three systems of socialization have some overlap, and differences. For example, the family and social work systems for pre-school children may share the task of providing nurturant and physical care. Similarly, teachers may work with parents in promoting cognitive skills development. Teachers and social workers may work with children who are failing academically or socially.

Being 'in need'

The Children Act 1989 recognizes that interdependence and mutual help are key aspects of caring for children. The Act is explicit about the role that SSDs should play with regard to working with parents and children. It confirms that children belong with (rather than to) their parents, that parents have responsibilities for caring reasonably for their children, and that social workers need to work in partnership with parents in providing or enabling care to take place. A large part of the Act therefore focuses on how social workers can and should prevent family breakdown where children in those families are 'in need'. Children are 'in need' if, broadly speaking:

• they are unlikely to achieve or maintain a reasonable standard of health (physical and mental) or development (physical, intellectual, emotional, social or behavioural), unless the local authority provides help in some way; or
• if they are disabled.

Help may take the form of a number of interventions or services, which all local authorities have the power to provide. Some of these are:

• financial help or 'assistance in kind'. Generally this means that families can turn to SSDs if they run out of money or food or clothing for their children

and when the children would endure unreasonable hardship by going without these things. Payments of small grants or loans can be made, and no family in receipt of Income Support or Family Credit is liable for any repayment;
- the provision of advice, guidance and counselling.

In their day-to-day work social workers may be asked to advise, guide and counsel people with a variety of problems. Gibbons (1991) showed that families experiencing child care problems who had been referred to social services were distinguishable from most families along a number of dimensions, in particular social disadvantage and deprivation, personal vulnerability and lack of social support.

In defining specific areas of work within these broad headings, social workers may directly intervene, refer to specialist help or work alongside specialist workers in other professions to achieve jointly identified goals. With regard to teachers, for example, the Act emphasizes that social workers should contribute to any special needs assessment initiated under the Education Act 1981 as well as to children's established social needs.

SSDs are encouraged to provide 'occupational, social, cultural and recreational activities' for children and their families. The guidance and regulations to the Children Act 1989, Volume 2, focus on family support, day care and educational provisions for young children (DoH, 1991). Here it is suggested that if local authorities are not already doing so a range of services should be provided in order to prevent children coming into care. These might include:

- day care offered by childminders or nurseries (which the SSD must inspect, register and support on a regular basis);
- befriending scheme, or parent and toddler groups for isolated parents;
- toy libraries;
- drop-in centres where people can meet;
- family centres where therapeutic work can take place to improve parenting skills;
- home helps or family aides who can offer parents practical help in running households, especially if parents are ill or if children have disabilities which place an excessive burden on parents;
- accommodation. In many ways this is a new and innovative provision. The Act recognizes that sometimes, perhaps for short periods, parents and children need to live apart from each other, particularly when the situation at home reaches a crisis point and living together may result in harm to or lack of care for children. Parents are encouraged to apply to local authority SSDs for respite from their task of parenting, but they can withdraw their children from this substitute care at any time they choose.

The Act requires local authorities to have 'due regard to the different racial groups to which children within their area who are in need belong' so that services reflect and are sensitive to any special needs that children from minority groups may have. For school-age children, the Act requires local authorities to regulate day care and supervised activities for those under 8 years old. The more general duty to provide such care and activities for all children in need means, in effect, that children aged over 8 years should be provided with some support after school and during school holidays via out-of-school clubs or holiday schemes.

Education supervision orders

It is worth noting that section 36 of the Children Act 1989 creates a new type of order aimed exclusively at cases of non-school attendance, the Education Supervision Order (ESO). Non-attendance at school by itself is no longer a sufficient reason for care proceedings. Significantly, an ESO must be sought and administered by education departments, and the order becomes available (at the discretion of the court) when children are of compulsory school age but are not receiving education suitable to their age, ability and any special educational needs that they may have. The SSD must be consulted before an application is made, as indeed must the child and those with parental responsibility. ESOs initially last for one year, but can be extended up to three years. It is expected that the supervising officer will be an educational welfare officer from the education welfare service of the local authority, although it is as yet unclear how those administering ESOs would link into the work of SSDs (Allen, 1990). It may be that their work complements the tasks of parents, teachers and social workers, as Robinson (1978) notes, by:

- helping to link home and school;
- bringing to light incipient social distress of which absence from school may be one of the early signs;
- ensuring that parents are fully aware of the benefits to which they are entitled under statute, for example those provided by the Education Act 1981 or the Children Act 1989;
- ensuring that the authority's statutory duties regarding school attendance and welfare benefits are carried out in accordance with the principles behind the legislation and in accordance with competent social work practice;
- helping to establish and maintain clear channels of communication between SSDS, schools, parents and other people important to children's welfare.

Issues and problems

In essence the Act suggests a working partnership between carers, teachers and social workers in providing a continuum of care. By identifying that one child in five returns to an empty house after school (DoH, 1991) and that over 40 per cent of mothers of school-age children go out to work, there is recognition that many children may become vulnerable or be without responsible adults looking after them. To help them remain with their families, the Act confirms that the sorts of provisions described above may be necessary. However, these provisions demand changes – partly in the quality of links maintained by or between workers and families, so that the recipients and providers of services can engage in the task of socializing children cooperatively and equitably. But to a substantial degree they also require an increase in material and financial resources which local authority education and social services departments may not have (Packman and Jordan, 1991).

Some commentators argue that the Children Act 1989 and the Education Reform Act 1988 may be pulling in different directions (Neate, 1992). There is some concern, for example, that publishing league tables on examination results and truancy levels under the Education Reform Act may weaken the resolve of some schools to hold on to pupils who do not achieve academically or have behavioural problems (Whitney, 1992). Children with special needs (as defined in the Education Act 1981) or children in need (as defined in the Children Act 1989) may suffer as a consequence. One recent National Union of Teachers survey indicated that pupil exclusions had increased by 20 per cent in the year prior to the publication of its findings (Children's Legal Centre, 1992). Some education authorities specified the reasons for exclusions as including disruptive or negative attitudes to school and school rules, refusal to obey instructions, defiance, insolence, verbal abuse, assaults on other people and staff, absconding from school and poor school attendance. Sone notes that:

> there is a definite connection between being excluded from school and coming to the attention of social services. Once a young person is not attending they become (for however brief a time) the responsibility of the carers. This places extra stress on the family. Relationships may deteriorate and the family may choose to bring in the social services. Or the young person may choose to spend increasing amounts of time on the streets and juvenile justice may become involved. Children out of school lose their cultural base and become alienated from their peer group. Either way there is a downward spiral. (1992, p. 12)

In a very real sense the preventive measures of one piece of legislation may be undermined by the effects of another. Collaborative efforts by parents and social workers to work together to care for children in need may suffer.

Child protection

Working together is central to investigating and dealing with children who have been abused or neglected. On the basis of recommendations made by the inquiry into the death of Maria Colwell, cases of child abuse and suspected child abuse are now entered on Area Child Protection Committee (ACPC) Child Protection Registers (CPRs). There has been a substantial growth in the past few years in the number of children who have been the focus of child protection investigation and registration. In 1986 there were 15,000 children's names on CPRs in England and Wales (Taylor, 1989), but the latest survey in England alone indicates that the total had reached 45,200 by the end of 1991 (DoH, 1992), a prevalence of just over four children per thousand aged 18 years or below. Of these approximately 28,000 were of school age and 16,000 had been registered in the year preceding the survey. Taylor (1989) suggests that although these figures may represent an increase in child abuse it seems as likely that they also reflect increased reporting due to greater public and professional awareness.

Categories of abuse

The *Working Together* guidelines give a definition of what abuse means for the purposes of registering children under the CPR (Home Office /DoH/DES/

Welsh Office, 1991). There are four broad categories which attempt to cover acts of commission and omission, and they emphasize the potential for harm as well as firm evidence of harm actually having taken place:

Neglect: the persistent or severe neglect of a child or the failure to protect a child from exposure to any kind of danger, including cold and starvation, or extreme failure to carry out the important aspects of care resulting in the significant impairment of the child's health or development including non-organic failure to thrive.

Physical injury: actual or likely physical injury to a child, or failure to prevent injury (or suffering) to a child including deliberate poisoning, suffocating and Münchhausen's syndrome by proxy.

Sexual abuse: actual or likely sexual exploitation of a child or adolescent. The child may be dependent and/or developmentally immature.

Emotional abuse: actual or likely severe adverse effects on the emotional and behavioural development of a child caused by persistent or severe emotional ill-treatment or rejection.

The process of investigation

Local authority SSDs are obliged to investigate any referral which suggests that a child is suffering or likely to suffer 'significant harm' (Children Act 1989). It is likely that any child abuse referral will be dealt with by a duty social worker at the SSD if the child is not already known to the department. The following steps are common to a full investigation:

- Seeing and interviewing the child to ascertain the extent of harm, the circumstances leading to its occurrence and the prospect of further harm occurring.
- Interviewing carers and other important people in the family. If prosecution of the perpetrator of harm is seen as likely, a police officer and a social worker carry out this interview jointly, as they would the interview of a child. These interviews, known as 'formal interviews', may be videotaped. Their main purpose is to gather evidence for prosecution.
- Arranging a medical examination if necessary. In many authorities a paediatrician from the Community Health Services would carry this out. The SSD would ordinarily expect this medical officer to supply them with a report.
- Convening a child protection case conference. A range of professionals can be present at this case conference, not all of whom would necessarily know the child or family. These might include health visitors, nursery workers, the police, doctors (from Community Health and/or the GP), teachers and education social workers. The conference is chaired by a senior manager in social services. The conference's purpose is to review evidence with regard to the categories of abuse and decide whether to place the child's name on the

CPR. In terms of further risk or harm to the child, conference members need to indicate what changes in behaviour or circumstances are necessary in order for the child's name to be removed from the register.

- Appointing a key worker. This is usually a social worker, whose services or tasks are specified by the case conference in order to help monitor the child's safety and provide the impetus for necessary changes. Decisions taken at the initial case conference are normally reviewed every six months.

Within the process of investigation further legal steps may need to be taken to provide care and protection. It should be noted, however, that the substantial majority of children whose names appear on the CPR are not the focus of further legal proceedings. A recent survey by the NSPCC estimates that in 67 per cent of cases where children's names appeared on the CPR in England and Wales between 1983 and 1987 no legal action was being taken. In other words, work was taking place on a voluntary basis with parents and other carers whilst the children remained at home (NSPCC, 1992).

Parental involvement in child protection

Parents can feel overwhelmed by the process of investigation and express feelings of alienation, anger and disempowerment about the decisions being taken (Brazil and Steward, 1992). The relationship between parents and social workers becomes one in which the possibility of care and cooperation is reduced and the probability of control and competition increased (Prosser, 1992). From social workers' point of view, investigations are also reported as being stressful and anxiety provoking (Glaser and Frosh, 1988; Dale *et al.*, 1986). Social workers' tasks are not simply to cope with strong feelings, but also to:

- clarify and be specific about the reasons for the investigation. They should be able to acknowledge the strength of feeling about the process of investigation with parents and children;
- explain their statutory responsibilities in a comprehensible way, either orally or in writing;
- explain the roles and duties of workers from other agencies;
- ensure that the parents' own legal rights are explored with regard either to making representations or complaints or to gaining access to official records;
- be open, honest and authoritative, particularly in stressing that the welfare of the child is the overriding factor guiding child protection work;
- inform parents about what is going to happen and how long it will take. The process of review and planning may need to be a continuous one;
- inform parents about their attendance at case conferences and discuss what help could be offered to them in putting their views across. If parents will not attend, arrangements need to be made to have their views expressed;
- help parents articulate their own abilities, strengths and solutions in relation to the protection and care of their child. In cases of sexual abuse the non-abusing carer (often the mother) is a vital contributor to the future safety and welfare of the child (Furniss, 1991).

Guidelines developed by a number of SSDs remind their staff that they should work in partnership with parents, reflecting the *Working Together* guidelines' comment that:

> it cannot be emphasised too strongly that involvement of children and adults in [child protection work] will not be effective unless they are fully involved from the outset in all stages of the process, and unless from the time of referral there is as much openness and honesty as possible between families and professionals. (DoH, 1991, p. 43, para. 6.11)

The role of teachers

Hallett and Stevenson (1980) note that until recently the role that teachers had in detecting, monitoring and dealing with child abuse had been underplayed. They attribute this partly to the focus having been, until at least the late 1970s, on injuries to pre-school children. Current understanding of child abuse is that it is likely to affect school-age children in substantial numbers (DoH, 1992), so further attention is being given to the importance of teachers' involvement in child protection. Hallett and Stevenson observe that:

> teachers are well placed by virtue of their close daily contact with pupils, and often their parents or the local community grapevine, to know about children and their families who are causing concern in the context of child abuse and neglect. (p. 46)

The *Working Together* guidelines confirm this view and state that although the education service in itself does not constitute an investigation and intervention agency:

- All staff in the service should be aware that investigative agencies should be alerted when they believe a child has been abused or is at risk of abuse.
- They should familiarize themselves with local procedures for reporting or referring cases. The area child protection committee information should be available via the headteacher of each school.
- The headteacher or a senior member of the teaching staff should be designated as having responsibility for working with the SSD and other relevant agencies.

There are also reciprocal expectations on SSDs:

- Formal notification should be sent to children's schools if their name is on the CPR, or where such children start or change school.
- Information about who to contact in the SSD about each child should be available. Normally this is the key worker nominated at the child protection conference.
- Close liaison between the key worker and the school should happen at all times, with absences and further concerns being monitored and reported as they arise.

These rules are designed to facilitate inter-agency cooperation and appear to be simple, yet beneath them lie some contradictions. As in the earlier example of the Education Reform Act 1988 and the Children Act 1989 pulling in different directions, it has been observed that teachers and social workers can also, perhaps unwittingly, work in mutually antagonistic ways. For example, children's difficult behaviour in the classroom may be experienced by teachers as a threat to authority given their general remit to create and maintain a culture of learning for all pupils. Jones (1974) writes:

> I remember as a teacher in a very difficult class of youngsters thinking 'I've got to survive; if anything goes under it's not going to be me'. I remember a whole range of techniques I used to maintain my own authority as a teacher in the classroom and the forms of defence I used to protect myself, and not help the disturbed child in the face of hostile, aggressive behaviour. (Robinson, 1978, p. 140)

The teacher's need to maintain equilibrium through the use of authority may lead to conflict with the social worker who is working for the welfare of an individual child. A gulf may appear between the educational and social needs of one child and those of his or her peers. In facing this sort of dilemma teachers and social workers may re-create between themselves the kinds of rivalries that they may have experienced in their relationship with the parents of children in need. Robinson (1978) observes that given the overlap in the tasks of parents and professional workers involved in socializing children, points of conflict about what is best for a child must emerge:

> teachers, like everyone else, have a deep need and motivation to do their job and . . . are often painfully aware that 'my child in my class' really 'belongs to' his or her parents who just do not give a tinker's curse for its education. (1978, p. 91)

This process of owning children who are vulnerable may simply be the other side of disowning them or their behaviour when this is experienced as uncomfortable. Teachers acting *in loco parentis*, like parents or like social workers, may be caught in this process without feeling that anyone else understands their particular dilemmas or their wider responsibilities. Questions about who has responsibility for what, who has the best solution to the child's difficulties and ultimately who cares the most do not easily diminish as a consequence of guidelines existing, as recent writings confirm (Furniss, 1991). The attempt to find a balance between control which is not coercive and care which is limited by resource constraints and wider responsibilities is always difficult. Perhaps for this reason meetings between parents and professionals focusing on the needs of the child and the problems and possibilities associated with those needs should always take place. Each party should delineate areas in which there are similarities and differences of views and actions. Where dissonance exists or potentially arises the impact of this on the child should be consciously attended to. The need for clarity, consensus and continuity of care for the child should not be obscured by the muddle which personal and professional fears and rivalries can generate.

Removing children from home

In the majority of cases services are provided while children remain at home. But in circumstances in which they are likely to suffer 'significant harm' they may need to be temporarily or permanently removed for their own safety and protection. As far as social workers are concerned a child can be removed from home under the new legislation in four ways:

- by obtaining a Child Assessment Order (CAO);
- by obtaining an Emergency Protection Order (EPO);
- by obtaining an Interim Care Order (ICO);
- by obtaining a full Care Order (CO).

The police also have powers to remove children to suitable accommodation, or under a Child Recovery Order.

Within the Children Act harm is defined as: 'ill-treatment or impairment of health and development'. But the Act is silent on what constitutes 'significant' within the phrase 'significant harm', and it is not yet clear how the courts will interpret it. It is likely to turn on a comparison of the child's health or development with 'that which could reasonably be expected of a similar child' – that is, one of the same age and other characteristics (Allen, 1990, p. 109).

The responsibilities of the courts

If an application for an order is made by the SSD or other parties, the court is duty bound within the framework of the Act to ask itself whether making an order is the only way to deal with the child's best interests, or indeed whether judicial intervention is necessary at all. The Act states that 'When a court determines any question with respect to the upbringing of a child, the child's welfare shall be the court's paramount consideration' [s. 1(1)].

The idea here is that the court should be child centred and act, as it were, as the ultimate good parent in settling issues where others may have competed and failed to agree. As such it would be reasonable to expect the court to scrutinize very carefully how child centred the parties represented in the case are or are prepared to be. The court would consider the following factors referred to as the 'welfare checklist' in making its decision about granting an order of whatever type:

- the ascertainable wishes and feelings of the child concerned, considered in the light of the child's age and understanding;
- the child's physical, emotional and educational needs;
- the likely effect on the child of any changes in his or her circumstances;
- the child's age, sex, background and any characteristic which the court considers relevant;
- any harm the child has suffered or is at risk of suffering;
- how capable each of the parents (and any other persons in relation to whom the court considers the question to be relevant) is in meeting the child's needs;
- the range of powers available to the court under the Act in the proceedings in question [s. 1(3)].

Allen (1990) comments that the checklist is not particularly novel, in that it is modelled on principles existing in previous legislation and current ideas about competent social work practice. Social workers, for example, will need to demonstrate in court that they have attended to these factors in their preparation for applications to court. They will ordinarily be expected to show the ways in which they have attempted to deal with the presenting issues on a voluntary basis with carers, how they have tried to develop partnerships, why this has not been possible, and the likely effect on the child of a court order not being made. They should also have discussed the implications of their actions fully with all relevant parties.

Continuity of care

A common perception, for those unfamiliar with social workers' use of statutory powers, is that they remove children at will, and for ever, on grounds which are spurious and against natural justice. To some extent this perception has been reinforced by media reporting of social work with children and families, where the profession as a whole or individual workers within it have been castigated for acting without accountability (Franklin and Parton, 1991).

Whether or not this is a real problem, good practice, and the Act, require a very different approach. Research into the experiences of children settling into substitute care has highlighted the significance to them of maintaining contact with their natural families and communities of origin (Millham *et al.*, 1986; Packman *et al.*, 1986). Other research has reinforced the message that children in need of care are not necessarily children whose parents were abusive or neglectful (Rowe *et al.*, 1989). Rather there is a strong link between admissions and material crises precipitated by homelessness, unemployment or financial debt. Admissions are also sometimes associated with behavioural problems on the child's part. In these circumstances the parents are often motivated by their children's welfare, and social workers respond in a supportive manner by negotiation and agreement. These needs for continuity of contact at a time of necessary change have been addressed by the new legislation. For example, the Act encourages social workers to place children with a person connected with the child, such as a family member or relative 'or other suitable persons'. It states that the accommodation offered should be near the child's home so far as this is reasonably practicable and consistent with the child's welfare, and that siblings should be accommodated together. If children have disabilities, arrangements need to be made to offer suitable accommodation, and due consideration needs to be given to how children's needs are best met in relation to religion, race, culture and language.

Competent social work practice for children in care involves continued consideration, by regular reviews, of the possibility of returning home. Once children are in care, no matter for what length of time, contact with parents or those with parental responsibilities should whenever possible continue, unless clear evidence emerges that this is detrimental to the children's well-being. The hasty removal of children by social workers to the care of people whom they do not know, and to an area which is unfamiliar to them, ought to be very rare but used knowingly and justifiably when circumstances dictate that this course of action is necessary.

The link with education

With regard to education, the Children Act's guidance and regulations governing the placements of children into families and into residential care identify and encourage good practice by asking social workers 'to act as good parents in relation to a child's education'.

There is recognition that the trauma of enforced separation, no matter how dire the circumstances from which children are removed, can worry and preoccupy them in a way which undermines their ability and educational potential. For children moved from one placement to another, the trauma can lead to their becoming disruptive and hard to care for. The regulations require local authorities to:

- notify the local education authority if children are based in its area;
- recognize that schools need to have as much information as possible about children;
- initiate contact between carers and the school if it does not already exist when children are being looked after by substitute carers;
- monitor children's educational progress and general welfare by maintaining direct contact with schools and carers, and via school reports sent to the carers. Social workers should be clear about access to specialist services within the local authority's educational provisions in order to enlist their help whenever necessary on behalf of the child;
- recognize that the natural parents may wish to contact the school or continue to play some part in the child's education. Social workers should work with schools and parents in establishing what this means in practice;
- help parents exercise their rights under the statementing process (see Chapter 1).

Residential workers in children's homes are reminded of their responsibilities to those in their care to provide 'support and encouragement beyond that which may be given by a caring parent'. These include:

- making rigorous efforts to counter low self-esteem and lack of confidence in children in their care;
- being alert to the possibility of these children being bullied or otherwise discriminated against at school and being prepared, in conjunction with the school, to deal with issues that arise as a consequence of this;
- giving information to children about as wide a range of educational, training and work opportunities as possible;
- providing a quiet space for children to study, including an appropriate selection of books and other reading material;
- helping children to cope with disappointments at not getting what they wish for, at a time when they need it in terms of academic success, training or employment (Jackson, 1989);
- finding out about their interests and attitudes and how these can be supported by schools, parents and others in guiding them to find employment, further education and training.

What the guidance and regulations do not comment on – and arguably this is beyond their remit – is the conflicts and contradictions inherent in the legislative framework that have already been discussed in relation to parents, teachers and social workers. These also include foster carers and residential workers. Robinson (1978) and Barclay (1982) both note that social workers should actively support substitute carers in their difficult task of helping children in need. Yet in many respects support may not be a straightforward process. Substitute carers, in building attachments to children, may compete with social workers in owning or disowning them. Like social workers they may pay more attention to care-giving and domestic tasks than to educational attainments (Prosser, 1978). It may be difficult for them to move away from being home centred to offering 'much intellectual stimulation . . . or [to] deal effectively with schools and teachers' (Jackson, 1989, p. 141). Berridge (1985) paints a graphic picture of children coming home from school bursting to recount the day's events, 'only to find adult attention firmly focused on the chip pan and the frozen fish fingers'. Bald (1982) describes how hard it is to persuade care staff to devote even ten minutes a day to helping children with their reading. Millham *et al.* (1982) note how few substitute carers have themselves had satisfactory or successful experiences of education. As Jackson summarizes,

> in these circumstances it is hardly surprising that staff may have difficulty in relating to school teachers or in asserting their own judgement of a child's ability and needs in the face of a presumed expert. In addition they may be inclined to play down the importance of school attendance and gloss over difficulties, not expecting that the children in their charge will do any better than themselves. (1989, p. 142)

Given these circumstances, specialist help may need to be made available to children in care in order to improve their educational abilities. Jackson (1989) describes one such effort – the recruitment by a residential home of a former teacher with intimate knowledge of local schools to act as an educational liaison officer. Jackson notes that:

> As a member of the staff group she played an important role in keeping school and education to the fore in decision making in the home. She arranged home tutoring (paid for by the LEA), helped to recruit outside teachers and volunteers to help with homework etc. . . . but her main task was to act as an intermediary and interpreter between care staff, children and teachers. In this her activities were similar to those which any concerned parent would take in support of their own children, with the difference that for children in residential care from disturbed backgrounds the monitoring and intervention required are almost continuous. . . . One measure of her success was the fact that no child had been suspended from school since her appointment, something which had previously been an almost weekly occurrence. . . . As a teacher herself she was equally concerned with matters of academic achievement and constantly alert for opportunities to help children from the home to make up lost ground. For those at secondary school great emphasis was placed on regular completion of homework, with an hour set aside each evening for this purpose during which two teachers were available to help any child in difficulty. This transformed the children's feelings about going to school, knowing that they could hand in acceptable pieces of work, and also changed the teachers' possible perception of the children's ability and potential.
>   The conception of education at the home went far beyond school work. Children were encouraged to participate in the life of the local community, to join clubs and take up hobbies and to acquire out of school skills such as riding, driving and playing

musical instruments. There was an attempt to make education fun and to associate it with pleasure and enjoyment. (1989, p. 148)

This type of innovative work is unusual, because extra funds need to be made available to sustain it. A more familiar scenario is that foster carers and residential workers feel undervalued and underpaid. The National Foster Care Association (NFCA) has recently drawn attention to the fact that foster parents are usually paid less than the cost of kennelling a dog, which can be £50 a week. At least 64 per cent of local authorities pay below the recommended weekly minimum of £47.76 for a 4-year-old outside London (NFCA, 1992). In substitute care, as much as in preventive work and in the protection of children from harm, issues of quality and quantity and of care and control go hand in hand. The inescapable conclusion that emerges is that the quality of care provided for children in need depends, to a large extent, not simply on guidance and regulations laid down by the Department of Health but also on an increase in the provision of financial and material resources.

LOOKING TO THE FUTURE

Considering what lies ahead in social work with children and families there is a growing sense of the profession going back to the future. On the one hand, the 1989 Children Act is clearly modelled on egalitarian principles; it confirms notions of working in partnership with carers and emphasizes the need to maintain children with their families. On the other hand, the decrease in resources since the late 1970s has resulted in the safety net of welfare provision looking threadbare. The ends defined within the Children Act may not be achievable given the means available. It is as if the profession is expected to deliver welfare as intended by the Beveridge reforms, by using the patchy and piecemeal provisions available to its nineteenth-century counterparts. Given this mismatch, there are uncertainties within the profession about its future.

Two questions remain difficult to answer. How well will social workers provide the services necessary, as defined in the Children Act, to promote the notion of families caring for their own children? And how well will social workers feel cared for by those who define what they should do?

There is after all a parallel between the ways in which social workers work with families, and the ways in which they feel supported by the state in the formulation of social policy and legislation. Within the framework of attachment theory, it may be argued that the state's lack of consistency and clarity in the provision of welfare has resulted, in part at least, in a failure in its role as *parens patriae*. This in turn has led to confusion and uncertainty within social work about how best to be a 'good enough parent' to those in need. The recipients of services would similarly argue that they have at times felt the profession to be abusive of its responsibilities. Parents of children who have been through child protection investigations have forcefully expressed this view (Prosser, 1992). All three parties – parents, professionals and policy makers – may continue to argue that they have the best interests of children at heart, but such a 'feel-good' argument may disguise the complex nature of their responsibilities to children in need, and the gaps between what they say ought to be done and what they end up doing.

Whilst these gaps exist, the positive impact that the Children Act 1989 can have on the lives of vulnerable children remains a matter of conjecture and debate.

REFERENCES

Ahmad, B. (1990) *Black Perspectives in Social Work*. Birmingham: Venture Press.

Allen, N. (1990) *Making Sense of the Children Act 1989*. Harlow: Longman.

Bailey, R. and Brake, M. (1975) *Radical Social Work*. London: Edward Arnold.

Bald, H. (1982) Children in care need books. *Concern*, Vol. 44: 18–21.

Barclay, P. (ed.) (1982) *Social Workers, Their Role and Tasks*. London: Bedford Square.

Berridge, D. (1985) *Children's Homes*. Oxford: Blackwell.

Blom-Cooper, L. (1985) *A Child in Trust: The Report of the Panel of Inquiry into the Circumstances Surrounding the Death of Jasmine Beckford*. London: Kingswood.

Bowlby, J. (1973) *Attachment and Loss:* Vol. 2, *Separation, Anxiety and Anger*. London: Hogarth.

Bowlby, J. (1979) *The Making and Breaking of Affectional Bonds*. London: Tavistock.

Bowlby, J. (1988) *A Secure Base*. London: Routledge & Kegan Paul.

Brazil, E. and Steward, S. (1992) My own flesh and blood. *Community Care*, 12 April.

British Association of Social Workers (1987) *Social Fund Guidelines*. Birmingham: BASW.

Byrne, T. and Padfield, C. (1978) *Social Services Made Simple*. London: Heinemann.

Children's Legal Centre (1992) School exclusions on the increase. *Childright*, July/August.

Curtis Committee Report (1946) *Report of the Care of Children Committee*. London: HMSO.

Dale, P., Davies, M., Morrison, T. and Waters, J. (1986) *Dangerous Families: Assessment and Treatment of Child Abuse*. London: Tavistock.

DoH (1988) *Protecting Children: A Guide for Social Workers Undertaking a Comprehensive Assessment*. London: HMSO.

DoH (1991) *The Children Act 1989 Guidance and Regulations:* Vol. 1, *Court Orders;* Vol. 2, *Family Support, Day Care and Educational Provisions;* Vol. 3, *Family Placements;* Vol. 4, *Residential Care*. London: HMSO.

DoH (1992) *Health and Personal Social Services Statistics for England*. London: Government Statistical Service.

Fahlberg, V. (1981) *Attachment and Separation*. London: British Agencies for Adoption and Fostering.

Finlay, R. and Reynolds, J. (1987) *Social Work with Refugees*. NEC/Refugee Action.

Franklin, B. and Parton, N. (eds) (1991) *Social Work, the Media and Public Relations*. London: Routledge.

Furniss, T. (1991) *Multi-professional Handbook of Child Sexual Abuse: Integrated Management, Therapy, and Legal Intervention*. London: Routledge.

Gibbons, J. (1991) Children in need and their families: outcomes of referrals to social services. *British Journal of Social Work*, Vol. 21 (3): 217–28.

Glaser, D. and Frosh, S. (1988) *Child Sexual Abuse*. Harlow: Longmans.

Glastonbury, B., Bradley, R. and Orme, J. (1987) *Managing People in the Personal Social Services*. Chichester: Wiley.

Hallett, C. and Stevenson, O. (1980) *Child Abuse: Aspects of Interprofessional Cooperation*. London: Allen & Unwin.

Home Office/DoH/DES/Welsh Office (1991) *Working Together under the Children Act 1989. A Guide to Inter-agency Co-operation for the Protection of Children from Abuse*. London: HMSO.

Jackson, S. (1989) Education of children in care. In B. Kahan (ed.), *Child Care Research, Policy and Practice*. Sevenoaks: Hodder & Stoughton.

Jones, D. (1974) The truant. *Concern*, Vol. 14: 12–24.

Jordan, B. (1984) *Invitation to Social Work*. Oxford: Martin Robertson.

Mack, J. and Lansley, S. (1992) *Breadline Britain in the 1990s*. London: HarperCollins.

Millham, S., Bullock, R., Hosie, K. and Little, M. (1986) *Lost in Care: The Problems of Maintaining Links between Children in Care and Their Families*. Aldershot: Gower.

Neate, P. (1992) Pulling in different directions. *Community Care*, 12 December.

NFCA (1992) *Foster Care Finance: Advice and Information on the Cost of Caring for a Child*. London: National Foster Care Association.

NSPCC (1992) *Child Abuse Trends in England and Wales 1988–1990*. London: National Society for the Prevention of Cruelty to Children.

Oppenheim, C. (1990) *Poverty: The Facts*. London: Child Poverty Action Group.

Øvretveit, J. (1986) *Improving Social Work Records and Practice*. Birmingham: British Association of Social Workers.

Packman, J. and Jordan, B. (1991) The Children Act: looking forward, looking back. *British Journal of Social Work*, Vol. 21: 315–27.

Packman, J., Randall, J. and Jacques, N. (1986) *Who Needs Care?* Oxford: Blackwell.

Parsloe, P. (1981) *Social Services Area Teams*. London: Allen & Unwin.

Pincus, A. and Minahan, A. (1973) *Social Work Practice: Model and Method*. Itasca, IL: Peacock.

Pearson, G., Treseder, J. and Yelloly, M. (1988) *Social Work and the Legacy of Freud: Psychoanalysis and Its Uses*. Basingstoke: Macmillan.

Preston-Shoot, M. and Agass, D. (1990) *Making Sense of Social Work: Psychodynamics, Systems and Practice*. Basingstoke: Macmillan.

Prosser, P. (1978) *Perspectives in Foster Care*. Windsor: NFER.

Prosser, P. (1992) *Child Abuse Investigations: The Families' Perspective*. PAIN.

Robinson, M. (1978) *Schools and Social Work*. London: Routledge & Kegan Paul.

Rowe, J., Hundleby, M. and Garnett, L. (1989) *Child Care Now*. London: British Agencies for Adoption and Fostering.

Satyamurti, C. (1981) *Occupational Survival: The Case of the Local Authority Social Worker*. Oxford: Blackwell.

Seebohm, F. (1968) *Report of the Committee on Local Authority and Allied Personal Services*. London: HMSO.

Sone, K. (1992) When school's out. *Community Care*, 16 April.

Taylor, S. (1989) How prevalent is it? In W. Stainton Rogers, D. Hevey and E. Ash (eds), *Child Abuse and Neglect: Facing the Challenge*. London: Batsford.

White, T. (1991) Running a campaign: appropriate strategies for changing times. In B. Franklin and N. Parton (eds), *Social Work, the Media and Public Relations*. London: Routledge.

Whitney, B. (1992) A time to act. *Community Care*, 6 June.

FURTHER READING

Marsh, P. and Fisher, M. (1992) *Good Intentions: Developing Partnership in Social Services*, York: Joseph Rowntree Foundation. Gives a very full account of the ways in which users and providers of social services can work towards mutually defined resolutions in dealing with jointly identified problems, particularly within the framework of new legislation.

Macdonald, S. (1991) *All Equal under the Act?* London: National Institute for Social Work. How can social workers and users put into practice the egalitarian principles of the Children Act 1989? This book provides practical help and advice in dealing with the question, focusing on developing competent practice with members of racial minority groups and children with disabilities.

PART 4

HEALTH SUPPORT

INTRODUCTION

The three chapters in Part 4 relate to various aspects of doctors' work with children. Whilst all parents will be aware of their GPs and the ways in which they treat illness, they may be less sensitive to the current issues facing GPs which influence both their capacity to meet the health needs of the community and the ways in which they are trying to develop preventive approaches to health care. Similarly, whilst parents and professional groups will know of the regular medical check-ups that take place within schools, they are less likely to be familiar with the professional and organizational issues within the School Health Service and how it might develop in the future. Chapter 9, on infection control, is different from the other two health chapters and the other chapters within the book. In it Donal O'Sullivan discusses how health and local authority staff work together to control infection within schools. However, many of the concerns about inter-professional relationships are similar to those explored in the rest of the book.

CHAPTER 7

The School Health Service

Moira Dick

A health service for schools has been in existence since the beginning of this century. Until recently the service had continued almost unaltered despite a dramatic improvement in children's health in the first half of the century and many changes in both education and health services. Legislation, particularly in health (the management changes recommended by the Griffiths Report (DHSS, 1985) and the 1990 NHS Act) but also in education (the 1981 Education Act and 1988 Education Reform Act), has led to a reappraisal of the school health service, the needs of schoolchildren and how best these needs might be met. There is general acceptance that school health services have to change but there are concerns that some of the changes that have already occurred have been driven mainly by cost and not by a consideration of all the issues. This chapter briefly describes the original aims and objectives of the service and the many organizational changes that have occurred, in order to give a background to current issues.

The chapter will mainly focus on the work carried out by doctors and nurses in mainstream schools whilst recognizing that the school health service is very involved in the health care of children in special schools and comprises other professional groups such as those in the fields of physiotherapy, speech therapy, occupational therapy and clinical psychology.

WHY THE NEED FOR A SCHOOL HEALTH SERVICE?

The School Health Service was set up in 1908 to help tackle the widespread malnutrition and disease that were preventing many children from taking advantage of school. Concern had also been expressed that the majority of recruits for the Boer War had been in a poor physical state and unfit for active service. The original aims were not only to detect disease in the early stages and provide necessary treatment, but to prevent disease through health education and immunization programmes and to advise the education authority of the implications of any child's illness or disability. These were described as 'the early detection of unsuspected defects, checking incipient maladies at their onset' and 'furnishing the facts that will guide education authorities in relation to physical and mental development during school life' (Board of Education, 1907). Children at that time had no access to general practitioners as we know them today.

The service was run by doctors and nurses, who carried out health inspections on every child at three statutory ages throughout their school life. Children were also weighed and measured regularly, hearing and vision were checked, teeth were inspected, immunization programmes were carried out and children's heads were combed for lice.

The inspections confirmed a high level of disease, and this led to a provision in the 1918 Education Act that local education authorities should provide treatment clinics for children. Special clinics were set up for the management of skin diseases and other minor ailments, ear, nose and throat conditions, orthopaedics and remedial exercises. The local education authorities provided treatment facilities and the local Medical Officer of Health (who at that time was the senior doctor in the local authority) organized medical and nursing input.

Improvement in children's health

Over the next twenty years children's health improved dramatically, in part owing to the general improvement in social conditions and the reduction in infectious diseases such as tuberculosis. The prevalence of malnutrition was 133 per thousand schoolchildren in 1915, and this had fallen to 12 per thousand children by 1931. Apart from dental decay the prevalence of other diseases had also fallen, and successive governments continued to see the value of routine medical inspections. More clinics were introduced to include child guidance, enuresis (bedwetting), audiology and speech therapy. Routine medical inspections were carried on until the 1959 Education Act allowed more selective arrangements to be introduced, but even then most authorities continued with the same system until at least 1985.

One of the consequences of improvement in physical health and increased recognition of diseases in the pre-school period was that health and educational professionals became more aware of the influence that social, emotional and developmental factors have on children's health and their ability to learn. Doctors and nurses have needed to be qualified not only to recognize physical disease but also to assess and manage children with emotional and behavioural problems, learning difficulties and those who are socially disadvantaged. There was a time, however, when doctors were still being required to carry out so many routine inspections, often repeatedly, on entirely normal children that there was no time to devote to the management of these important problems or to liaise with teachers.

When the National Health Service was set up in 1946, every family had access to a general practitioner and it was intended that there should be a reduction in the number of clinics provided by the education authorities. But the range and number of clinics continued to rise, reflecting the change in the nature of children's medical problems and also the general practitioners' reluctance to take on the recognition and management of developmental problems in children.

Assessment of child development and behaviour had always been part of the medical examination, and originally the school doctor had prime responsibility in deciding on the educational placement of handicapped children. Following the 1974 NHS reorganization, more qualifications were required of the medical officers who examined children for special schooling. Multidisciplinary assessment became accepted practice (DES, 1975) and since the 1981 Education Act the school doctor is now only one of three professionals required to report on children's special educational needs. In the process, the school doctor's contribution has been minimized and attention is given only to the doctor's comments on medical factors.

BACKGROUND TO THE PROFESSION

The doctors and nurses working in the School Health Service were originally employed by the local authority and this continued until the first NHS reorganization in 1974. So from the beginning of the NHS there was a tripartite structure of public health, general practice and the hospital sector. It should be pointed out that the terms 'public health' and 'public health medicine' have now acquired quite different meanings. Public health at that time encompassed the School Health Service, which was seen as being mainly preventive, whilst general practice provided treatment services at a primary care level. Hospitals were of course mainly concerned with treatment. Even after integration of public health into the NHS in 1974, this tripartite structure largely remained. Recently attempts have been made to combine preventive and treatment aspects of care, particularly within general practice, and this area is explored further in Chapter 8.

Medical posts within the three sectors have had very different levels of status. Medical students have mainly been taught in hospitals by consultants, and until recently achieving a consultancy post was considered the pinnacle of a medical career. General practice was seen as being only for those who had failed to stay on the hospital career ladder, and public health doctors were often regarded as not being 'real' doctors in that they did not see 'real' illness and were hardly involved in treatment.

There was no specific training requirement to be a school doctor and, unless the doctor was following a career with the intention of being a medical officer of health, no real career prospects. It was one of the few medical posts that could be done on a sessional basis, so it often attracted women with domestic commitments or doctors with other part-time jobs. Consequently, although many competent doctors worked for years in school health and gained enormous experience as well as the respect of health and education colleagues, the service never received much recognition from the rest of the NHS and had very little influence on decision-making bodies. This lack of prestige and influence, and the development of general practice from the 1960s, has made the service extremely vulnerable to the most recent NHS reforms.

Coming in from the cold

At about the same time that attempts were being made to integrate all the health services through the 1974 reorganization, a committee was set up to look at integrating child health services and to rationalize what were seen to be the parallel services of school health and general practice. The report, *Fit for the Future*, later known as the Court Report (Court, 1976), recommended that there should be general practitioner paediatricians who would be able to combine preventive and treatment aspects for children, their families, and schools. These GPs would be backed up by consultant community paediatricians who would coordinate programmes of child health surveillance and also take on the assessment and management of children with handicaps and chronic disorders.

Although the post of general practitioner paediatrician was never created, most districts now have a consultant community paediatrician who is responsible for managing pre-school and school health services. The school doctor is now either part of a community child health department led by a consultant community paediatrician or part of a combined hospital and community paediatric department. Having started off life as a public health doctor, the school doctor is now seen as a paediatrician. The posts are increasingly becoming part of training programmes for those going into paediatrics or general practice, rather than career posts in themselves. However, there is still a large mix of doctors – some who have been employed prior to the changes and have permanent posts, and junior doctors who stay for one to two years. For those taking up posts now, there is usually a requirement to have had at least six months' hospital paediatric experience. In-service training is provided on all aspects of school health work such as child development, screening procedures, immunization, child protection procedures, working in multidisciplinary teams and preparing reports on children who are thought to have special educational needs.

No specific training is required for school nursing apart from being registered as a general nurse, and no mandatory in-service training, although there is a school nursing certificate, which an increasing number of school nurses now hold.

Further changes in the NHS affecting the delivery of the service

Following the 1974 NHS reorganization, health services were managed by area health authorities which usually had the same boundaries as local authorities. In a less extensive reorganization in 1982 these were abolished in favour of smaller district health authorities, which in some instances were not coterminous with local government boundaries. This led to difficulties in effective joint working when some county councils or boroughs had to relate to two or more health authorities, or one health authority to more than one borough or council.

In 1984 the introduction of general management into the NHS (the Griffiths reforms) led to more formal management structures within health authorities. Often these were organized around particular client groups, often termed 'care groups' in the NHS. Perhaps because of the uncertainty as to what the School Health Service actually provided, school nurses and doctors found themselves organized into different management units, and this caused problems in maintaining the concept of a school health team.

FUNCTIONS OF THE SCHOOL HEALTH SERVICE

Despite all the reorganizations in health and changes in children's health needs, the aims and objectives of the School Health Service have remained remarkably unaltered. One of the main aims is still to detect any problem that may have implications for children's health or education. The service still has responsibilities to the child, the school and the education authority, and has a statutory duty to comply with the requirements of the 1981 Education Act in preparing medical reports for those children who are thought to have special educational needs. Prevention of infectious disease through immunization programmes remains one of the aims. More emphasis is now placed on providing health information to help children make healthy choices as adults, and also to promote a healthy environment in which children can grow and develop. As fewer children with special needs, such as physical disability or learning difficulty, go to special schools, and more are integrated into mainstream schools, so the role of the school doctor and nurse has changed to help in the management of these children. The term 'special needs' is used in this context to mean children with physical, sensory or learning disability who are also likely to have special educational needs. There are also children who are identified in school as having special educational needs but who may not have a permanent disability.

The functions of the School Health Service that are generally accepted by those in the profession (Faculty of Community Child Health, 1990) are:

Health surveillance

An attempt is made to look at every child's health and development when he or she enters school at the age of 5 years. How extensive this review is depends on the nature of the pre-school programme. Some authorities simply review the pre-school records with or without a parental questionnaire and then offer medical examinations where necessary. Others continue with a medical and neurodevelopmental assessment for all children. This consists of a neurological examination that includes gross and fine motor skills, hearing and vision, and a number of screening tests that aim to pick out delays in cognitive abilities such as language comprehension and perceptuomotor skills that are likely to affect children's ability to learn. Measurement of visual acuity and a screening check for hearing impairment may be repeated at intervals throughout school life. A routine medical examination is not offered for older children, but those entering secondary school will usually have their health records reviewed.

Immunization programme

The immunization status of every child entering school is reviewed and steps are taken to ensure that those who have not completed the pre-school programme do so. Later immunizations are carried out according to local and national schedules. They are usually done in school to ensure that coverage is as high as possible and they usually include rubella for girls and BCG (for protection against tuberculosis) for everyone. School-leavers are offered a booster against polio and tetanus.

Medical examination

An open referral system usually operates so that anyone can refer a child if there is concern. This may be the child, parent, teacher or another health professional.

Coordination of medical and therapeutic care of children with special needs

Children with special needs such as hearing impairment, language delay or physical disability may already be known prior to entering school. Others may be identified at the first school medical or later on during their school career. The school team has a duty to ensure that all the relevant services know about the child, and it should regularly review the child's progress.

Compliance with the 1981 Education Act

Most children with special needs who are also thought to have special educational needs will have been notified by the health authority to the education authority before entering school, under section 10 of the 1981 Education Act. If the education authority decides to proceed with a formal assessment of the child's special educational needs, there is a statutory requirement for a doctor to complete a report outlining the child's needs from the doctor's perspective. Once a statement has been agreed, the child's progress is reviewed formally on an annual basis with a complete reassessment at 13 years. The doctor has similar responsibilities if a child is found to have special educational needs after starting school, the only difference being that the notification is usually made by a member of the teaching staff.

Liaison

The effectiveness of a school health team depends on how well it communicates with parents, teaching staff, social services, the local child development team and other health professionals, particularly the general practitioner.

Medical advice

Teaching staff often request discussions and information on the management of common disorders such as epilepsy, asthma and diabetes. Teachers often feel that their care role in relation to children with such problems is difficult, so this medical advisory and support function can be very important for both the child and the teacher.

Health promotion and health education

The school health team can be a useful resource for teachers in preparing lessons or taking part in discussions with groups of children. School nurses see health promotion as one of the main parts of their work in schools. The sorts of areas they may be involved with include smoking, alcohol, drug misuse and sex education.

Treatment service

School doctors often manage straightforward problems such as bedwetting or sleep disorders. Health authorities frequently run vision clinics and secondary audiology services. A bedwetting service is sometimes provided for cases which do not respond to simple advice or interventions based an behavioural approaches. Because of the way the School Health Service came into being, school doctors rarely, if ever, prescribe medication, and children with acute medical problems are referred to the general practitioner.

Adolescent services

Counselling services and walk-in clinics for adolescents are held in some schools. These tend to focus on the psychosocial and sexual problems or worries of adolescents.

Child protection

The school health team works closely with other agencies to monitor children already on the 'at risk' register, and attempts to attend all case conferences. The School Health Service can usually respond to requests for medical examinations of children thought to have been non-accidentally injured.

Policy and planning

The school health team collects data on the numbers of children seen and on the nature of referrals made to enable the health authority to plan resources in the best way. Many use a computerized database designed to their own specifications or use the pre-school and school modules of the National Child Health System, a standard nationwide computer system.

ORGANIZATION OF THE SERVICE

There are local variations in how the service is organized, and management structures differ greatly from place to place. However, there is general agreement on the core structure needed (Faculty of Community Child Health, 1990). The key principles behind this structure are as follows:

Relationship with community child health services

School health is normally part of the community child health services and provides integration of surveillance for all children from birth to 19 years. This allows for continuity of record keeping and of the staff who see children and their families. Doctors in school health gain experience in working with children of all ages and become aware of the wide range of normality. The school health team, as part of the wider service, has easy lines of communication with health visitors, who usually offer important pre-school support for families, and also with the child development team, which comprises professionals working with children with special needs. There is normally a senior doctor in the child health service who has responsibility for coordinating the work of school doctors and arranging training when needed.

Geographical factors

Many services divide their community child health services into geographical patches so that close working relationships develop between staff working in the same geographical area. The same school doctor and nurse may visit a number of schools and the school doctor may also run pre-school clinics and visit day nurseries in the same area.

Named doctor and nurse

For every primary and secondary school there are usually a named doctor and nurse with a programme of visits organized at the beginning of each term. Depending on the size of the school and the extent of the surveillance programme, medical examinations may be carried out on a weekly or fortnightly basis. School nurses tend to be more flexible and are often in more regular contact with the school.

Appointments and confidentiality

Invitations to come for a medical examination are usually sent out with children from the school. Parents are requested to be present and children are not examined without their parents' consent, except if the child's health or safety are felt to be at risk. Notes may be kept in the school or in a local health centre depending on the space available, but are always kept locked and are not available to teaching staff except with the parents' consent.

Communication

Knowledge about the School Health Service varies from school to school. Some parents are made aware of it and are encouraged to use it as soon as their children start school. In other schools, teaching staff themselves are unaware that there is a health service that they could use. Some school health teams have regular meetings with the headteacher and some may have multidisciplinary meetings that also include the educational psychology and educational social work services. Communication with teaching staff after a school medical varies and information about children is shared only with the parents' and child's consent.

CURRENT ISSUES

As has been outlined, the organization of the service has changed several times in the past twenty years, leading to wide variation in service provision, organization and delivery. An audit carried out of 130 health authorities in the UK in 1986 concluded that variation in practice 'reflects an uncertainty within district health authorities about what a school health service should be doing and how it should be organised. And this in turn reflects central indecision' (Harrison and Gretton, 1986). The different strands in the history of the profession – public health and more recently paediatrics – and the low level of influence on decision-making bodies were noted earlier. To compound this, doctors working in the School Health Service continue to be divided. They are represented by two main bodies: the Faculty of Community Child Health, which is part of the Society of Public Health, and the Community Paediatric Group, a subgroup of the British Paediatric Association. This division reflects a difference in emphasis between those who relate more closely to the historical link with public health and those who see themselves primarily as paediatricians.

Managers are increasingly having to take decisions on priorities in order to keep within budgets to find cheaper ways of delivering the service. Professional issues can become clouded by expediency rather than being based on what is accepted as good practice. Some of the major current issues are as follows.

Extent of coverage – should all children be seen?

One view is that there is no longer a need to carry out routine, comprehensive developmental screening checks and that only a limited number of screening checks for hearing, vision and physical abnormalities should be undertaken. This view is expressed in *Health for All Children* (Hall, 1991), a major report on child health surveillance. It points to the low yield of problems that are not known about prior to school entry and argues that parents are the best people to draw attention to children's difficulties. The report recommends that for all children at school entry the School Health Service should:

• enquire about parental and teacher concern;
• review pre-school records, including immunization status;
• measure height, and plot on chart;
• check vision using Snellen chart;
• check hearing by sweep test.

It does not address other aspects of school health such as who does the check and who should be responsible for ensuring that the school entry review is carried out. It does emphasize the importance of good pre-school records and good communication between the pre-school and school part of the service. Parent-held records, which have been recommended on a national basis, and the keeping of pre-school information on a computerized database should lead to better integration of school and community child health services.

The other view, expressed cogently by Whitmore and Bax (1990), is that it should be every child's right to have a medical examination and that parents often welcome such an examination even if they expect it to show that their child is normal. Bax and Whitmore feel that a selective system can easily become arbitrary and exclusive rather than carefully selective about whose health should actually be checked, and point out that adult concern is not a foolproof pointer to childhood disorders. They also advocate continuing neurodevelopmental assessments (Bax and Whitmore, 1987), showing a significant association between early difficulties and subsequent learning difficulties. They feel that this knowledge helps children rather than stigmatizes them, and that to wait for problems eventually to come to light in school may be rather too late for individual children.

Who should be providing the service?

General practitioners are now taking on more pre-school surveillance and there is a view that it would make sense for GPs also to take on school surveillance. As explained earlier, school doctors are unable to prescribe and GPs are likely to know the family situation better. This move would remove the service from schools and would lead to the loss of the good communication that often exists between the teaching staff and the School Health Service. However, using GPs in this way would allow school doctors to focus on the management of children with special needs, who are increasingly being integrated into mainstream education. Extending the workload of GPs in this way may be unacceptable and there are implications for the training requirements of school doctors, as such a post would probably not be suitable for junior doctors on short-term contracts who are just beginning their training in community child health.

Another option is for school nurses to carry out more of the routine health surveillance and screening checks and to implement the immunization programmes. There are arguments for and against this option. School nurses are tending to see themselves as independent practitioners who are able to carry their own caseload rather than being dependent on doctors for defining their work. It is also seen as a cheaper option by managers, since nurses' salaries are lower than those of doctors. However, Whitmore and Bax (1990) costed the likely savings for a school with an annual intake of 37 'rising five' children. They compared a joint doctor–nurse interview and examination, and a nurse-only interview with subsequent medicals for those children thought to need them. The annual difference was only £55. Organizing school nurses and school doctors in different management units has led to decisions being made concerning one part of the service without due reference to the other. This has affected the nature of the school health team and undermined its ability to work *as* a team of nurse and doctor with common aims and objectives. Increasing the role of school nurses could compound this problem.

Working together

Recent papers on teachers' and parents' understanding and use of the School Health Service point to a lack of awareness of what the school health team can offer and what it is trying to achieve (Fitzherbert, 1982; Perkins 1989; Fox *et al.*, 1991). Not surprisingly, given the uncertainty of the school doctor's role within the medical profession, it is not always clear to teachers and parents how school doctors differ from GPs. Conversely there may be undue expectations of the service that school doctors can deliver and frustration at their inability to deal with social problems. Where doctors are experienced they are frequently used to sort out a variety of different problems from medical and developmental to social, behavioural and even educational. There is an overlap of expertise in assessing children's development and behaviour with that of the educational psychologist, clinical psychologist and educational social worker and this can lead to confusion. There may also be different perceptions of what the different professionals' roles are, which can lead to conflict. One of the conflicts that emerges is the extent to which the school doctor can comment or give advice on children's learning difficulties. At the age of 5 children suddenly become the exclusive province of the educational establishment and not that of health, as they had been until they were 5. Health education and promotion is another area where both education and health think that they own the expertise and where joint working would be beneficial. Much lip service is paid to multidisciplinary and inter-agency working but greater effort is needed to make it work effectively. Education and health authorities could combine their limited resources to work as a team in schools with enormous benefit to children and staff.

Who is the client?

There is uncertainty, or perhaps unclarity, in defining the client of the School Health Service. Is it the child and his or her family? Is it also the school? The statutory requirements of health, education and social service authorities may conflict with professional responsibilities to the family. It is possible that one of the reasons that adolescent services have not become widespread is partly the reluctance of adolescents to use a service that is thought to be closely associated with the educational establishment. There is also a duty to the whole community, particularly in relation to immunization programmes and health and developmental surveillance. If these different duties and responsibilities were clear to all it would make the work of the school doctor more effective.

Quality measures

The 1990 NHS Act has placed great emphasis on auditing health services and measuring output. Various studies have been undertaken, usually at a local level, to see what sorts of problems present to the School Health Service, how many medical problems are diagnosed, whether neurodevelopmental problems at the age of 5 are significant for learning and what perceptions parents and teachers have of the service. One study, the North Paddington Primary School Health

Project (1978–80) (Whitmore, 1984), looked at a range of activities undertaken by the school health team over a three-year period. There is a need for nationally agreed standards for the service and outcome measures that can be used as a basis for audit. There is also a need to try to define quality measures, particularly as the part of the school health team's work that is valued most is communication and liaison between parents, the school and other health professionals.

Manpower and training issues

It has already been stated that doctors and nurses working in the School Health Service should have the necessary qualifications and training to be able to assess and manage a wide range of children's problems from physical and sensory to behavioural and developmental. No national training programme has been devised and most school doctors and nurses acquire skills in a haphazard fashion. Posts of six months' or one year's duration, the norm for junior doctors training to be GPs or paediatricians, do not allow sufficient time for familiarization with the complexities of the School Health Service and the duties and responsibilities required. Health service managers looking to making savings argue that pre-school surveillance is now being carried out by GPs, so it is possible to abolish community child health posts. A reduction in medical establishment results in fewer doctors being available for school health work and tends to have an adverse effect on recruitment. If GPs were to take on school health work they would require training and list sizes would have to be adjusted to account for this extra work. The North Paddington Primary School Health Project (1978–80) calculated that medical time needed was not less than one hour per week per term and for the school nurse 20 minutes per week. The medical time is equivalent to one full-time doctor during school terms for 3500 children and one school nurse for 900 children. Current figures are not available, but in 1980 the national figure was one doctor for 6750 pupils and one nurse for 1950 pupils, and the trend has certainly not been to increase the numbers of medical and nursing staff in schools. Urgent consideration needs to be given to the sort of school health service needed, the optimum number of medical and nursing staff to run it, and training requirements. Without a conscious decision to maintain a school health service there is a real risk that the service will dwindle to a point where it cannot be recovered.

IMPLICATIONS OF THE LATEST LEGISLATION IN HEALTH AND EDUCATION

There have been recent major legislative changes in health, education and social services. It is too soon to know what implications this legislation will have for the School Health Service, so the following comments are speculative:

The 1990 NHS Act

This Act has radically altered the way health services will be delivered. District health authorities now have the responsibility to identify the needs of their population and to purchase health services to meet those needs. The provision of service will mainly be from independent NHS Trusts, though some 'directly managed units' will continue to exist (see Chapter 1). The implications for school health services are as yet unknown, but there are anxieties that this more explicit approach to what health services do will create difficulties for services such as school health, which are seen by some as marginal.

GP fund-holding

GPs have been given the option to manage their own budget and decide what services to purchase for their patients. At the present time hospital referrals are the only services that can be purchased by GP fund-holders. There are plans to allow community nursing services to be purchased directly, but it is not clear whether GP fund-holders will eventually be responsible for all the services needed for their patients. If this were the case, GPs could decide whether they wanted to spend part of their budget on a school health service or on some entirely different service.

Local management of schools

The future of the School Health Service is dependent on whether purchasing health authorities (or possibly GP fund-holders) continue to pay for it. It is likely that the present local arrangements and agreements between health and education authorities will continue and be respected by locally managed schools. It is not certain whether this will be the case for opted-out schools that are no longer accountable to the local education authority.

1989 Children Act

The 1989 Children Act imposes no new responsibilities on the School Health Service, but does emphasize the importance of all the agencies working together, especially for children defined as being in need. Children with disabilities are children in need, as are those who are socially disadvantaged or at risk of abuse or neglect. Any decisions that were made to cut back on school health services would have to take into account the statutory requirements laid down by the Children Act.

THE FUTURE OF THE SCHOOL HEALTH SERVICE

The School Health Service met obvious needs in the school population when it first began, and it continued to be valued for many years. There is still the potential for a health service that is primarily for schoolchildren, whether they are from the inner city or rural areas, which can meet their needs at various ages through their school career. The Court Report defined educational medicine as the study and practice of child health and paediatrics in relation to the process of learning. Perhaps if educational medicine were recognized as a paediatric speciality and given the necessary resources, the School Health Service could become as relevant for schoolchildren at the end of the century as it was at the beginning.

REFERENCES

Bax, M. and Whitmore, K. (1987) The medical examination of children on entry into school: the results and use of neurodevelopmental assessment. *Developmental Medicine and Child Neurology*, Vol. 28: 40–55.

Board of Education (1907) *Memorandum on Medical Inspection of Children in Public Elementary Schools* (Circular 576). London: HMSO.

Court, S.D.M. (1976) *Fit for the Future: Report of the Committee on Child Health Service*. London: HMSO.

DES (1975) *The Discovery of Children Requiring Special Education and the Assessment of Their Needs* (Circular 2/75). London: HMSO.

DHSS(1985) *NHS Management Inquiry* (The Griffith Report). London: HMSO.

Faculty of Community Child Health (1990) *The School Health Service*. (Available from Dr P.A. Gardner, The Society of Community Health Ltd, 31 Battye Avenue, Crosland Moor, Huddersfield HD4 5PW.)

Fitzherbert, K. (1982) Communication with teachers in the health surveillance of school children. *Maternal and Child Health*, Vol. 7(3): 100–3.

Fox, T., Rankin, M., Salmon., S. and Stewart, M. (1991) How schools perceive the School Health Service. *Public Health*, Vol. 105: 399–403.

Hall, D.M.B. (1991) *Health for All Children. A Programme for Child Health Surveillance*. Oxford: Oxford University Press.

Harrison, A. and Gretton, J. (eds) (1986) School health: the invisible service. In *Health Care UK: An Economic, Social and Policy Audit*. London: CIPFA.

Perkins, E.R. (1989) The School Health Service through parents' eyes. *Archives of Diseases in Childhood*, Vol. 64: 1088–91.

Whitmore, K. (1984) The past, present and future of the health services for children in school. In J.A. Macfarlane (ed.), *Progress in Child Health*, Vol. 1. London: Churchill Livingstone.

Whitmore, K. and Bax, M. (1990) Checking the health of school entrants. *Archives of Diseases in Childhood*, Vol. 65: 320–6.

CHAPTER 8

General practice

Paul Booton

INTRODUCTION

The doctor in general practice is the first point of contact for most children needing medical care. General practitioners control access to much of the rest of the National Health Service, which for better or worse makes them very important in children's lives. It is, therefore, essential that those with responsibilities for children, such as parents and teachers, are well informed about the role of general practitioners and the services to which they have access. This chapter examines the history of general practice, the work that GPs do and the organizational structures under which they do it. It tries to identify what a good general practice looks like and ends by looking to the future of the service. Although there are some specific links between education and general practice, the most important relationship is the most general one – that is, children. Accordingly, the chapter concentrates on the services GPs provide for children and does not really explore large areas of GPs' work in relation to adults and the elderly.

WHAT IS A GENERAL PRACTITIONER?

General practitioners are, as the name implies, doctors who have a general responsibility for their patients' problems. They are aware that illness is not only physical in nature but psychological, and that social problems have an important bearing on illness. A general practitioner needs to have training across the whole spectrum of medicine and health care, but without necessarily having great depth at any one point. Many general practitioners now undertake a degree of specialist training – quite frequently in child health, which makes up a large part of the work of general practice. This is separate from the more generalist training they have to be GPs.

General practitioners are also known as family practitioners, the name highlighting the responsibility they have not just to individuals but to family groups. General practitioners value the relationships that develop with their patients and families over a long period of time and it is common for GPs to look after several generations of the same family.

GPs are also referred to as 'primary care' doctors because they are often the first contact for patients within the health service. It is the GPs' job to find the appropriate way to help patients with their problems, which may be by the GPs themselves or may involve finding the agency or medical specialist who is best equipped to deal with these problems. For this reason GPs are sometimes known as the 'gatekeepers' of the health service. Most GPs work as part of a primary health care team with other health workers, an aspect of their role discussed more fully later in the chapter.

THE HISTORY OF GENERAL PRACTICE

General practice has emerged as a distinct discipline over hundreds of years. The name 'general practice' was in common use by the middle of the nineteenth century, when an abortive attempt was made to found a college of general practitioners. In terms of current practice, general practice started at the turn of this century.

The situation at the end of the nineteenth century

At the end of the nineteenth century the disparity between the rich upper classes and the poor working class was as marked in terms of access to medical care as it was in relation to all other aspects of life. Treatment by local doctors could impoverish families or be entirely beyond their reach. For the poor, access to medical care depended upon the charity of doctors or employers, the crude and humiliating provisions of the workhouse or, for a few, entry to one of the great charitable teaching hospitals of the major towns.

The medical 'clubs'

Perhaps the first step towards modern general practice can be found in the evolution of medical 'clubs'. These acted as a kind of insurance scheme for those who could not afford to pay for their consultations with doctors in the usual way. Doctors received a small fee for each person in the club (the per capita payment of today's general practice discussed later) and club members had access to the doctor's limited services as and when they needed them. It gave the poor limited access to the lowest level of health care at an affordable price, and gave a living to those doctors working in areas where there were few opportunities to earn an income from what we would nowadays refer to as private practice.

The 1911 National Insurance Act

The first glimmerings of a national service came in 1911 with Lloyd George's National Insurance Act. This Act effectively turned the medical clubs of the late nineteenth century into a national system of insurance, whereby working men (but not women or children) had access to both doctors and sickness benefit for periods of illness. In practice sickness benefit was the more significant of the two. Before the Act, illness of the breadwinner could quickly impoverish a working-class family. The Act recognized that this was the beginning of a vicious spiral of ill-health leading to poverty, and thus to vulnerability to further ill-health.

The doctor, whose medical interventions were often of little or no value, was part of the scheme mainly as an adjudicator of entitlement to receive sickness benefits – a role the doctor still possesses. This successful reform gave rise to the GP and his or her 'panel patients' (as patients were known under the provisions of the Act), who were crammed into surgeries at the beginning and end of the day. The middle of the day was devoted to visiting 'proper' patients who were able to pay their own way. The model of busy surgeries with short consulting times (still only about 8 minutes per patient on average in the UK) held at the beginning and end of the day is a direct descendant of this scheme.

The National Health Service

The Second World War demonstrated the need for a national, planned system of health care, and also raised widespread enthusiasm for it. The 1946 National Health Service Act, pioneered by the postwar Labour government, aimed to provide a comprehensive health service available to all regardless of their rank in society and free at the point of contact. It was perhaps the most radical innovation ever in the organization of health care, but it was not brought about easily. The medical profession was initially deeply opposed to it and the hospital consultants were bought off by Aneurin Bevan, the Labour Party's Minister of Health, who 'choked their mouths with gold'; that is, their opposition was bought off by generous salaries and financial incentives. GPs continued recalcitrant and fought a bitter campaign against the government through the British Medical Association (the 'doctors' union'). The solution eventually accepted by GPs was a compromise whereby they remained as independent contractors to the health service. This meant that they continued as private doctors, with a contract with the government to provide a range of health care services to the public, instead of being government employees as the hospital consultants now became.

To an extent GPs were right to be apprehensive. From their point of view the changes were aimed almost entirely at the hospital service, and left them in much the same position as before. In the early discussions there was much talk of new health centres, staff and equipment; in the event there were none of these and GPs were left with their generally poorly resourced premises and lack of administrative or support staff. For patients there were two important benefits: first, the Act removed the anomaly whereby only working men were entitled to benefits and extended it so that everyone had access to free primary health care. But the greater change was that secondary health care (i.e hospital care), which previously had been available only to those who could pay or obtain charitable help, was now available to everyone, unrestricted and free of charge.

Paradoxically, as the health service expanded over those first few years and became a model for health care provision worldwide, so the status of GPs within the medical profession declined. The National Health Service had given them a role only as gatekeepers to the rest of the service, and the profession's perception of GPs was that they were failed hospital doctors whose job was to sift the trivia and send the 'real' problems on to the hospital specialists.

The 1968 GPs' Charter

The impetus for change into today's pattern of service came from two directions. First, concerned GPs formed their own Royal College (along the lines of the ancient colleges of physicians and surgeons) to monitor and improve standards. Secondly, in 1968 Harold Wilson's government recognized the problems of general practice and wanted to limit the growth of expensive hospital medicine. The General Practice Charter was negotiated. It allowed GPs to build adequate surgeries and employ administrative and nursing staff. It encouraged doctors to work together in group practices and encouraged the development of post-graduate training schemes for general practitioners. However, it did not nationalize general practice in the way that the NHS Act had nationalized hospitals; GPs remained as private subcontractors to the health service. This status persists, which is why GPs generally own their premises and employ their own staff. They undertake to provide a range of services to the general public, for which they receive payment.

In practice, the vast majority of their income is from this source, the remainder coming from signing certain certificates and producing reports for insurance companies and the like. For the most part this system works surprisingly well, allowing GPs enough independence to develop in ways appropriate to their communities, whilst exercising sufficient control to prevent excesses developing. That said, it fails to reward excellence and permits some very poor GP services to continue.

The Thatcher health service reforms

The major reforms of 1991 were set in train by the Conservative government following widespread concern of the general public and health workers about the poor state of the service. The Royal Colleges of the medical and nursing professions believed that this deterioration was due to the inadequate and declining funding of the service. Prime Minister Thatcher ordered a review of the health service, and following a rather brief overview offered not money but reforms. These were informed by a view that money was being wasted within the NHS which could best be dealt with by allowing market forces to operate. The ensuing competition between service providers would reward those who offered the best services at the lowest costs. However, there were concerns that this was the first step in privatizing the health service and doubts about whether market forces were capable of providing the best rather than merely the cheapest service.

Under the reforms, hospitals became 'providers' of a range of services bought on behalf of patients by health authorities acting as 'purchasers', or directly by the new breed of fund-holding GPs who controlled their own finances. General practice was also reformed by imposing a new contract on GPs. The speed with which these changes were imposed, their untested nature and the addition of new tasks of unproven benefit to patients aroused massive and almost unanimous opposition among GPs. The protests varied from valid intellectual and pragmatic criticisms to emotional and sometimes hysterical denunciations. Despite all this the changes went through Parliament with little modification. Since then GPs have learned to live with them, the worst of the reforms have been quietly dropped and the better ones have found their place in the life of the practice and the NHS.

THE TRAINING OF GPs

Becoming a doctor

Before entering postgraduate training for general practice, medical students have to qualify as doctors by obtaining an undergraduate medical degree and become fully registered with the General Medical Council (GMC), the organization that regulates the profession. Undergraduate training takes place in medical schools, which are part of universities, though students also spend a lot of time in the teaching hospitals which are closely related to the medical schools. At this stage, training follows traditional lines, stressing doctors' role in curing diseases and dealing with physical problems. Students are taught a great deal about physical illnesses, how they arise and how they can be treated.

After qualifying, doctors have to work in hospitals under supervision for a year as house doctors before becoming fully registered with the General Medical Council.

Becoming a general practitioner

At this stage doctors are free to specialize. To do so in general practice involves a minimum of three years' additional training. Of these, two are spent in hospital, working in a range of specialties (one of which usually includes paediatrics) with the third spent working in a general practice under the supervision of a GP trainer. In practice many GPs do more than this minimum, some choosing to acquire a degree of specialization in a specific medical area or in a related discipline such as counselling.

This training aims to give GPs the breadth of knowledge necessary for general practice work. Through working in hospital specialties they acquire a broad knowledge of medicine. In the general practice part of their training they consider how the physical, the psychological and the social aspect of patients' problems interrelate to produce the whole picture. They think about the context and meaning of illness, not only for patients, but for their families, their homes and their jobs. They also learn how their own feelings can help or hinder their relationships with their patients, and how to develop appropriate communication skills to cope with their work. During and at the end of this training they may take postgraduate diplomas and examinations, and at the end they are fully accredited as general practitioners and may join or form their own practice.

THE WORK OF THE DOCTOR IN GENERAL PRACTICE

GPs' work has a number of dimensions which relate to their skills as carers and in running the practice. First, doctors are there to see, treat and offer advice to their patients. Traditional medical care is reactive in that it concentrates on curing diseases after they have arisen. GPs increasingly try to work proactively or preventively, dealing with diseases by preventing their occurrence in the first place. The effects of tobacco and alcohol on health are traditional targets for this preventive practice with more recent ones being screening for high blood pressure and high cholesterol to prevent heart disease and strokes. The GP's brief is, however, much wider than this and the work often involves counselling and frequently a degree of what might be seen as social work.

Secondly, GPs are increasingly having to be business managers. A modern general practice works as a small business with a sizeable number of employees, and an annual turnover of £250,000 would not be unusual. This comes about partly through GPs' status as self-employed subcontractors, but the development of the new fund-holding practices makes it even more pronounced. In these circumstances not only are they paying the usual staff bills but they are using funds to purchase hospital care directly for their patients.

A visit to the doctor

Let us take as an example a parent bringing a child with a problem to the doctor. The GP has two main options in dealing with the problem. The doctor may decide to deal with the problem himself or herself, or may seek the help of some other agency for the child's problem and refer the parent and child there. The vast majority of consultations in general practice do not involve referral, but it is impossible to give cut and dried rules about which problem comes into which category. There are often a number of equally valid ways of dealing with problems which may be chosen for a variety of reasons in different situations. The approach selected will be influenced by:

- the GP's training, experience and personality;
- local facilities: these vary widely, and a service which is well provided for in one area may be poor or non-existent in another;
- patients' views: a patient may find one solution much more acceptable than another theoretically equally good one.

So GPs with experience of counselling or child psychiatry may be perfectly happy to tackle complex psychological problems without outside help, but may refer a child to a specialist for something relatively straightforward but about which they are uncertain. Allergy problems may be dealt with swiftly and efficiently by a special clinic in one area, but in another the absence of such help will throw GPs back on their own resources. Some mothers may be incapable of accepting reassurance about their child's condition until a specialist appointment is arranged, whilst others in similar situations may find that a brief chat with the GP resolves things.

The primary health care team at the surgery

GPs usually work as part of a primary health care team composed of a variety of other health workers, some of whom are directly employed by the practice and others who work alongside and within the practice but are not employed by it. Many GPs work in group practices where they have access to other general practitioner colleagues. There is a tendency nowadays for GPs to specialize in different areas, so they may call in a colleague from the next consulting room for a second opinion, either because that doctor has specialist knowledge of the area or more simply because collaborative work is often more effective than working alone.

Practice nurses are now a part of many primary care teams, though their role varies between practices. Sometimes they carry out relatively mundane but important tasks like vaccinations and changing dressings, whilst in other practices they run specialized services such as asthma or family planning clinics. Some work alongside GPs as nurse practitioners diagnosing and treating a range of conditions.

Increasingly, the primary care team includes workers with special skills such as counsellors, physiotherapists and dietitians who work for a few sessions a week in the surgery. Non-professional staff are an important component of a modern practice. Receptionists can make or mar the smooth running and atmosphere of the practice, and behind the scenes most group practices have a practice manager and secretaries to deal with the administrative burden. The GP is very much part of the team, but is often its leader or coordinator.

The primary health care team in the local community

The members of the primary health care team discussed above are all employed directly by the practice. There are other team members who work in or around the practice but are employed by other agencies related to the practice in different ways. These include health visitors, district nurses, community midwives and sometimes social workers. The origins of this lie in the historical development of different parts of the health service. These additional team members may be attached to the practice or to a group of practices and may be responsible only for those practices' patients. They may work in a geographical location or 'patch' where the patch and the area covered by the practice partly or wholly overlap, or they may have responsibilities to individual patients rather than to an area. This mish-mash of agencies clearly makes for difficulties in coordinating health care, but conscientious GPs are at pains to try to liaise with each agency to provide effective and efficient care for their patients. This is much more easily achieved if the general practitioners and the other agencies all work from the same building.

The wider community service

Beyond the confines of the surgery the GP has access to a range of other services to which children can be directed. The most important of these are the community health services. These are run by the health authority or are part of an NHS Trust, and they usually provide a variety of services. Health visitors, clinical medical officers and district nurses are usually employees of the community health services. Children may be referred for advice on physical growth and development, mental development, tests of hearing and vision, speech assessment and therapy and other services which vary considerably from district to district. Patients can attend these clinics directly without referral from a GP, particularly for the less specialized services and for vaccinations. Increasingly, GPs are taking responsibility for developmental screening – the routine assessments of children's mental and physical development. Where GPs do not provide this service, the screening is carried out by the clinical medical officers (CMOs) at the community health clinics.

There is a degree of overlap between the GP, the community services and the hospital. For example, routine childhood vaccinations are given by the community services, by many GPs and in a few hospital settings. The community services have a responsibility to provide this for the whole childhood population but they have no obligation to ensure it is taken up. GPs have no obligation to provide the service but have financial incentives to make sure their children are vaccinated. Hospitals offer vaccination on an *ad hoc* basis to the comparatively small percentage of children that they look after. Similar considerations apply to developmental screening. This complex area of parallel and competing responsibilities and services is explored further in Chapter 7.

Relationships with the hospital

Referral to community services can be made by GPs, health visitors or hospital staff, but referral to the hospital specialist is almost exclusively the province of GPs. As outlined earlier, referrals can be made for a variety of reasons which do not always relate to the severity of the disease or the problem the patient brings to the doctor. Historically GPs had a free choice as to where to refer patients, but since the 1991 reforms this choice is limited to those hospitals with which the health authority has a contract. Generally this provides an adequate choice, and when referrals have to be made to highly specialist centres other arrangements exist. This might happen with very rare or complex problems.

Relationships with schools

Although GPs rarely have formal relationships with schools, in a number of circumstances this does happen. Sometimes GPs act as 'school medical officers', though this usually happens only with private schools. In some parts of the country GPs may be employed as school doctors by the community health services (see Chapter 7).

More informally teachers may suggest that parents take their children to the GP about problems that in other parts of the country, or in other circumstances, may be referred to other professionals. This might happen for example if there are concerns about speech difficulties, or if the teacher suspects that a child has visual problems. There is no correct answer as to which professional parents and teachers should go to but it is important to realize that many routes are possible, and that inter-professional communication is important.

WHAT ARE GPs' OBLIGATIONS TO THEIR PATIENTS?

GPs have a number of legal and contractual obligations, which identify the minimum service they are expected to provide. The details of these are given below; in practice good GPs offer a great deal more and their services are reviewed in the following section.

GPs in the NHS work under contract to the local Family Health Services Authority (FHSA), which places various obligations on the GP and can take action if the GP is in breach of any of these requirements. Complaints about doctors' behaviour or practice are investigated by the FHSA, which recommends disciplinary action if the complaint is upheld. The contract between the FHSA and the general practitioner is used throughout the UK, although Scotland's is agreed separately and with some minor differences. It requires doctors to provide a full range of general practice services. They can opt out of family planning or maternity work if they wish to, but few actually do.

The few GPs who work privately are not bound by these conditions, but make their own arrangements with their patients. However, all doctors are bound to certain standards by the requirements of their regulating body, the General Medical Council. The GMC, whose powers and responsibilities are defined in law, is responsible for standards of conduct and discipline in all doctors, and in extreme circumstances doctors can be struck off the list of registered medical practitioners. One criticism of the GMC is that it can act only when there has been serious malpractice. There are suggestions it should be allowed to consider less serious offences, and to focus more on clinical quality.

When patients join an NHS general practice list the GP agrees to provide certain services for them. These services require the GP to be easily available during surgery hours. GPs are also responsible for providing services for their patients 24 hours a day, 365 days a year. This on-call work can be, and nowadays usually is, shared between the doctors in a group practice. In many areas, especially cities, it is contracted out to commercial deputizing services. GPs are required to be available to their patients but exercise their own discretion in what needs to be done. So patients can request a visit, but it is up to the doctor to decide how to respond. That said, if patients suffer as a result of a poor decision the doctor is answerable.

GPs work in a practice area whose borders are decided in conjunction with the FHSA. They are obliged to care for any patient in that area if requested to do so by the FHSA, but they may take on patients from outside the area if they wish. Once GPs have taken a patient on to their list they are obliged to provide them with full services. GPs have to be available to visit patients at any address within the practice area and to visit those they have agreed to take on from addresses outside that area.

When someone is away from home and requires medical help (whether as an emergency or more routinely) he or she can register with a nearby doctor on a temporary basis. GPs have an obligation to provide this care when such patients are within their practice area, and as a result the public have access to primary medical care wherever they are, and at all times. Patients can leave the doctor's list at will and without giving a reason. Similarly the doctor can – again without reason – have patients removed from his or her list by a request to the FHSA. There is a mechanism, for which the FHSA is responsible, which allows the FHSA to place patients on a GP's list when they are unable to find a GP.

When GPs undertake to provide necessary medical advice and treatment, this includes referral to a specialist for help when appropriate. Patients have no rights, as such, to see a specialist, but GPs have been advised by the British Medical Association (which acts as a trade union and a source of advice on professional matters) that they should agree to any 'reasonable request' for a second opinion. The NHS Patients' Charter (1991) also includes a right to a second opinion in some circumstances. Good GPs have no problems with this advice as they wish their patients to feel confident that the right thing is being done. This may sometimes mean referral to a specialist for reassurance. The NHS Patients' Charter has clarified some of these patients' rights.

THE GOOD GENERAL PRACTICE GUIDE

The question of choice does not arise with many services. For instance, with social services there is one agency in each area, so there is no choice as to which to use. Whilst it is true that in relatively isolated country areas there may be only one general practice that patients can realistically attend, for the most part there is usually a choice of two or three local practices that are convenient for the patient. In view of the importance of GPs in the lives of children and the variability in the quality of services, it is important to have some idea of how to choose a satisfactory practice. Giving such advice is difficult since there is enormous variety within general practice, and each practice style has its strengths and weaknesses. Nevertheless, it is also true that some practices are far more committed to quality of care and to serving the interests of their patients than others, and it is worth seeking out one with these virtues. To find out about local practices, the FHSA or the local community health council (CHC) can be contacted. The CHC acts as a consumer watchdog for local health services and has an obligation to provide information about local practices – even though it is often of a fairly basic nature.

Informal contact with neighbours and friends gives extra information about local practices. However, people's perception of quality varies and may differ from that held by professionals. A practice that makes antibiotics freely available for conditions which do not really need them may be popular with people who (incorrectly) believe that the practice is providing a good service.

Finally, GPs are obliged to produce a practice leaflet describing their services. This can give a useful insight into the attitudes and organization of the practice, but it may become a triumph of optimism and advertising over truth.

So what does the good general practice feel like?

You should expect reasonably comfortable surroundings, courteous staff, not to have to wait an unreasonably long time for an appointment, and access to doctors when you need them. Once with a doctor you should feel you are being given enough time, that you are being listened to and that your problem has been understood. Conscientious GPs believe that patients' problems should be understood in physical, psychological and social terms, so you should not expect to leave with a prescription each time, but rather should feel that the problem has been dealt with, or that a plan has been made which will deal with it. This may be by referral to a specialist, by waiting to see how the problem evolves, by carrying out tests, by trying a specific treatment or by visiting another member of the primary care team.

Out of hours, better GPs prefer to do their own visits or join up with other practices they respect to share the burden. However, in some inner city areas it is too dangerous to visit at night and these practices often use a deputizing service. There is pressure from within the profession to end the requirement for GPs to offer 24-hour care to their patients, but changes are likely to be many years away.

Of course, even the best GPs can have bad days and problems in getting access to all the resources that they would like to be able to use. Good practices can suffer staffing difficulties and have problems with inadequate premises. The problem with general practice is not just that one can't always tell the book by the cover, but that the contents are not easy to assess either.

What services might be offered in a good, well-organized modern practice?

Since it is difficult to get a picture of what can reasonably be expected from a good general practice, what follows is an imaginary account of a typical well-organized, forward-looking, modern general practice.

At the Feelgood Medical Centre there are three male partners and one female partner looking after 8000 patients in a suburb of a large city. They practise from a large old Victorian house which was extensively enlarged and modernized five years ago. Patients coming into the surgery are met by reception staff who courteously (but if necessarily firmly) deal with enquiries. They make routine appointments for patients to see the doctor or practice nurse, or arrange for patients to see a doctor more urgently if required. The partners have agreed that children will always be seen urgently at the request of parents.

In surgery sessions the doctors give comparatively long 10-minute appointments to each of their patients. This accords with their philosophy that many problems are dealt with more effectively by talking them through than by prescribing medicines. Accordingly they prescribe comparatively few antibiotics for children, but are not afraid to prescribe when there are good reasons. A good example of this is that their anti-asthma prescribing has soared since the practice nurse started running an asthma clinic.

They refer comparatively few patients to hospital, but make extensive use of the community health services and have a close relationship with the two health visitors who are based in the practice. They frequently phone the social services department, which is based at the other side of the town. They run a vaccination clinic, which, because of their good links with the health visitors who contact those who haven't attended, means that over 95 per cent of their patients are fully vaccinated. One of the partners has extra training and a special interest in children's problems and runs a developmental screening clinic to check on physical and mental development. Those whose progress causes concern are referred to the community health services for more detailed assessment, or in certain cases to a hospital specialist.

The GPs make extensive use of their practice computer to keep well-organized records of preventive care, such as details of which patients are due for a cervical smear or vaccination. The computer is also used for repeat prescriptions, but the GPs are careful to control the number of prescriptions that may be ordered before patients have to be reviewed by the doctor. They take an interest in medical education, both for themselves and for others. There is usually a GP trainee in the practice, students from the local medical school visit the practice and the doctors all take several weeks' leave each year to attend courses and keep up to date.

FUTURE DEVELOPMENTS IN GENERAL PRACTICE

Since the formation of the Royal College of General Practitioners and the implementation of the General Practice Charter, the development of general practice has been rapid and positive. Premises have improved and staffing levels are better, but the changes that may be expected for the future are less visible but perhaps more profound.

Moving care into the community

Developments in hospital medicine and pressure on financial resources meant that patients are now spending much less time in hospital, and this trend will certainly continue. GPs need to be able to cope with the new challenges of providing increased care in the community. This is likely to have support from a government concerned to save money, since community care is seen as a cheaper alternative to hospital care. Whether of not this is true is not clear, as providing it effectively requires adequate community-based resources. This is a point of some concern, as something similar has already been tried in the closure of the old mental asylums. All too often, the promised accommodation in the

the community has failed to materialize or has been inadequately staffed or funded. Inadequate and highly vulnerable individuals are now swelling the numbers of the homeless.

Not only will GPs look after more patients who have come out of hospital, they will also be able to prevent them from going there in the first place. Investigations and tests are becoming more refined so that patients often have no need to be admitted to hospital to have investigations carried out. Enthusiastic and well-trained GPs can now diagnose and treat conditions which previously would have involved hospital outpatient visits or even hospital admissions.

Preventive care

Medical science is becoming more able to understand the causes and natural history of illnesses, giving the possibility of identifying and correcting the underlying problem before it has become obvious. GPs are ideally placed within the community to identify 'at risk' patients and offer them appropriate preventive advice and treatment.

Medical education

The approaches GPs use in dealing with problems and the teaching skills that have developed to train GPs are beginning to be seen as ways of improving the education of undergraduate medical students. In progressive medical schools general practice is now seen as a way of providing experience for medical students that they could not obtain elsewhere, in preference to the traditional teaching experiences and methods used in hospitals.

The doctor as manager

As practices grow in size and complexity GPs' role may be to plan and coordinate the work of the primary care team members with the hospital and other agencies. This coordinating role will develop to the extent that some doctors will become full-time managers of what will be significant small businesses, particularly if the present scheme for fund-holding turns out to be successful.

Whether GPs will become distanced from their patients, as directors rather than family doctors, or whether they will use their increased resources as an opportunity to develop their caring skills and improve their ability to deal with their patients' needs, we must wait to see.

CONCLUSION

General practice has developed substantially over the past twenty-five years. But despite real anxieties about the implications of the 1991 NHS reforms it remains central to the organization of health care, and especially important for children's health. There continue to be significant overlaps with the work of health and other professional groups, but the development of strong primary care teams with good relationships with other agencies should ensure that potential problems are overcome. The nature of general practice varies considerably throughout the country, but it seems likely that there will continue to be improvements in both scope and quality.

FURTHER READING

Surprisingly little information is available on the topics covered in this chapter. Information on choosing and using general practitioner services is produced locally and can be obtained by contacting the local Family Health Services Authority or Community Health Council (numbers in the telephone directory).

Gann, Robert (1991) *The Health Care Consumer Guide*. London: Faber & Faber. An excellent consumer's guide to health care services with a good section on primary care.

Hart, Dr Julian Tudor (1988) *A New Kind of Doctor*. London: Merlin. The author argues passionately for radical changes in general practice, and as part of the argument gives a fascinating account of the history and current problems of the service.

Which Way to Health: the magazine of the Consumers Association's College of Health. This produces general articles on health care including those on general practice services. It is available on subscription and in some local libraries.

CHAPTER 9

The control of communicable disease

Donal O'Sullivan

INTRODUCTION

Communicable diseases are caused by specific infectious agents, such as bacteria or viruses, and they occur when the agent is transmitted from an infected person or the environment to a susceptible individual. Although many people believe that communicable diseases are largely problems of the past, this is not the case. Human immunodeficiency virus (HIV) is an obvious example of an infectious agent which has wreaked havoc among certain populations, and which may be the most important threat to public health in the UK. Many older diseases also remain a threat to the health of individuals and to that of the population. The decline in the incidence of tuberculosis, for example, has stopped, and it is likely that it will become a more common problem over the next few years.

The surveillance and control of communicable diseases in schools is important not only because of the threat to the health of individual children, and the disruption which such disease may cause to their education, but also because of the large numbers of children at risk in most schools. Schools may also act as a focus for the spread of infection into families and the community at large. Outbreaks of communicable disease – that is, a sudden increase in the numbers of people affected by a particular illness – may lead to a considerable burden for schools and education authorities. The commonest example of this is probably diarrhoea and vomiting due to food poisoning.

Recent changes in the health and education services and in the organization of the professions involved in the control of communicable disease in schools mean that local structures and policies may vary considerably. Teachers and parents should, as far as possible, know the local arrangements, but it is particularly important for headteachers and governors to be aware of them.

As with all activities in schools, teachers, parents, and indeed children are the most important individuals in the control of communicable disease. Others involved include the consultant in communicable disease control, the community paediatrician, school nurses and environmental health officers. This chapter describes the role of each of these professionals, including some brief background to their involvement. Arrangements for the control of communicable disease in schools, an explanation of the sorts of problems that can arise and specific examples which serve to illustrate the implications for schools will be discussed.

THE PROFESSIONALS INVOLVED

Almost all professionals who have a role in the control of communicable disease in schools perform this role only as part of a much wider remit. Consultants in communicable disease control (CCDCs), however, have an executive responsibility to the health authority for the control of communicable disease in the community at large. They are usually the most important relevant individuals outside the school, though in some areas CCDCs may have made arrangements with other doctors, usually community paediatricians, to fulfil this function in schools. Whatever the local arrangements, successful control of communicable disease in schools depends on the cooperation of a large number of individuals, often employed by different organizations.

Consultants in communicable disease control

Since the publication of the Acheson Report (1988) – the report of a committee of inquiry into the development of the public health function in England – every district health authority is required to employ a consultant responsible for the control of communicable disease. The CCDC may be a consultant in public health medicine or a consultant microbiologist, but will normally be accountable to the director of public health of the local health authority. CCDCs are responsible for the surveillance of communicable disease, for drawing up plans for dealing with outbreaks and for taking action when outbreaks occur. The CCDC also works with others to coordinate programmes aimed at the control and prevention of disease, one of the most important being the immunization of children. As well as advising the health authority, the CCDC is also responsible for providing medical advice to the local authority on control of communicable disease. Although most of this advice is given in an informal capacity, most CCDCs are also appointed as 'proper officers' to their local authority. Under the Public Health Act, the proper officer has a variety of powers in relation to the control of communicable disease. These include powers to keep people away from work, and to admit people to hospital and to examine them. Whilst these powers are rarely used, they form the legal basis on which local authorities control communicable disease. CCDCs therefore act as officers of health authorities and local authorities, and can act as law enforcers in a way which is quite different from their normal professional investigative and advisory role. Each borough or district council in England should, therefore, have access to a consultant whose responsibility is to control communicable disease in the community, including schools. However, most county councils do not have access to one named individual for advice on this function. Schools in areas where education services are organized on a county basis may need to turn to their local council for relevant advice. Arrangements similar to these exist in Scotland, Wales and Northern Ireland.

The role of CCDC has replaced that of medical officer for environmental health (MOEH), though this title persists in many parts of the United Kingdom, and may still be used as an alternative to that of CCDC, especially by local authority employees.

Community paediatricians

The role of the community paediatrician and its development are discussed in Chapter 7. Changes in child health services, and the increasingly specialist nature of the work of doctors employed by community child health services, mean that there is considerable variation in provision of school medical services in different parts of the country. Usually, a community paediatrician acts as manager of the school health service, which is staffed by senior clinical medical officers and clinical medical officers, more commonly known to schools as 'school doctors'. The school doctor may well be the only doctor in contact with schools on a regular basis and he or she may be the obvious point of contact for advice in relation to communicable disease control problems. With the school nurse, the community paediatrician is the person responsible for running immunization programmes in schools and for giving medical advice to schools on any issue on a day-to-day basis. CCDCs may rely on community paediatricians for help in dealing with outbreaks in schools.

In many areas of the country CCDCs have devolved their responsibilities, in relation to schools, to a community paediatrician. In other areas, consultants in communicable disease control collaborate very closely with their consultant community paediatrician colleagues in formalizing structures and policies necessary for the control of communicable disease in schools. Many people find the lack of a standardized approach confusing, but the intention is that locally negotiated arrangements are the best way of meeting local needs from whatever resources are available. Different levels of interest in the control of communicable disease among community paediatricians are also relevant.

Medical officers of schools

Independent boarding-schools usually appoint a medical officer (who is often a local GP) to provide the school with medical advice as necessary. Such advice usually covers the control of communicable disease. Medical officers of schools should consult with their local CCDC about the structures and policies in place in other local schools so as to identify how the arrangements in independent boarding-schools may best be integrated with those of the local education service. They should, in any case, report any cases of the many diseases notifiable under public health law to the CCDC (these include meningitis, food poisoning and tuberculosis) as well as any outbreak that occurs in the school.

General practitioners

It is important to remember that children should be registered with a general practitioner (GP) whose responsibility is to examine, diagnose and treat them as appropriate. CCDCs or community paediatricians may advise GPs on any aspect of individual children's care, but only the GP can prescribe medication. Like any other doctor, the GPs must notify the CCDC of cases of any one of the listed diseases notifiable under the Public Health Act. Despite their central role in the management of individual cases of infectious disease, it is inappropriate for GPs to offer advice on exclusion of children from schools unless this advice is based on local policies and procedures. Advice on exclusion should be sought from the school nurse, the community paediatrician or from the CCDC.

School nurses

Like community paediatricians, school nurses are also in regular contact with schools. As well as providing a range of child health services, school nurses may give guidance in matters of health and hygiene. Indeed, many take on a more direct educational role. School nurses also take part in immunization programmes, and may offer advice on control of communicable disease. Finally, and not least importantly, the school nurse may act as an invaluable resource in the event of outbreaks in schools.

There is an active debate about the role and function of school nursing services, and this is explored further in Chapter 7. Such services have often been undervalued with school nurses relegated to a relatively minor role. In many parts of the country school nursing services are underfunded and understaffed, and the consequent decline in the quality of service and in staff morale have led to a poor image and difficulties in recruitment. This situation is a real problem and there are good reasons for believing that the role of school nursing services should be strengthened rather than diminished, so as to avoid the loss of a focus for health-related activity in schools. In the absence of adequately funded school nursing services, health visitors may take on the role of school nurses and assist in the control of communicable disease in schools.

Environmental health officers

Environmental health officers are local authority employees and have a wide range of responsibilities. They are among the most important professionals involved in the protection of the environment and public health. Together with the CCDC, the local director of environmental services (or chief environmental health officer) has responsibilities to draw up plans for the control of outbreaks of communicable disease in the community. He or she also has a role in investigating and taking action in any such outbreak. The safety of food and of water supplies in schools is another responsibility in collaboration with the local education service. CCDCs may ask for his or her help in investigating outbreaks in schools, particularly if they are thought to be due to contamination of food or water.

Environmental health officers are also responsible for other aspects of the environment within schools, such as problems caused by asbestos and lead.

ARRANGEMENTS FOR THE CONTROL OF COMMUNICABLE DISEASE IN SCHOOLS

As already discussed, arrangements for the control of communicable disease in schools vary considerably between different parts of the UK. Whatever the arrangements, CCDCs have an executive responsibility to the health authority for the control of communicable disease but they are also the proper officer of the local authority for powers in public health law. CCDCs also act as a source of specialist advice to any member of the population, and parents, governors or teachers can contact their local CCDC via the local district health authority.

Despite this central role, the numbers of other professionals involved means that local negotiation about the detailed arrangements for the control of communicable disease in schools, and clarification of the roles and responsibilities of the various individuals involved, is essential. Certain aspects of communicable disease control need to be agreed as part of local policy. These are:

- surveillance;
- outbreaks and their control;
- disease prevention;
- action necessary to control transmission of specific diseases.

Surveillance

In order to be able to control and prevent the spread of communicable disease it is necessary to know how much of it there is in any particular community. It is necessary to be able to answer questions such as: how many cases of food poisoning have there been in the last month? What are the ages of the cases of meningitis over the last year? Is there more measles around? Surveillance may be defined as the routine, systematic monitoring of the incidence of disease, and an effective surveillance system facilitates the identification of changes in the frequency of diseases and the evaluation of preventive measures. It also alerts the relevant authorities to take the necessary appropriate action in relation to individual cases or outbreaks.

Surveillance requires the commitment of many people to report cases of diseases; systems therefore need to be developed on a collaborative basis, must allow the information that has been collected to be interpreted meaningfully, and must include ways of feeding the information back to those who need it. Many surveillance systems fail, or do not live up to their potential, because of a failure to obtain the continuing commitment of reporters to the system at an initial stage, or to maintain that commitment by providing continuing incentives such as useful information derived from data collected by the system. There is little incentive for GPs or teachers to inform CCDCs of cases of measles unless they get some feedback.

As already discussed, any doctor who diagnoses a 'notifiable disease' is required, by law, to notify the CCDC. This requirement forms the basis of an important local and national surveillance system, and is often referred to as the notification system. Unfortunately, in most areas this system does not result in complete or accurate information. Many CCDCs attempt to improve matters, but they also need to add to the information from this system by other means. One way is to develop a system whereby headteachers are asked to report individual cases of certain diseases to the CCDC or the consultant community paediatrician. Indeed, such systems are already in existence in some parts of the country.

Outbreaks and their control

An outbreak is defined as a greater number of cases of disease than would be expected in a particular population in a given time period. A small number of cases of food poisoning over a fortnight or more may not constitute an outbreak in a large school, whereas a single case of diphtheria may be regarded as an outbreak in any setting in the UK. Outbreaks of communicable disease are major events in the life of a school. Because of this, disease prevention and the control of transmission of disease in schools are very important, but with even the best efforts at prevention and control, outbreaks do occur.

In the event of an outbreak, especially if it involves a serious disease or a large number of children, the efforts of many individuals may be required to investigate and control it. The CCDC and local environmental health officers already have a plan for dealing with outbreaks in any setting and the CCDC decides whether this plan should be called into operation. One of the essential elements of the plan is to convene an outbreak control group, the membership of which should include all the key people involved in dealing with the outbreak. The headteacher, and other staff members, may be invited to become part of this group.

The outbreak control group has a number of responsibilities. These include:

- deciding what information to give to parents and the public;
- investigating the outbreak;
- controlling the outbreak. School closure is only rarely necessary, but keeping affected individuals away from school is common – particularly with food poisoning outbreaks.

Outbreaks in schools often mean an increased workload for staff, and this can cause problems if large numbers of staff become ill. Education services and schools should bear this in mind in contingency planning.

Disease prevention

As implied above, efforts to prevent disease minimize the numbers of outbreaks and the resulting disruption to school life and to individual children. The essential elements of prevention of communicable disease in schools are education, immunization, and hygiene; but as with disease prevention generally, education is the key. Educational measures aimed at the prevention of such diseases should be part of an integrated health education programme, and, as such, be part of the school curriculum. They should relate in particular to those parts of the curriculum dealing with hygiene and sexual health.

Immunization of children against specific diseases is one of the most effective ways of preventing disease. Much of the immunization programme occurs before school, but some vaccines are administered in the school setting. These include:

- pre-school boosters against diphtheria, tetanus and polio;
- rubella vaccine for 10–14-year-old girls;
- BCG for all 10–14-year-olds;
- boosters against tetanus and polio for 15–18-year-olds.

Teachers and parents often feel that the organizational efforts necessary for the immunization of children in schools are something of a chore, but the importance of the programme cannot be overemphasized.

Hygiene, or sanitary science, is a rather out-of-date term. This does not, however, obviate the need for sound structure, maintenance and cleaning of schools. Legislation exists in relation to the provision of sanitary facilities in schools, but despite this, concern has been expressed about the quality and cleanliness of toilets in primary schools in parts of the UK.

Action necessary to control transmission of specific diseases

There are a number of measures specific to the control of particular diseases. These include:

- exclusion of affected children or staff from school;
- immunization of children and staff;
- administration of antibiotics to prevent illness in children or staff;
- specific hygiene measures;
- supervised personal hygiene for children.

Many of these may be required to control transmission from even a single case of communicable disease. The amount of work necessary to implement some of them is similar to that necessary to control transmission in the event of an outbreak. Since adopting these measures often generates a high level of anxiety amongst staff and parents, it is important to give out as much information as possible on the disease involved and on why such measures are necessary. In many parts of the country, handbooks have been produced which give detailed guidance on how to prevent the transmission of specific diseases. These handbooks also incorporate other aspects of policy, an explanation of the roles of the different professionals involved and a list of contact numbers.

POSSIBLE PROBLEMS IN COMMUNICABLE DISEASE CONTROL

A number of issues can cause problems in the control of communicable disease in schools. Some of these are general and are likely to cause problems for most schools in most areas, whereas others may affect only certain schools, education services or health authorities.

Fear and stigma

Despite misconceptions about the declining importance of communicable disease, many people's instinctive response to meningitis, dysentery or other diseases is fear. This is usually due to lack of knowledge or information, and may result in stigmatization of the affected person. It can also cause anxiety, which may range from the imperceptible to an acute state of panic. Teachers, other education staff, parents and pupils are often no different from the general public in this respect.

The stigma which a pupil or teacher may suffer because he or she has a communicable disease can be enormous. Given the well-known response to head lice, for example, the reaction of many people to someone known to be infected with HIV is likely to be much worse. Because of this, it is vital to ensure the confidentiality of all information which may result in the identification of any affected individual. However, even when schools, education and health services have dealt with information in a strictly confidential manner, the identity of people affected by communicable disease may become known to others. This may be for a variety of reasons, but the resulting situation needs to be dealt with in as sensitive a way as possible. A full explanation of the nature of the disease concerned, how it is transmitted, what steps have been taken (or are planned) to prevent transmission, and the extent of the risk to people in contact with the affected person should serve to allay fears. This explanation may be given in a letter, or often more profitably (because it more easily allows questions to be answered) at a meeting of those concerned. A similar approach should also be adopted when it is necessary to inform parents and staff of the existence of a case. This may happen because of a need to involve them in the steps necessary to prevent other cases. However, even in these circumstances it is not necessary to break confidentiality and reveal the names of affected individuals. CCDCs are able to advise schools on what information should be issued and how this might be done.

Whether or not to give parents or staff information is often an important and difficult question when only a single case of disease has occurred. Important factors to consider in answering this question should include the purpose of issuing information, and the likelihood that, if it is issued, the affected individual will be identified. The elimination of stigma and the need to involve people in control measures are the only real reasons for issuing information of this kind, except where it is given as part of a planned educational programme.

School premises, maintenance and compulsory competitive tendering

The condition of school premises is very important in relation to the spread of disease in schools. Many older buildings have kitchens, toilets or water systems which are not of a suitable standard; local education services should examine improvements required as part of their capital programme.

Maintenance and cleaning are also relevant. The introduction of compulsory competitive tendering in relation to such services may, in some instances, have resulted in a decline in standards and increased potential for disease transmission. Specifications for catering services should address the control of food-borne illness.

Professional relationships

Because many professions have a role to play in the control of communicable disease in schools, the potential for inter-professional conflict exists. Even within the single profession of medicine there is also potential for conflict. In this chapter four different types of doctor have been identified as having a role in this area. Generally, there are good professional and personal relationships between doctors, and between doctors and other relevant professionals, and these should minimize the potential for conflict. Often, the source of problems is a failure of communication, so the clarification of roles and responsibilities locally is essential. In the end the CCDC has responsibilities to the health authority and the local authority for this function, but CCDCs cannot meet these responsibilities in isolation from others.

Roles of the health authority and the local authority

Just as there may be dispute about the role of different professions, there is also the possibility of problems arising because of confusion over the relative roles of the health authority and the local authority. Generally this does not happen, as CCDCs often act as a bridge between the two, but when a dispute does occur it is usually about resources and who should provide them. This might happen when a CCDC – who is a health authority employee – makes recommendations about a school that the local authority has to implement. Such disputes may occur not only between authorities but also between different departments of the local authority, such as the education and environmental health departments. The exact responsibilities in relation to these issues are not clear.

SOME PRACTICAL EXAMPLES

This section looks at a number of specific diseases and problems which schools may well experience and which illustrate the practical implications of communicable disease control in this setting.

Hepatitis B and HIV

The revelation that a staff member or pupil is infected with a blood-borne agent such as hepatitis B or HIV often gives rise to considerable concern amongst parents and staff and this may result in an extreme example of the stigmatization referred to earlier. As many people who are infected by such agents do not know they are infected, and as all educational settings may have some such pupils or staff, procedures for control of these infections should be followed for all children and adults at all times. They are not a reason for the exclusion from school of anybody who is well, nor are there any specific measures which are usually necessary in relation to any school in which HIV or hepatitis B infection is known to exist. The names of affected individuals should never be disclosed.

In general the control of such blood-borne infection in schools depends on precautionary hygiene measures, and proper procedures for waste disposal and for dealing with accidents which involve bleeding. Educational programmes designed to promote sexual health and personal hygiene may be more important as a means of avoiding these diseases. Immunization against hepatitis B is not necessary, except perhaps in schools for children with learning difficulties, where bites (which can transmit the hepatitis B virus) are a common cause of injury.

The problems for schools in relation to HIV and hepatitis B include:

- how to adopt the necessary procedures;
- how to deal with conflicting advice;
- how to deal with fear;
- how to prevent stigmatization.

As described earlier, the levels of stigmatization, fear and anxiety that head-teachers or governors may need to deal with in relation to these issues are far greater than they may otherwise encounter. These problems can be dealt with only in the way already described: by informing people as far as possible about the disease and how it can be prevented. Counselling of certain individuals may also be required.

Meningitis

Meningitis is another medical condition capable of generating fear. Although it may be caused by a number of agents, the only form of meningitis which requires action to control transmission when a single case occurs in an educational setting is a form of bacterial meningitis known as meningococcal meningitis. Such action is necessary only when a case occurs in a *pre-school* setting (because children under 5 have more intimate contact with one another than older children), or when a case occurs in a boarding-school where children share the same dormitory. Unless specific action is necessary, it is debatable whether or not parents or staff should be told of a single case. But if it is already common knowledge that a case exists, it is certainly wise to inform parents and staff.

When action is necessary, this consists of informing parents about what has happened and what they need to do, and excluding selected children and staff from school until they have received a short course of antibiotics. This exercise may place a substantial administrative burden on the school.

Where more than one case of meningitis occurs, then further action may be necessary. This varies depending on the agent involved and the nature of the school – but it may involve a large number of children being excluded, having samples taken and receiving antibiotics. It is important that headteachers and CCDCs collaborate closely in dealing with any such situation.

Food poisoning

Generally, a small number of cases of food poisoning in a school does not require action other than the exclusion of affected people from school, as advised by the CCDC or an environmental health officer, and an increased awareness of the importance of hygiene. Further action may be required in the event of more serious illness or when many children or staff are affected. If this occurs, then an outbreak control group, as described earlier, is established to investigate and control the outbreak. The investigation of the outbreak and the control of further transmission may require a great deal of activity by the school and have major staffing and other resource implications. The providing of information to parents is again important when this happens.

CONCLUSION

The control of communicable disease in schools involves a large number of individuals and rather complicated arrangements, which vary considerably between different parts of the UK. Reviewing these arrangements and ensuring the appropriate participation of all individuals poses a challenge to those responsible for the control of communicable disease in the community and in schools in particular. Fear, stigma and misunderstanding are often greater problems than the diseases themselves.

FURTHER READING

DES (1981) *The Education (School Premises) Regulations*. London: HMSO.

DHSS (1988) *Public Health in England*. London: HMSO.

Jewkes, R.K. and O'Connor, G.H. (1990) Crisis in our schools: survey of sanitation facilities in schools in Bloomsbury Health District. *British Medical Journal*, Vol. 301: 1085–7.

Joseph, C., Noah, N., White, J. and Hoskins, J. (1990) A review of outbreaks of infectious disease in schools in England and Wales 1979–88. *Epidemiol. Infect.*, Vol. 105: 419–34.

PART 5

SERVICES FOR SPECIFIC PROBLEMS

INTRODUCTION

This part concentrates on three support services that focus on particular difficulties experienced by children: hearing, vision, and speech and language. Whilst the scope of the problems discussed here is narrower than elsewhere in the book, similar themes emerge.

CHAPTER 10

Hearing impairment

Alec Webster

This chapter begins by considering some important background issues in the field of hearing impairment which determine how special needs are defined. There then follow some major distinctions: hearing losses are caused by different factors and interact in an unpredictable and largely uncharted way with many other aspects of children's development. It is important to be clear from the outset about the relative impact of a mild conductive hearing loss occurring alongside common childhood illnesses such as colds or flu, in contrast to more severe hearing impairments caused by permanent damage to hearing. Recent research on how deafness interferes with important processes, such as adult–child interaction, has also changed views on how children can best be helped in the early years and supported through school.

The next section in the chapter considers some of the complex theoretical arguments which have been used in favour of one kind of intervention for severely hearing-impaired children versus another. Education of the deaf has a very long history and has always been surrounded by controversy. Questions are often raised about whether children should be taught through the medium of sign language or speech, whether deaf adults should be involved in their education, and whether an integrated mainstream class offers a better learning environment than a special school for deaf children. The following sections in the chapter outline the range of support services available in health and education, how contrasting professional views may emerge, and how services for the hearing-impaired can work together to meet the individual needs of families and children.

Finally, the chapter considers the current context of educational reform and how children and their supporting services are likely to be affected by the policy changes which lie ahead.

BACKGROUND

Deafness and special needs

The term 'hearing-impaired' spans a very wide continuum. The needs of hearing-impaired children are defined only partly by physical factors, such as degree of hearing loss. For this reason care should be taken not to assume that all profoundly deaf children will inevitably have difficulties in acquiring language or literacy. Similarly, there are some children with mild hearing losses accompanying periodic ear infections who are markedly affected in their development of speech, language, school attainments and behaviour. Obviously, children with severe and permanent hearing losses have many more obstacles to contend with, but there are other factors which influence individual development, such as motivation, family environment, personality and determination.

Whether or not we describe the needs of hearing-impaired children as 'special' depends in part on our assumptions. Are deaf children basically just like all other children, but with additional difficulties to face, which may result in lower levels of educational achievement relative to hearing children of the same age? This assumption would lead us to judge the success of any interventions that are made in terms of how far a deaf child is equipped (or 'rehabilitated') to participate in a hearing society. Success might be judged on the basis of speech intelligibility, number of hearing friends, and participation in social or work settings with hearing people.

On the other hand, we may view deaf children as distinctive and different, rather than 'damaged', following a developmental path which is unique. (For this reason, deaf people prefer the term 'deaf' to 'hearing-impaired'.) Lacking access to sound, deaf individuals may develop discrete ways of perceiving, processing and thinking about the world. This assumption would shape intervention towards realizing a child's identity in relation to deaf language and culture. Deaf people usually see themselves as a minority cultural group with inequalities of opportunity in relation to issues such as employment. Deaf parents who have deaf children will have different expectations as compared with hearing parents of deaf children. A deaf family with a richness of deaf culture and sign language may not measure success in terms of whether they are considered 'as though' hearing. Hearing parents, however, may strongly wish their deaf children to speak intelligibly and compete alongside hearing peers.

It should be noted that more than 90 per cent of deaf children have hearing parents, whilst very few education professionals (such as specialist teachers or psychologists) are deaf themselves. This is an important point to grasp in order to understand why expectations of deaf children held by hearing adults may be very different from those held by deaf individuals themselves or the organizations that represent their interests (for example the British Deaf Association).

To some extent the history of educational intervention for the deaf has also been shaped by important developments in techniques of detection and diagnosis. Developments in microtechnology have enabled many children to make use of residual hearing through powerful hearing-aids, such that the presence of a profound loss does not preclude the development of intelligible speech. These are some of the reasons why the field of deaf education is characterized by strongly expressed opinions and beliefs about the kind of support and intervention which should be offered to deaf children and their families, not all of which are supported by evidence. For many parents it can be difficult to know what advice to listen to and which decisions are sensible, especially when those who work in the field disagree amongst themselves.

In fact, recent research (Webster and Wood, 1989) suggests we should move away from arguments about teaching methods, which have preoccupied deaf education for three or four centuries, towards a more careful analysis of the learning context in relation to individual needs. No method of communication holds guarantees for all deaf children and there are positive and negative consequences of all approaches. It can be seen that at the heart of most of these controversies lie some fundamental differences in the way in which hearing-impaired individuals are perceived, the images which are held of deaf children as learners, and the roles they can take up in society as adults. Undoubtedly, the way forward is to focus attention on the quality of education that deaf children receive (rather than methods or philosophy) and whether the individual's needs are being met. It is in recognition of this that research has begun to focus on more finely grained aspects of teaching and learning, such as how adults interact with hearing-impaired children in conversational exchanges and whether the curriculum is sufficiently challenging to promote cognitive development (Webster and Wood, 1989).

The nature of hearing impairment

A distinction is normally drawn between deafness which arises from the faulty transmission of sound across the conductive mechanisms of the middle ear, known as 'conductive deafness', and deafness which arises from damage to the nerves in the cochlea or auditory pathways, known as 'sensori-neural deafness'.

Conductive deafness

Conductive deafness is often associated with ear infections or the accumulation of fluid in the middle ear, and its effects are generally much less severe than those of a sensori-neural loss. Many conductive problems are transitory and can be treated in order to restore hearing. Even so, there is a wealth of evidence to show that conductive hearing difficulties are associated with developmental delays in speech and language, together with poor attainments in literacy and other aspects of school functioning (Webster *et al.*, 1989).

How far conductive hearing loss actually causes these difficulties, as opposed to simply occurring alongside other developmental immaturities, is hard to say. Whatever the precise link may be, it is important that adults are vigilant to the possibility of a child suffering from a conductive hearing loss, so that appropriate medical treatment and educational measures can be organized. Conductive problems are very common in early childhood and may affect up to one in five children at any one point in time. Children most likely to suffer developmental consequences associated with conductive hearing loss are those whose hearing problems onset during early infancy, with persistent recurrence, and in combination with other adverse factors such as disadvantaging economic or social circumstances.

Sensori-neural deafness

The prevalence of sensori-neural deafness in children is far lower than that of conductive hearing loss. About one child in every thousand will be identified as having a sensori-neural loss. A proportion of children with sensori-neural impairments will also suffer from additional conductive hearing difficulties. Until very recently, surveys showed that maternal rubella (German measles during pregnancy) was the most common cause of deafness (Newton, 1985; Martin, 1982). This pattern is changing owing to the impact of an immunization programme designed to protect all pre-pubescent girls from rubella, together with careful screening and follow-up of expectant mothers. Hereditary factors account for approximately 10 per cent of deaf children, whilst meningitis accounts for approximately 6 per cent of cases of acquired deafness in infancy. In a very large proportion of cases (about 40 per cent) the precise cause of deafness is unknown.

Certain factors predispose children to suffer a hearing loss and these may be known before birth. Deafness may be anticipated because of genetic factors in the family's history and there may be hearing-impaired relatives or siblings. Contact with rubella or other infections during the mother's pregnancy, prematurity or a difficult delivery should alert professionals to the possibility of deafness. Babies in special care units are approximately ten times more likely to be hearing-impaired than other babies, and paediatricians who work in special care baby units will monitor babies' development and alert audiological services when any factors potentially harmful to hearing have arisen. Some health authorities focus a hearing surveillance programme on certain children, according to criteria such as family history, prematurity, facial abnormalities, or consanguinity in a marriage. 'At risk' babies are usually closely monitored, including children with cerebral palsy, Down's syndrome or cleft palate. Since in no more than about half of the instances of sensori-neural deafness can the exact cause be pinpointed, the monitoring only of 'at risk' children would still leave many cases undetected. Hence the need for effective early screening of all children.

Identifying a hearing loss: early screening

The sooner a hearing loss is detected, the sooner the impact of deafness can be reduced at source. This applies to children with mild conductive hearing losses and to those with sensori-neural impairments. Professional opinion is unanimous on this issue: the earlier that deafness is identified and diagnosed, the more quickly can appropriate steps be taken to support the child and the family. In rare circumstances a child with a severe sensori-neural hearing loss may escape detection until 2 or 3 years of age. Occasionally, moderate or high-frequency deafness comes to light on entry to school, perhaps as a result of a vigilant teacher observing a child's listening behaviour and then taking steps to arrange a hearing check.

Detection depends in the first place on suspicion. Often parents are the first to suspect that their child has a hearing problem, and it is important that professionals take these concerns seriously. In order to provide appropriate medical treatment or fit hearing-aids, to expose the child to a facilitating language and learning environment, and to maximize the range of experiences necessary for social, emotional and intellectual growth, early diagnosis of deafness is critical, if possible within the first year of infancy. In the UK, community health services generally organize early screening and testing procedures for all infants to try to identify children with hearing losses as early as possible. The success of infant testing is very variable.

The 'Distraction Test' used by health visitors to screen every baby around the age of 7 or 8 months, either at home or in a child health clinic, is by no means fail-safe. In order to do the test babies have to be able to sit up, with good back and head control, so that they can turn to locate a sound stimulus out of the field of vision. The baby is usually encouraged to sit forward on the parent's knees, supported at the hips and facing one of the examiners, who engages the infant with a toy. A second examiner presents a sound stimulus, which the baby must not be able to see or feel. High- and low-frequency sounds are presented separately at about 35 decibels in quiet conditions to both ears a number of times. If no response is observed at these levels the sounds are made louder until a definite response is shown. A baby who does not turn to locate high and low sounds until they are presented at a 60-decibel level may be suspected of having a 60-decibel hearing loss. Distraction testing is difficult to carry out. There are many babies with normal hearing who fail to respond in the expected way. Conversely, a hearing-impaired child may respond to the smallest visual clue and persuade the tester that the sound has been heard. There are added difficulties in giving this test when babies are developmentally delayed, although these children are more at risk of a hearing loss.

Good practice indicates that the early identification of hearing loss in young infants requires a number of coordinated strategies rather than relying on one method (Scanlon and Bamford, 1990). In the section on health services to follow, a programme of surveillance will be described, including 'at risk' registers, neonatal screening, family questionnaires and follow-up interviews.

Changing perceptions of the hearing-impaired

The impact of the more severe forms of deafness affects a wide range of developmental processes, such as adult–child relationships, social and emotional adjustment, speech and language, together with educational and intellectual achievement (Webster, 1986). Over the past decade our thinking has shifted to include the effects of deafness on the patterning of adult behaviour, for example in conversational interaction or in styles of teaching (Webster and Wood, 1989; Wood et al., 1986).

Some of the most important insights, for example in child language development, have begun to emerge from studies in which parents figure highly, identifying ways in which parents capture children's attention, tailor linguistic input to the child's level of competence, sustain engagement on a topic of mutual interest, and use strategies such as paraphrase and commentary to promote shared meanings (Webster and McConnell, 1987). This research has also provided us with evidence of how inhibiting certain adult styles can be to children learning to talk, such as overuse of direct questions, frequent correction of children and asking for the repetition of model or grammatically 'correct' structures.

In other words, there is a greater awareness that not all the developmental obstacles associated with deafness are located within the child. In some instances there are secondary consequences evoked by, but not dependent on deafness, which lead to less facilitating adult strategies. To some extent these effects can be modified, for example through the in-service training of teachers. A great deal can also be achieved by empowering parents: providing accurate information, supporting how they interact with children, enabling them to contribute more positively to their children's development, and basing decisions on the evidence gained by implementing particular teaching strategies and evaluating outcomes in relation to meeting an individual's needs.

THEORETICAL PERSPECTIVES UNDERPINNING PRACTICE: THE ORAL–MANUAL DEBATE

The story of deaf education over the past three or four centuries shows there has never been a time when people agreed on the best educational approach to hearing-impaired children. At the heart of the controversy is a three-cornered struggle between those who want the deaf to speak and integrate with hearing society; those who argue on behalf of the deaf community for the active teaching of sign and recognition of deaf culture; and those who feel there are bridges to be made between the two. A common-sense and pragmatic approach to these issues accepts that what works for some children, their families and teachers may not work for others. A good local education authority may well be judged on the range of opportunities it provides, permitting a flexible response to the needs and circumstances of the child and family, and identifying with parents the criteria by which the success of a particular approach may be judged (Webster and Ellwood, 1985).

The oral perspective

One point of view is that if a child's hearing loss is diagnosed early enough and good hearing-aids provided, with appropriate counselling and educational experiences, then even very severely deaf children can be encouraged to make the best use of residual hearing to develop speech. To support this 'oral' position professionals can usually point to a number of successful, although very deaf, children who became good lip-readers and developed intelligible speech, attended the local school and became fluent readers, later going on to high academic achievements among hearing peers. In its traditional form the oral approach emphasized lip-reading and a structured approach to language teaching, reducing visual clues other than lip patterns and writing, to the extent that teachers were advised to keep their hands in their pockets.

Natural auralism

More recently, 'natural auralism' highlights the need for children to acquire language naturally through listening and conversational interaction rather than structured teaching. The very best amplification is required, with frequent monitoring, to promote the full use of residual hearing. However, gesture, visual and contextual clues are permitted, with writing used to support a child's emerging language. Natural auralists believe that most hearing parents of deaf children would prefer their children to be part of a community of language-users based on listening and speech (Tucker and Powell, 1991).

Not all severely deaf children are successful enough with this approach to be able to speak intelligibly and take part comfortably in hearing society. Some children find speech, even with lip-reading and powerful hearing-aids, a very difficult mode of communication, which they come to reject. There are many possible reasons for this, including late diagnosis of deafness, poor hearing-aid provision, or quite simply that the auditory information around which the child is trying to build a language structure is too degraded and distorted.

The manual perspective

Proponents of signing methods argue that exposure to sign can lead to much richer and earlier patterns of language interaction, less frustration and isolation, and better school progress. British Sign Language (BSL) refers to the communication system which deaf people in the UK use among themselves. It is now recognized that BSL is a language governed by grammatical rules which are different from but no less complex than the syntax of spoken languages. A strong case has been argued for the 'first language' teaching of deaf children from deaf families in sign, in the same way that 'mother tongue' teaching is often recommended for bilingual hearing children whose home language is different from that of the host culture. In both situations, fluency in the first language is felt to enable second language learning. Very few LEAs offer sign teaching within ordinary schools and BSL is largely associated with schools for the deaf and the deaf community.

Several manual systems have been devised to support the teaching of English. Cued speech uses a set of hand configurations around the mouth to differentiate speech sounds which look alike or are unseen on the lips. Finger spelling uses hand positions to form the 26 letters of the alphabet, which can be used to spell out English words. In Sign-Supported English some of the spoken features are supplemented by signs to indicate key words, preserving English structure but adding additional clues to aid understanding. In Paget Gorman and Signed English, a complete visual representation can be given alongside speech, marking features such as tenses and plural endings. Paget Gorman uses invented signs, whilst Signed English adopts signs from BSL. Makaton is a much simplified version of BSL used mainly with children and adults who are very slow to learn. Total Communication uses as many systems of access to language information as possible: speech, residual hearing, lip-reading, a manual sign system and finger spelling, gestures and written language. Not surprisingly, Total Communication covers a wide range of practices and is more a philosophy than a distinct method. It has thus proved difficult to carry out effectively and to evaluate, and is again frequently associated with special schools for the deaf.

SUPPORT SERVICES FOR THE HEARING-IMPAIRED – HEALTH

The very first contacts a family has with support services, once a hearing loss is suspected or has been diagnosed, are crucial in terms of defining attitudes, expectations and confidence in what the future holds for a child. Support networks for very young children are usually funded by either health or education departments and will be managed accordingly. It is particularly important for the families concerned that key professionals establish clear lines of communication between health and education to determine key contacts and coordinate plans (Webster *et al.*, 1985).

Health visitors

Health visitors routinely visit the families of pre-school children, give advice on care and management, and are well placed to make developmental observations. They are often the very first professionals to whom parents express their concerns, they have oversight of siblings and are able to link up with other medical agencies. Their continuity of contact with families puts health visitors in a good position to recognize when a child is slow to react to sounds, producing a limited range of vocalizations, or delayed in speech. They screen all babies at around 8 months for hearing, vision and general development. Some of the problems of early screening techniques have already been highlighted. Apart from the technical problems of carrying out the test, making sure that only auditory stimuli are presented at the correct intensity, much of health visitors' training emphasizes clinical intuition, whilst distraction testing can succeed only through absolute objectivity of judgement.

Because of the problems of distraction screening, health visitors take account of other information as they visit families. They have an important role in the surveillance programmes operated by many health authorities. In some areas a questionnaire is used by health visitors asking for details of every child's history and including the question: 'Have you ever been worried about your child's hearing?' Where 'at risk' factors had already been identified the health visitor would conduct in-depth interviews with families and be vigilant about a child's progress, particularly in early speech and language. Concerns about a child's hearing at this stage would normally be passed on to the family doctor, who might then refer a child directly to a hospital ear, nose and throat (ENT) department. In some areas, senior community medical officers with a specialism in audiology might see children for assessment in a clinic. In other areas a family might be referred to a regional centre for advice, such as the Nuffield Hearing and Speech Centre. Depending on location, there may be a wide range of referral options, including self-referral by families to some hospital departments.

Clinical medical officers

Doctors who have a key role in identifying children with hearing losses are the clinical medical officers who work in well-baby clinics, schools and other community services. The precise role varies from area to area, but will include liaison with other medical and nursing colleagues, health visitors, consultants and family doctors. Clinical medical officers examine most children on school entry, when a 'sweep' hearing test is usually given, although often in unsatisfactory conditions. Teachers' concerns about children's health can usually be discussed with the school medical officer, who may decide to refer a child on, for example, to a community health audiology clinic, staffed by doctors trained in audiology. The next step may then be to refer a child to the specialist team in a hospital audiology unit. In some areas parents can refer themselves to a hospital department, or arrange appointments through their GP.

One of the community medical officer's responsibilities is to indicate the significance of any medical findings to the education authority. Doctors who work in schools have an ongoing role in identifying undiagnosed hearing losses which may result from mumps, measles or other infections. They also contribute to the multiprofessional assessment and review of children whose needs are reported formally under the 1981 Education Act. Clinical medical officers are important members of the core team of professionals involved with the families of hearing-impaired children. The period of early identification, diagnosis, ENT examinations, and in some cases the fitting of earmoulds and hearing-aids, can be very traumatic. Clinical medical officers and GPs are often able to explain procedures and offer support to families, whilst the diagnosis and treatment of hearing impairment can be seen as the more specialized responsibility of a hospital department.

Audiology/ENT departments

In hospitals, the audiologist, medical specialists and community health services will work in close collaboration. The audiologist is an expert in testing hearing and provides important information towards the diagnosis of deafness, and the prescription and monitoring of hearing-aids. The ENT consultant is a surgeon whose medical speciality is the diagnosis and treatment of disorders of the ear, nose or throat. Consultants work closely with audiologists and other colleagues in deciding the best way of intervening when a child has a hearing loss, including the prescription of hearing-aids. If a 'whole child' approach to supporting children with special needs is to have any meaning, it is important for decisions about hearing-aids, for example, to take into account factors such as the child's progress and responses in school. This underlines the need for all professional agencies to share their own specific knowledge of the child in different social and learning contexts when plans are made with parents.

Speech therapy and the hearing-impaired

Speech therapists have an important role in assessing, diagnosing and treating communication difficulties in the widest sense of the word, in children and adults. Some speech therapists specialize in working with families with deaf children, or with teachers of the hearing-impaired, and have additional training or experience in this field. Employed mainly by health authorities, speech therapists accept referrals from doctors, teachers, other professionals and parents themselves. They are usually able to give detailed assessments of a child's speech and language abilities and may carry out a programme of treatment. Speech therapists contribute advice to the overall management of the communication environment. In the field of hearing-impairment, specialist speech therapists may work closely with teachers of the deaf in units and special schools and be proficient in sign.

EDUCATIONAL SERVICES AND PROVISION FOR THE HEARING-IMPAIRED

Because of the potentially damaging impact of deafness on children's development, all LEAs in the UK provide services for hearing-impaired children and their families. Most services are staffed by teachers holding a specialist qualification to teach the deaf, whilst some employ staff who are also qualified audiologists. Services for the hearing-impaired may be part of a larger organization concerned with supporting children with special needs generally. Such services will usually have as their 'mission statement' that they aim to identify and meet the individual needs of children and families, through a combination of assessment, advice, planning, liaison and direct teaching of children.

Increasingly, specialist teachers work indirectly in an advisory capacity, handing on strategies to those who have day-to-day contact with a hearing-impaired child, such as parents and mainstream class teachers. They will give advice on issues such as use of hearing- or radio-aids, acoustic conditions and noise reduction, strategies for promoting listening and conversation, and modifications to teaching style which are likely to promote access to the curriculum for a hearing-impaired pupil. Most peripatetic (visiting) teachers work within a service for the hearing-impaired, which in some LEAs operates in parallel with teachers employed in special resources, such as units or schools for the deaf. All specialist teachers of the hearing-impaired must now have a background in normal classroom experience followed up by further training, or a qualification pursued whilst employed in a school or resource for the hearing-impaired. Many have clinical competence and are qualified to carry out audiological assessments.

Parent guidance and counselling

The first educational support for the pre-school hearing-impaired child will usually come from a peripatetic teacher of the hearing-impaired who visits the home. All LEAs in the UK make provisions for pre-school deaf children, including home visiting, nurseries and playgroups. Even when deafness has been anticipated or suspected by parents, a great deal of information and support may be necessary to help families come to terms with their child's hearing loss. It has been said that parents of a deaf child grieve for the 'normal' child they have lost and must be helped through the stages of coming to terms with such a loss. If this is so, then teachers working with pre-school children must be sensitive family counsellors as well as sources of practical advice. It is axiomatic, if teachers are to work successfully in parent guidance, that they are well trained. One potential problem, in view of our changing insights into how children acquire language through interaction, is that many teachers may view early work with deaf children in 'rehabilitation' terms and concentrate their visits to families on working with the child, such as on aspects of pronunciation or vocabulary.

Good practice in this respect requires teachers to focus more on promoting an environment in which learning and development are enhanced, rather than attempting to produce short-term changes directly in the child's language or behaviour. Counselling demands flexibility and empathy, an understanding of family systems and processes of adapting to conflict. In his book on the counselling of hearing families with deaf children, Luterman (1987) argues that deafness complicates the already hazardous course of parenting, but that some parents become so wrapped up in the deafness that they 'forget the child underneath'. Teachers who are able to help families meet their psychological needs and deal with stress, guilt, resentment, feelings of inadequacy and conflict must be very skilled indeed.

For deaf families of deaf children, it is becoming more widely recognized that deaf adults have a role to play in supporting families and advising on aspects such as interaction and communication strategies with young children. Deaf adults are often able to receive help from LEA social workers trained to work in this field, and who will represent the entitlements, welfare and social interests of deaf individuals. Specialist social workers are usually contacted through local authority social services departments, through local deaf clubs or national organizations such as the Royal National Institute for the Deaf. Many families who have hearing-impaired children join local support groups organized within the National Deaf Children's Society, which again aims to promote awareness, welfare and educational interests.

These first contacts with counselling and guidance services are important in setting realistic expectations and in preparing both parents and children for the point at which children enter school. In some LEAs pre-school home visiting is undertaken by teachers who also work part time in nursery or infant schools which are resourced for hearing-impaired children, thus providing a valuable link. Most LEA support services have strategies for introducing hearing-impaired children to school, such as a series of visits, enabling social contacts between families with children entering the same class, or preparing scrapbooks, showing videos and photographs about school.

The role of the educational psychologist

Until recently, few educational psychologists had training or experience in working with hearing-impaired children, although many more psychologists are now aware of the needs of such children, and indeed a number have prior experience working as teachers of the deaf. Some LEAs and special schools employ specialist psychologists for the deaf, many of whom are familiar with sign languages. Whilst psychologists are often associated with testing children, in the field of hearing-impairment psychologists now recognize the pitfalls of IQ scales and other standardized tests when used with deaf children, and are much more likely to act in a coordinating or facilitating role, mediating the needs of children *vis-à-vis* LEA resources.

Educational psychologists are available for advice on issues such as managing behaviour, strategies for promoting play, conversation and literacy, together with drawing up an educational programme plan in collaboration with teachers and parents. They may be asked about realistic attainments for deaf children in relation to their abilities, to make suggestions about how the classroom can be organized and additional in-class help utilized, to suggest resources and ways of presenting information, together with strategies for evaluating whether the learning environment is meeting a child's needs. An important role of LEA psychologists is to contribute information to multiprofessional assessments when the needs of hearing-impaired children, their strengths and weaknesses are detailed together with appropriate resources, school placements, additional teaching help, or vocational training requirements at the post-school phase.

It has already been said that perceptions of hearing-impaired children have changed recently away from an exclusive focus on children and their disabilities, and towards the learning context and how this can be modified to create a more effective learning environment. Educational psychologists are skilled at assessing learning as well as children. Many specialist psychologists now advocate a profiling approach to the assessment of deaf children's skills and competences, collecting a range of evidence from different contexts over a period of time, involving the child and familiar adults in the process, and using a framework such as *Profiles of the Hearing-Impaired* (Webster and Webster, 1991a) as a basis for observation and planning.

Integration of hearing-impaired children in mainstream schools

Statistics published by the National Deaf Children's Society (1987) show that, out of an estimated 31,081 children with significant hearing impairments, including those with conductive hearing losses, some 64 per cent are educated in local schools and visited by peripatetic teachers. Fourteen per cent are placed in units for hearing-impaired children attached to mainstream schools, whilst 12 per cent attend special schools for the deaf. About 7 per cent of this population are pre-school children, whilst 3 per cent are supported in full-time further education. The majority of hearing-impaired children, therefore, receive their education in ordinary school settings without any specialist facilities, or in units attached to mainstream schools.

Whilst many of the children in integrated settings have mild or moderate hearing losses, surveys carried out by the Department of Education and Science in the 1960s (DES, 1967) show that a third of the children supported by teachers of the deaf in units or mainstream schools had severe to profound losses. This trend towards integrated provision, even for children with profound deafness, has gathered momentum for a number of reasons: changes in philosophy reflected in the 1981 Education Act; technological developments which have facilitated earlier diagnosis of deafness and the provision of sophisticated hearing-aids, including radio aids; parental expectations; and economic pressures on LEAs.

The integration of hearing-impaired children in ordinary schools is by no means a soft option. A number of factors will determine how effective this turns out to be, remembering that it is the quality of a child's experience which is important, with integration a means to that end. It is critical that a school feels a sense of ownership of an integration programme, where all staff take some responsibility for meeting children's needs. In a school community where hearing-impaired children are simply imposed on a school or treated as visitors, an attitude of 'our' and 'their' children arises between mainstream and specialist support staff, and children are in danger of being merely located, rather than integrated, in a school setting. A 'whole-school' approach, especially where a unit or resource has been attached to a school, is fostered by the appointment of specialist teachers to the mainstream school, rather than their belonging to a separate service; physical location of the unit within the main body of the school, rather than in a 'terrapin' at the edge of the playground; communal hours, playtimes, lunch breaks, uniforms, assemblies, report systems, parents' events; and a commitment to regular in-service training for non-specialist staff.

Where a child is supported by a visiting teacher, the role is likely to take the form of advising colleagues about teaching strategies, hearing-aids and listening conditions, classroom layout and organization, use of visual aids, cueing and key-wording systems, appropriate language, interaction and questioning styles, together with helping to monitor children's progress, passing on information about resources and materials, and giving additional tutoring, in-class support or companion teaching. Increasingly, schools are looking to support staff for advice which can be applied practically in the classroom, rather than, for example, a fortnightly visit when a child is removed from the class group for an individual session, which can prove more disruptive than helpful. The first question on everybody's lips when hearing-impaired children are integrated in mainstream is the provision of additional resources, usually in the form of extra adult help, to make it feasible.

Figure 10.1 illustrates the range of possibilities for educational provision available in most LEAs which can be used flexibly to meet an individual's needs. It can be seen that the amount of specialist teacher of the deaf support available for an individual generally decreases outside of special schools or units.

Units for hearing-impaired children

Varying degrees of integration of hearing-impaired children into mainstream class environments are often achieved by the resourcing of primary and secondary schools with a special unit. It pays dividends, when parents are moving from one area to another, to find out what unit support is available, since this varies so widely from one LEA to another. In the UK some 4500 children (14 per cent) attend units in mainstream schools. In some units, one teacher and an assistant may be responsible for a group of about six to nine children of all ages, who spend almost all of their time in a self-contained setting with only brief social contacts with mainstream. In other units a policy of full integration is operated with in-class support. The function of this kind of resource may be to offer a safe social haven. Other units collect children together for specialist teaching, combined with support in mainstream groups and, perhaps, reverse integration when hearing children come in to work with the hearing-impaired.

163

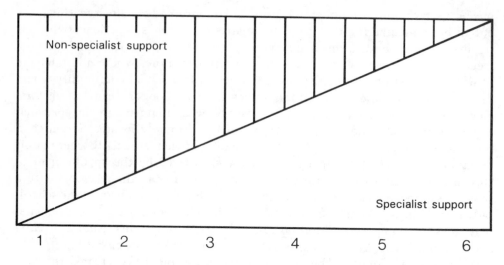

Figure 10.1 A continuum of provision for hearing-impaired children:

1. **Mainstream class: largely unsupported, occasional monitoring and advice from visiting specialists.**
2. **Mainstream class with help: regular visits from special needs or specialist support agencies.**
3. **Mainstream with tutorial help: withdrawal or companion teaching across curriculum.**
4. **Resource unit in mainstream: varying degrees of integration and a reduced curriculum.**
5. **Special school as a base: part-time integration with support.**
6. **Full-time special school: intensive specialized teaching.**

For younger children it is now commonplace for profoundly deaf children to be placed in a unit in mainstream, and some children and parents may be introduced to a supportive sign system. There are, however, restrictions in the utility of this approach if other children and staff in mainstream are not also familiar with the system. The advantage of unit provision is that some of the social and emotional consequences of very young children having to travel a long distance to get to a special school, or having to live away from home, are avoided. Even so it can prove difficult to sustain friendships and participate in after-school activities if units serve a wide geographical area, with long taxi-rides extending the school day at both ends. The small scale of most units means that teachers are able to make close relationships with all members of the group and are on hand to sort out any problems that arise in mainstream. Ideally, a balance can be achieved for most children between time spent in demanding situations in larger class groups with hearing children, and time spent on more personalized, intensive work with a specialist teacher.

Curriculum resource centres

Many units, particularly at secondary level, see themselves as curriculum resource centres. Booklets are sometimes produced setting out the role and aims of the unit, examples of schemes of work followed by specialist teachers, together with strategies for communication and use of hearing-aids. Ideally, all the teachers involved with hearing-impaired children will meet regularly to discuss individuals' needs, areas of the curriculum where extra help is required, how the unit can resource a teaching programme, advice and training required by mainstream staff, as well as appropriate materials, communication strategies and modifications to any course materials or textbooks. As the term implies, a 'whole-school' approach to meeting special needs in ordinary schools demands much time for planning, negotiation and sharing of resources between all staff.

Special schools for the deaf

Another kind of provision within the continuum depicted in Figure 10.1 is the special school, which may operate on a day, part-time or residential basis. Some 4000 children (12 per cent) attend special schools for the deaf. Many special schools for the deaf have closed in the past few decades and not all LEAs have such provision. However, there will be a special school within reach of every LEA, several of which have charitable status (Royal Schools for the Deaf) and operate independently. Special schools are usually recommended on the basis that a child's ability to learn, personality, confidence and communication needs would be best met in an environment where all teachers are trained, experienced and well motivated to work with the hearing-impaired. Many special schools are associated with signing methods and employ deaf adults. The main advantage of the special school, for some children, is the intensive, individualized curriculum that can be offered: a whole signing community, for example.

Residential special schools tend to cater for more severely hearing-impaired children, children with additional special needs, or children in family circumstances that militate against the child's living at home. There are two exceptions in the form of selective residential schools which admit children on the basis of outstanding abilities and attainments. These selective schools are usually recommended on the basis that they offer academic opportunities to deaf youngsters who would be unable to reach their full potential in an integrated setting. Their main advantage is that they are staffed by teachers who are recruited as subject specialists with additional qualifications to teach deaf children.

Parents may more readily accept the reasons for recommending a residential placement at the secondary or further education stage, when the social and academic demands are greater and when youngsters are more mature. It could be argued that children placed in a special school at a young age will benefit from more intensive help early on, with the prospect of returning to mainstream. However, the advantages of a special school environment must be weighed carefully against the drawbacks, such as distance from home, loss of contact with local children, difficulties in preparing pupils for life after school in their local communities through, for example, work experience, and possibly a more restricted educational curriculum.

A fundamental question about special schools for the deaf arises in relation to the issues raised at the beginning of this chapter regarding images of children as learners, expectations of what academic success can be achieved, and whether education should aim to prepare children for life in a 'hearing', as opposed to a 'deaf', society. Should we measure the success of deaf children in competition with their hearing peers? Is special school placement opted for as second best, when all else has failed, rather than as a positively planned opportunity? Many deaf adults support special school provision for deaf children because it represents an important vehicle for the transmission of deaf culture and sign language, but this view is not necessarily shared by hearing parents or specialist teachers.

It should be noted that special schools which have independent status are not subject to the regulations imposed on LEA schools under the Education Reform Act, although most special schools are taking note of developments associated with ERA, such as the National Curriculum.

CURRENT ISSUES AND THE EDUCATION REFORM ACT

National Curriculum and assessment

Recent government legislation has imposed complex and multiple changes on the school system, many of which have far-reaching implications for hearing-impaired children. Undoubtedly, many children, including those with hearing losses, will benefit from the introduction of the National Curriculum with its aims to provide an explicit account of what children are entitled to be taught, whilst the new reporting arrangements should lead to greater involvement of children and parents in assessment, and much more detailed awareness, if not raised expectations, of the achievements of children. In some areas of the National Curriculum, however, many severely hearing-impaired children may be working at levels well below what is expected, thus engendering a sense of failure, whilst important aspects such as personal and social development are neither core nor foundation subjects.

Problems have already been anticipated by some teachers in relation to the withdrawal of children from mainstream class groups for support work, as they would then miss National Curriculum work: the statutory syllabus. In fact there should be no conflict between more individualized approaches and what is taught in mainstream, with considerable flexibility in how teachers cover topics and the amount of time that must be devoted to prescribed subjects at each Key Stage. The real question is how to determine what is worthwhile and relevant study for an individual within the National Curriculum framework. For example, requirements such as the learning of a foreign language by hearing-impaired children at the secondary stage could be interpreted as a strait-jacket, or as an opportunity to 'learn about France' whilst also developing listening, writing and reading. Where necessary, children who are the subject of statements under the 1981 Education Act can be exempted from parts of the National Curriculum, but this could lead to a rash of statements in those schools which are not prepared to adapt how they teach to the needs of individuals.

Some of the possibilities and pitfalls of the National Curriculum are described in more detail by Webster (1990), who also discusses what is perhaps the most controversial aspect for hearing-impaired children: assessment and testing arrangements. It is a well-established fact that hearing-impaired children are often compromised in formal testing situations. This may be because the 'carrier' language of test instructions is more complex than the concepts assessed, or because of the adult's interaction with the child during a test session, with questioning, directive and managerial styles likely to result in the child becoming much more inhibited and unresponsive. Many support services have responded to the new assessment and reporting arrangements of the National Curriculum by rethinking how evidence of achievement is collected as an integral part of the teaching process, with many teachers basing their assessments of hearing-impaired children on the 'Profiles' (Webster and Webster, 1990, 1991) mentioned earlier. It is still the case, however, that the results of formal tests, or SATs, take precedence over teacher assessment, even when formal testing can prove a misleading exercise destined to expose the child repeatedly to failure.

Conflicts are bound to arise with the implementation of the ERA in relation to many of the issues and principles stated earlier on effective education for the hearing-impaired. ERA is essentially a language of accounts applied to education: setting targets, collecting evidence of performance and publishing results. Far less emphasis has been placed on processes of teaching and learning than on developing test materials. Earlier I suggested that most recent advances in teaching of the hearing-impaired have come from close-grained studies of the way in which adults and children interact in learning encounters. Programmes of study linked with formal and frequent testing of deaf children are unlikely to be an effective mechanism for raising quality of education, unless attention is also paid to the learning process.

LMS and the future of support services for the hearing-impaired

In the immediate future it is the nature of educational support which is likely to undergo drastic revision. Because of the pressure on mainstream schools to publish results and compete in a market economy, some schools may become reluctant to have low academic achievers on roll, or to develop integration programmes for children with special needs, and LEAs may reverse the trend to place fewer children in special schools for the deaf. Under LMS, mainstream schools are inevitably going to be careful about services which are bought in. If support services such as peripatetic teachers are not paid for centrally by LEAs, as they are currently, then schools will be evaluating the contribution made by costly specialist services, and whether there are cheaper alternatives, such as lower-paid non-teaching classroom assistants.

Some support services for the hearing-impaired have seized the opportunity provided by educational reform to rethink their policies and services to schools, particularly in relation to their work on assessment and in-service training. As services themselves enter the market economy it is inevitable that those which will survive and flourish will be the professional groups which are responding to new challenges and making known what they can offer to families and schools. What remains to be seen is how support services will be funded under LMS and in schools that have opted out of LEA control, and whether parents of hearing-impaired children will have a powerful voice in determining how their needs are met. Certainly, any hopes that parents would have a wider choice of schools their hearing-impaired child might attend will fade as schools themselves become increasingly selective of the children they want to admit.

SUMMARY

This chapter began by drawing attention to the fundamental differences that exist in the way hearing-impaired children are perceived and the expectations of achievement which are held by different groups. Some important distinctions have been made between different kinds of hearing loss, and the relative impact of various degrees of hearing loss on development. Educationalists continue to disagree about methods of communication and how best to teach deaf children. These views have been explored in some detail, whilst current research suggests we move away from arguments about methods and look more closely at the quality of learning contexts, including how adults interact with deaf children.

From early infancy onwards, parents of a hearing-impaired child will find a richness of opinion and advice, not all of which is coherent, from professionals who work in different agencies, with contrasting training backgrounds, status and focus. In their encounters with doctors, audiologists, speech therapists, teachers and psychologists, parents may sometimes have a difficult job to steer an appropriate course of action, especially when professionals cross the boundaries of their particular spheres of knowledge and responsibility. This is not to say that many services do not have excellent lines of communication and good inter-professional liaison. Parents will need to weigh advice from different professionals carefully before making decisions about how they think their child's needs can best be met. The chapter has looked at the roles of different professional groups, together with the kind of support provisions available through health and education authorities. Finally, some consideration has been given to the changing educational context and how this may affect the quality of education for the hearing-impaired.

REFERENCES

DES (1967) *Units for Partially Hearing Children* (Education Survey No. 1), London: HMSO.

Luterman, D. (1987) *Deafness in the Family*. Boston, MA: College-Hill Press.

Martin, J.A.M. (1982) Aetiological factors relating to childhood deafness in the European Community. *Audiology*, Vol. 21: 149–58.

National Deaf Children's Society (1987) *For All Deaf Children*. London: NDCS.

Newton, V.E. (1985) Aetiology of bi-lateral sensori-neural hearing loss in young children. *Journal of Laryngology and Otology*, Vol. 99, Supplement 10.

Scanlon, P. and Bamford, J. (1990) Early identification of hearing loss: screening and surveillance methods. *Archives of Disease in Childhood*, Vol. 65: 479–85.

Tucker, I. and Powell, C. (1991) *The Hearing Impaired Child and School*. London: Souvenir Press.

Webster, A. (1986) *Deafness, Development and Literacy*. London: Methuen.

Webster, A. (1990) Hearing-impaired children and the National Curriculum. *Journal of the British Association of Teachers of the Deaf*, Vol. 14, No. 2: 46–53.

Webster, A. and Ellwood, J. (1985) *The Hearing-Impaired Child in the Ordinary School*. Beckenham: Croom Helm.

Webster, A. and McConnell, C. (1987) *Children with Speech and Language Difficulties*. London: Cassell.

Webster, A. and Webster, V. (1990) *Profiles of the Hearing-impaired*. Bristol: Avec Designs.

Webster, A. and Wood, D. J. (1989) *Children with Hearing Difficulties*. London: Cassell.

Webster, A., Scanlon, P. and Bown, E. (1985) Meeting the needs of hearing-impaired children within a local education authority. *Journal of the Association of Educational Psychologists*, Supplement to Vol. 6, No. 5: 2–10.

Webster, A., Bamford, J., Thyer, N. and Ayles, R. (1989) The psychological, educational and auditory sequelae of early, persistent secretory otitis media. *Journal of Child Psychology and Psychiatry*, Vol. 30, No. 4: 529–46.

Webster, V. and Webster, A. (1991) Assessment, hearing-impaired children and the National Curriculum: the state of the art. *Journal of the British Association of Teachers of the Deaf*, Vol. 15, No. 5: 126–39.

Wood, D. J., Wood, H. A., Griffiths, A. J. and Howarth, C. I. (1986) *Teaching and Talking with Deaf Children*. Chichester: Wiley.

FURTHER READING

Fletcher, L. (1987) *Language for Ben: A Deaf Child's Right to Sign*. London: Souvenir Press. A parent's personal account of the struggle to have Total Communication accepted and resourced: makes an interesting contrast with Tucker and Powell (1991) advocating natural auralism, in the same Human Horizons series (see references).

Webster, A. and Webster, V. (1992) *Supporting Learning: Hearing Impairment*. Bristol: Avec Designs. This is a comprehensive set of materials, trialled in a number of UK services for the hearing-impaired, designed to enhance learning support for pupils in primary and secondary schools. It includes planning and recording forms, INSET resources, handouts, and many teaching ideas: most useful for visiting support teachers and other advisory agencies.

Wells, G. (1987) *The Meaning Makers: Children Learning Language and Using Language to Learn*. London: Hodder & Stoughton. An entertaining account of some of the new insights about adult–child interaction drawn from research, showing how adults facilitate or inhibit language and learning in hearing children.

Wood, D. J. (1988) *How Children Think and Learn*. Oxford: Blackwell. A stimulating book which looks at changing perspectives on how children learn and how these could influence teaching; this is an interesting complement to Wood's writing on deafness and development (see references).

CHAPTER 11

Speech and language therapy

Jannet A. Wright

This chapter describes the profession of speech and language therapy, whose members provide assessment, intervention and information on developmental and acquired communication disorders. The way the service is organized and the theoretical frameworks which influence practice are outlined. The chapter concludes by discussing current issues that influence service delivery, relationships with other support services and preventive measures.

THE NATURE OF CHILDREN'S SPEECH AND LANGUAGE DIFFICULTIES

Children with language difficulties are a varied group. Aram and Nation (1982) believed that trying to conceptualize children with language difficulties as a homogeneous group was 'an exercise in unreality'. Speech and language problems can be conceptualized as a continuum. A mild disturbance in the sound system such as substituting 'w' for 'r' as in 'wabbit' might represent one end of the continuum. A severe and specific language disorder such as an inability to understand spoken language which requires specialized therapeutic and educational provision can be seen to represent the other end of the continuum. Speech and language problems can coexist with other sensory, cognitive and physical problems. However, where children appear to have only a communication problem, a description of their difficulties includes the term 'specific'. This variety of problems requires speech and language therapists to have considerable knowledge in many areas.

BACKGROUND TO THE DEVELOPMENT OF THE PROFESSION

Pre-1944

The speech and language therapy profession is relatively young. Saint Bartholomew's Hospital opened the first speech therapy centre for adults and children in 1911. Four speech clinics for young stammerers were opened in 1918 by the London County Council and the staff were called 'remedial teachers of speech', 'curative speech trainers' or 'stammering instructors'. There were limited training opportunities, though by 1935 four schools of speech therapy were offering a two-year training course.

1944-74

The year 1945 was a significant one for children with communication problems and for the speech therapy profession. The term 'those with speech defects' was included in the eleven categories of the Handicapped Pupils and School Health Service Regulations (1945) which followed the 1944 Education Act. Thus children with speech and language problems were categorized as a separate group and local education authorities now had the responsibility of making provision for them. The regulations went on to say that 'aphasic' children (those with very severe language problems) should be educated in schools for the deaf. Children with other speech defects should attend ordinary schools with the expectation that they would receive treatment at local clinics and be 'cured'.

The professional body, the College of Speech Therapists, was also formed in 1945. It was an amalgamation of the British Society of Speech Therapists, a medically orientated group which had the backing of the Medical Advisory Council, and the Association of Speech Therapists, whose background was in speech training and elocution. In 1991 it was renamed the College of Speech and Language Therapists.

Between 1944 and 1974 there were two speech therapy services in Great Britain. The Education Speech Therapy Service was organized under section 48 of the Education Act 1944, as part of the School Health Service. The other was hospital based and formed part of the National Health Service. The majority of therapists were employed in the School Health Service.

The Quirk Report (Quirk, 1972) made 48 recommendations covering speech therapists' work, organization, training and research. One of the most significant was that speech therapy services should be unified and organized under area health authorities in England and Wales and health boards in Scotland. It also recommended an average caseload of no more than 100 people and the development of more training courses – but at degree level.

1974 onwards

The 1974 National Health Service and local authority reorganization unified the two speech therapy services into the NHS. The newly created area speech therapist was responsible for developing a cohesive policy for provision across the area health authority.

A further NHS reorganization in 1982 led to smaller units of responsibility – district health authorities – and the area speech therapist was replaced by one or more district speech therapy managers (DSTMs). A major implication was that specialized services for children with particular difficulties such as hearing impairment or language disorder might not be available in a district. Such families would be referred to another district which could offer appropriate specialist services and could possibly face delays while this referral took place.

Unfortunately health service reorganization has not always led to improved service delivery. Vocal (Voluntary Organizations Communication and Language) published the results of a survey (Cox, 1987) which revealed that of the district health authorities included in the survey 75 per cent had staff : child population ratios worse than those recommended by the Quirk Report, with some therapists having caseloads of over 300.

The speech and language therapy profession now has all-graduate entry with a published code of ethics and professional conduct. Voluntary registration by members of the professional body is occurring with a commitment to continued education. The majority of speech and language therapists continue to be employed by NHS Trusts or health authorities but they also have to respond to legal changes in the education system as well as developments in local authorities.

SPEECH AND LANGUAGE SERVICES

Qualifications and career progression

There are two routes to qualifying as a speech and language therapist. One is at undergraduate level and the other at postgraduate level. When students have successfully completed a course they can apply for a licence to practise from the College of Speech and Language Therapists. Successful graduates are qualified to work with both adults and children, though first jobs usually involve a mixed caseload but with opportunities for more specialized work with a specific age group or communication problem as they gain experience.

The College of Speech and Language Therapists recently published *Communicating Quality: Professional Standards for Speech and Language Therapists* (1991), which described three levels of professionally qualified therapists:

- *Specialist speech and language therapists* have additional qualifications, well-developed skills and an in-depth knowledge of a particular client group and/or disorder. These therapists act as advisers within the profession and to other related professional groups.
- *Generalist speech and language therapists* see a mixed population of clients and have good assessment, diagnostic and intervention skills but have not acquired specialist knowledge of any particular group or disorder. They are not specialists.

- *Specialized speech and language therapists* provide specialized services to a designated location, client group or those with a specific disorder. These therapists do not have the additional training or knowledge of a specialist therapist but they may work towards this in their professional development.

Career progression within the speech therapy profession is usually based on some degree of specialization or a move into management. To specialize, speech and language therapists increase the amount of time they spend with a chosen client group and receive ongoing practical guidance from a more experienced/specialist therapist in that area. In addition, they develop their expertise through local, regional and national in-service courses.

Over recent years the demand for therapists has increased, as they are now offering their skills to those with psychiatric problems, adults with learning difficulties, parents of young babies with feeding problems, pre-school children, adults with degenerative diseases and the elderly. There is also increased interest in and use of a range of alternative communication aids including synthesized speech products. These changes raise issues about future training needs. Current health service training budgets are very small so there is a problem for therapists who want to keep up to date. It may mean that therapists will have to fund their own further training – not a popular idea.

There are also two levels of unqualified support to the therapist. On one level is the speech and language therapy assistant, who has been trained to do a variety of tasks ranging from preparing equipment to implementing certain therapy programmes. On the other is the unpaid volunteer who is involved in a range of activities. Speech therapy assistants exist as a recognized group within the profession, and the College of Speech and Language Therapists keeps a register of assistants. The profession has identified certain skill and competence levels an assistant should reach, and discussions with the Department of Health about levels of training continue.

Referral

The majority of children seen by speech and language therapists are referred by their teacher, parent, doctor or health visitor. Many pre-school referrals arise out of childhood developmental checks. A hearing assessment will usually be carried out before the child begins therapy, and the child is likely to be seen for a first appointment within four to six weeks of referral.

Assessment

Children referred for a speech and language assessment are seen for an initial assessment period by a therapist. This may mean several appointments at a clinic or a combination of clinic and home or nursery/school visits. The assessment takes account of a variety of individual factors. These include:

- communication skills, language structure and use;
- developmental history;
- play ability and pattern;

- interaction with peers and family;
- expected development at that chronological age;
- early illness;
- any known cognitive or sensory deficits;
- parental concerns.

The results of the assessment can lead to different outcomes:

– Despite a slow start the child is making rapid linguistic progress, which is unlikely to be further improved by therapy. In such cases, the child may be placed on review.
– The child's progress is delayed and the therapist feels that linguistic skills will improve by working with the family. In this case therapy is offered for a period.

Patterns of intervention

The local arrangements are the responsibility of the manager of the speech therapy services, who appoints speech and language therapy staff and plans service delivery for both education and health service establishments.

The main service delivery mode is peripatetic with the intensity varying between daily, weekly and monthly intervention. Each appointment can last from 30 to 90 minutes. Some health authorities offer intensive courses for older children during the school holidays. This has been particularly popular with children who lack fluency or stammer. For some teenagers attendance at such a course on a daily basis has been a more acceptable form of therapy especially if parental attendance is also required.

Organization of speech and language services

Services are usually provided by NHS Trusts or community units. The organization of the service varies from one area to another with the service offered being based on a number of factors. These might include:

- the age of the children;
- the most effective way of meeting the needs of children placed in special schools and mainstream settings. Typically, one team of therapists sees all the children with identified special needs placed in special school settings, whilst another deals with those in mainstream settings;
- the particular needs of individual children and the availability of specialist staff.

Specific intervention programmes are usually implemented in one of the following types of centre.

School-based centres

In the past, children attending mainstream schools have usually attended a local health centre for speech therapy, but there has been a recent increase in the number of therapists working with children in the classroom. This helps the development of functional communication skills, is clearly more convenient for children and helps the development of strong links between teachers and therapists. In some authorities all the therapists are now based in schools.

Unit-based centres

Historically, special schools usually had a therapist based at the school or one working there on a part-time basis. Now special schools and language units have regular visits from a therapist who sees the children in the school. The therapists spend several days at a time in a school or in some instances may still be based there. During the school holidays these therapists may carry out home visits, run intensive courses or carry out reviews at nearby health centres.

Clinic based

Children may be seen on a twice-weekly, weekly or monthly basis at a clinic in a health centre or within a hospital department or child development centre. At least one parent usually attends the session and joins in the therapy. The work that the speech and language therapist does with the child can be continued at home, and strong links with the parents should develop. This pattern of intervention is seen by many NHS managers as cost-effective. A therapist who spends a whole morning in a clinic can see three or four children on an individual basis for 45–60 minutes. A whole morning spent visiting a school may involve seeing only one child and one teacher. It also allows pre-school children to be seen in the same place as school-age children.

THEORETICAL BASIS FOR PRACTICE

So far this chapter has reviewed aspects of the organization of speech and language therapy services; it now turns to the theoretical perspectives which underlie practice. Three major theoretical models have influenced speech and language therapists' practice with children with communication problems, and most therapists draw on all three at some point in their work.

Medical model

Speech and language therapists working in educational settings are often identified with a medical model and this in part may be because therapists have used terms such as 'patient', 'diagnosis', 'intervention' or 'treatment'. Within this model an assessment of children's communication problems involves gathering information from the child, the family and school. The features of the individual's problem are compared with those of particular communication problems so that a diagnosis can be made.

Evidence of organic factors will lead therapists to make a referral to a doctor. Such evidence might include the information that the child is a mouth breather, has constant colds and likes the television turned up loud – indicating possible hearing problems. Within the medical model an attempt is made to establish the cause of a communication problem, to try to eliminate or reduce the influence of any organic factors.

The advantage of such a model is that medical or organic factors can play a significant part in the overall explanation of some communication problems such as in children with cerebral palsy. However, this 'within-child' model is marked by a lack of any description of children's language impairment. Although it is important to know whether an organic cause exists for a problem – such as damage to the auditory nerve leading to a severe hearing loss – this information gives no indication of the child's communicative strengths and weaknesses or where intervention may begin. Therapists need criterion-referenced assessment which describes what children can do and helps to inform them of how best to help facilitate further progress. Most speech and language therapists would use this model as and when necessary, but rarely as the only approach.

Linguistic model

Earlier research (and clinical work) in linguistics focused on language structure but this was invariably divorced from the context in which it was used. The emphasis moved towards examining the social contexts of language learning and use (Wells, 1981; McTear, 1985), and a linguistic model was adopted. This model had a revolutionary effect on the work of speech and language therapists when it was introduced into speech therapy courses in the mid-1970s, as it offered a means of describing language breakdown.

Speech and language therapists who use this model collect samples of spontaneous conversation from children, using audio or video recorders. They transcribe the tapes and analyse them using a linguistic framework. Both expressive language and understanding/comprehension are considered at the following levels:

Phonology – the range of sounds used in a given language. These sounds, together with intonation, voice and fluency, may be referred to as 'speech'.

Syntax – the ordering of words into phrases and sentences.

Semantics – the study of how meaning is structured in language.

Pragmatics – the 'study of factors that govern users' choice of utterance, arising out of their social setting' (Crystal, 1987).

The linguistic model led to the label 'language disorder' being used to describe children's communication problems. The epithet 'specific' has been added to the term 'language disorder' to indicate that the language disorder is the primary problem and does not appear to have been caused by any other factors.

The model gave rise to a range of assessment procedures and an increase in linguistic terms in therapists' work. Such assessments include:

- the Phonological Assessment of Children's Speech (PACS) (Grunwell, 1985), a procedure that uses pre-selected pictures to collect a sample of 200–250 words for analysis;

- the Language Acquisition Remediation and Screening Procedure (LARSP) (Crystal *et al.*, 1976), which provides therapists with a framework for analysing the syntactic structures of spoken language samples at word, phrase and clause level;
- with the focus now on language use, an interview schedule has been developed to use with parents (Dewart and Summers, 1989) which collects information about the way children use language in the home environment.

The weakness of the linguistic model is its lack of reference to psychological factors that influence children's learning. It has been a major advance to be able to describe what children can say and understand, but many children fail to acquire their linguistic skills because of poor attention and limited memory skills. It is for this reason that linguistics and psychology have been brought together in the psycholinguistic area.

Psycholinguistic model

The use of a psycholinguistic model enables language disability to be described in linguistic terms, but also allows psychological factors such as attention, perception and memory to be considered. Thus all aspects of children's strengths and weaknesses are included.

Psycholinguistic assessment includes all the areas assessed within the linguistic model, but information is also gathered about children's ability in areas such as auditory discrimination, sequencing skills, short- and long-term memory and learning style. This enables the therapist to target the next linguistic goal as well as to consider how to teach children these abilities in the light of their learning strategies and the teaching methods used in a school.

The advantages of this model include:

- a more holistic approach to assessment;
- an opportunity for therapists to discuss the children's strengths and weaknesses with teachers and educational psychologists who are more familiar with the vocabulary of psychology than that of linguistics;
- intervention procedures which relate more directly to the classroom environment.

CURRENT ISSUES

There are a number of issues facing speech and language therapists which arise from both health and education reorganization, as well as from the nature of therapists' work.

Educational and health reforms

One of the most controversial issues in the past ten years has been whether or not speech therapy is seen as special educational provision under the 1981 Education Act. It is provided by professionals employed by the health service and is often viewed as medical rather than educational provision.

Recent High Court rulings have done nothing to clarify the situation about whether speech therapy is educational or non-educational provision. This was highlighted but not resolved in the DES Circular 22/89: 'In the case of speech therapy provision LEAs should be aware that the High Court case of *R.* v. *Lancashire County ex parte CM* (March 1989) ruled that speech therapy provision could be considered as either educational or non-educational provision' (DES, 1989, para. 63).

One implication of this ruling has been to encourage LEAs to provide speech and language therapy and where necessary to employ therapists to do so. As a result some authorities have employed dually qualified therapists who have both teaching and speech and language therapy qualifications. These staff have been employed on the same salary and conditions of service as teachers to work with children who have a statement of special educational need. Other LEAs have hired speech and language therapists from the health authority. In some areas education, health and social services have jointly funded posts in settings such as social services day centres, day nurseries and language units. These variations in arrangements have often been the result of LEA policy which emerged in response to the 1981 Act.

Like most professionals, speech and language therapists write reports and keep records. They write an initial report after assessing a child and interim reports as intervention continues. One of the reports that has given them the most concern has been the statement of educational need. Until recently the speech and language therapist's report prepared for a statement of need was often not seen in full by headteachers and class teachers. However, paragraph 42 of DES Circular 22/89 states that advice about all therapy services provided by the district health authority should be passed 'in full' to the LEA and attached as Appendix G.

The 1988 Education Reform Act introduced both the National Curriculum and local management of schools (LMS) and left therapists facing benefits as well as problems. Speaking and listening are Attainment Targets in the English curriculum; this was a positive move. Many therapists working in schools were involved with curriculum planning, had access to specific details about the curriculum and were able to alert teachers to pupils with communication difficulties. However, there is concern that as speaking and listening are not included in the Standard Assessment Tasks (SATs) they will become marginalized.

LMS raises many possibilities for speech and language therapy. Schools may decide to buy enough time from the health authority for therapists to be on the premises for most of the week, giving time for them to collaborate fully with teaching staff. Alternatively, they may want therapists to minimize contact time and thereby costs. If speech and language therapists are working for the school the issue of who manages them, the headteacher or a speech therapy manager, will also need to be clarified.

The 1991 NHS reorganization and the introduction of general management during the 1980s have also had a number of effects on both speech therapy services and the speech and language therapy profession. Many of these changes are ongoing, and it is only possible to speculate on their implications.

Decisions about how resources are allocated are less in the control of speech and language therapists now. Purchasing health authorities and provider unit managers will have varying, but often substantial, influence. Perhaps more of a problem is the question of accountability. Speech and language therapists have in general been accountable to their line manager or district manager, though they have obviously had a looser kind of accountability to the school head if they are based in a school. But increasingly, general management has led to therapists being accountable – at least in managerial if not professional terms – to a non-therapist manager. This is a real issue for all therapists in hospitals and a growing one for those in educational establishments. It raises issues of power, status and future relationships between different professional groups. Management by someone who is not a member of your professional group may provide many opportunities for misunderstanding. The person concerned may have no knowledge of training, intervention style or client population. Everything that the professional does has to be made explicit, justified and evaluated by someone who may be using different criteria from those of the profession. At worst it could lead to a breakdown in communication and loss of services felt to be important by therapists. At best, it does offer an opportunity for innovation and development. It does not offer peace and calm.

The 1991 NHS reforms will probably mean that most speech and language therapists employed will be employed by NHS Trusts. Some of these will be hospital trusts, and others more community focused. There will probably be some services run by directly managed units which remain as part of the health authority. It is unlikely that these changes will have immediate consequences for the day-to-day work of therapists, but they may be managed in smaller units than they have been recently. This could aid the development of teamwork as more therapists may be part of a multiprofessional acute or community team and will be managed as such on a day-to-day basis.

Relationships with parents and other support services

Therapists know that without a partnership with parents and teachers children are unlikely to make effective progress. A speech and language therapy session either once a week or every day in term time will be successful only if the therapy is fully integrated into children's lifestyles. Parents need to be involved as much as possible from the point of referral.

However, working with other professional groups can lead to problems as a result of limited knowledge of each other's specific skills, knowledge and intervention strategies (Norwich, 1990). Tensions mainly arise with other support services when colleagues from other professions make recommendations about an individual child's suitability for speech and language therapy, often based on misinformation. This leads to confusion and distress for children and parents, and should be avoided. To compound this, teachers and therapists have different contracts, employers, holidays and school duties, and all of these can influence professional relationships.

Speech and language therapists' relationships with other support services also reflect where they work and the client group they work with. For example, those who work with pre-school children may be working jointly with a clinical psychologist, a clinical medical officer or a consultant paediatrician. The therapist may be a member of a loosely knit team which comes together as and when the needs of an individual child necessitate it. On the other hand, the team may be well structured – such as a hospital-based team dealing with children born with cleft palates or a community team supporting children with severe learning difficulties at home via a Portage project.

There is hope that with the change of name to 'speech and language therapist', colleagues in other professions will see the therapist's role as being broader than just 'speech'. In particular, many therapists have been frustrated by colleagues in education who do not refer children to the speech and language therapist because of a perception that speech therapy deals only with speech. Despite these problems it seems that in general there is increased evidence of professional collaboration at the intervention stage (Wright, 1992) – but this needs to be improved at the assessment and planning stage.

Children for whom English is not a first language

There has been an increase in the number of children whose first language is not English. Children are not offered speech and language therapy unless a language difficulty is identified in their first language as well as in English. However, in order to carry out assessments in languages other than English the service needs to use interpreters and translators. Tests and procedures have been devised for assessing such children but it takes time to produce and standardize any new assessment procedure. To deal with this there have been efforts to attract multi-lingual students on to degree courses. In some areas the service has attempted to resolve the problem by employing co-workers who are fluent in languages other than English.

CONCLUSIONS

The speech and language therapy profession is experiencing significant changes in both the education and health fields. Whilst these present major problems of accountability, resources, teamwork and role, they also create possibilities and challenges. The strength of the profession lies in its strong theoretical under-pinning, the commitment of its members and a strong understanding of the importance of inter-professional work, inter-agency work and of the role of parents. It is likely that these will see the profession and the service through what appears to be a difficult time.

REFERENCES

Aram, D.M. and Nation, J.E. (1982) *Child Language Disorders*. London. C.V. Mosby.

College of Speech and Language Therapists (1991) *Communicating Quality. Professional Standards for Speech and Language Therapists*. London: College of Speech and Language Therapists.

Cox, D. (1987) *Survey of Speech Therapy Services for Children with Particular Reference to Special Education*. Report prepared by the Voluntary Organizations Communication and Language (Vocal).

Crystal, D. (1987) Concepts of language development: a realistic perspective. In W. Yule and M. Rutter (eds), *Language Development and Disorders*. Oxford: MacKeith Press.

Crystal, D., Fletcher, P. and Garman, M. (1976) *Language Acquisition Remediation and Screening Procedures (LARSP)*. London: Edward Arnold.

DES (1944) *Education Act*. London: HMSO.

DES (1945) *The Handicapped Pupils and School Health Service Regulations*. London: HMSO.

DES (1981) *Education Act*. London: HMSO.

DES (1988) *The Education Reform Act (ERA)*. London: HMSO.

DES (1989) *Assessment of Statements of SEN Procedures within the Education, Health and Social Services* (Circular 22/89). London: DES.

Dewart, H. and Summers, S. (1989) *Profile of Pragmatic Function*. Windsor: NFER-Nelson.

Grunwell, P. (1985) *Phonological Assessment of Child Speech*. Windsor: NFER-Nelson.

McTear, M. (1985) *Children's Conversations*. Oxford: Basil Blackwell.

Norwich, B. (1990) *Reappraising Special Needs Education*. London: Cassell.

Quirk, R. (1972) *Report of the Committee of Inquiry into Speech Therapy Services*. London: HMSO.

Wells, C.G. (1981) *Learning through Interaction: The Study of Language Development*. Cambridge: Cambridge University Press.

Wright, J.A. (1992) Collaboration between teachers and speech therapists with language impaired children. In P. Fletcher and D. Hall (eds), *Specific Speech and Language Disorders in Children*. London: Whurr.

FURTHER READING

Byers Brown, B. and Edwards, M. (1989) *Developmental Disorders of Language*. London: Whurr. Provides detailed information on communication disorders and possible intervention strategies.

Crystal, D. (1986) *Listen to Your Child*. Harmondsworth: Penguin. An accessible book about early language development.

Webster, A. and McConnell, C. (1987) *Children with Speech and Language Difficulties*. London: Cassell. Comprehensive coverage of communication difficulties – a good buy for the staffroom library.

CHAPTER 12

Visual impairment

Juliet Stone

Disabilities of sight range from temporary, minor visual difficulties along a continuum of problems ranging to total blindness. Whilst special schools exist in some parts of the country for children with more severe problems, education advisory services for the visually impaired work on a peripatetic basis to support children and young people who have a range of disabilities. This chapter describes the development of such services, their roles and functions and the issues they are currently facing. It begins by examining the background to the development of advisory services for the visually impaired.

BACKGROUND TO THE DEVELOPMENT OF ADVISORY SERVICES

Braille was universally adopted as the reading medium of the blind in the latter part of the last century. As a result segregated provision became the norm for educating the visually impaired and until around twenty years ago education for the blind was largely provided in special schools for the blind; most of these were, and still are, run by independent foundations. There have, however, been small pockets of support for visually impaired pupils in ordinary schools since the end of the last century.

In contrast to those with more severe visual disabilities the complex difficulties faced by pupils who have low levels of vision were not recognized by legislation until the 1944 Education Act, when the partially sighted were mentioned as a separate category of handicap. Provision for these pupils was then established in special schools for the partially sighted. During the 1960s, Barraga's work (1970) in the United States demonstrated that many children described as blind had residual vision that could be improved through training. In the United Kingdom the opportunity to assess and train the residual vision of children through the 'Look and Think' project (Tobin and Chapman, 1978) further blurred the categories of blind and visually impaired. Schools began to change their designation to schools for the visually impaired.

In the early 1970s advisory services for visually impaired children started to develop. These were primarily peripatetic services designed to support children, parents and teachers in a variety of ways. The first was started by the Birmingham Royal Institute for the Blind and was later taken over by the Royal National Institute for the Blind. It was a response to reseach by Langdon (1970), who found that parents were expressing a deep-felt need for support in the immediate period after the birth of a visually impaired baby. At about the same time an LEA special school for the visually impaired in Sheffield and one or two in shire authorities began supporting the severely visually impaired in their local mainstream schools (Lewis, 1981).

The Vernon Report (DES, 1972) on the education of the visually impaired recommended, mainly as a result of Langdon's findings, that every LEA should be responsible for securing an adequate number of staff with training and expertise who could support visually impaired pupils in the ordinary school, together with their teachers and parents. Although this report gave impetus to the development of advisory services, only 23 had been established by 1975.

Further services were established in response to:

- the Warnock Report (DES, 1978) recommendation that LEAs should set up fully comprehensive advisory and support services;
- the 1981 Education Act, which indicated that the statementing procedure for children with visual problems should include information given by teachers trained in visual impairment.

However, by 1991 not all LEAs had an advisory service supporting visually impaired pupils and it remains difficult to establish a cohesive national picture of support for visually impaired pupils. Only a small minority of LEAs have no provision at all, but the structure, staffing and resources of those that do exist differ widely. There are many reasons for this, including historical and geographical factors.

THE STRUCTURE OF SERVICES

There is considerable variation in both the structure and location of teams supporting visually impaired pupils. Where special schools exist, it is likely that they will be the focus of provision for the visually impaired within an LEA. In such circumstances pupils with more severe visual disabilities attend special schools, with advisory provision being available for the less severely impaired who remain within the mainstream sector. Where there is no special school it is likely that advisory services will support pupils with a wide range of visual impairments, including the educationally blind (i.e. those children without residual vision).

Approximately 90 per cent of advisory services for the visually impaired are based in an LEA centre, such as administrative offices or a school, with only a few being based in special schools. There are advantages and disadvantages of both systems. Advisory staff see the advantages of being based in special schools as:

- the easy access to resources and the expertise of other specialized staff;
- a feeling of belonging;
- the ability to offer a range of provision.

In contrast the advantages of working from an LEA base are:

- being part of a large influential organization;
- being part of a cohesive policy on special educational needs;
- easy access to other professionals, for example educational psychologists, teachers of the hearing-impaired;
- parents perceiving the service to be outside the special school system and therefore more open to mainstream education.

Differences in the *structure* of services are demonstrated by the job titles used by teachers. These include: support teacher, peripatetic teacher, visiting teacher and advisory teacher. On the whole, these terms are interchangeable and the *functions* carried out by teachers of the visually impaired are invariably similar.

The structure of individual services depends on many local factors including geographical area and the presence of a special school dealing with this disability in the region. There is great variation in how long services have been in existence. Fewer than twenty LEA services have been established for as long as twenty years. These offer a comprehensive service to the whole age and ability range and generally have good staff:pupil ratios. Others are still in the very early stages of developing an effective response to meeting children's needs.

Urban conurbations with large school populations are likely to have a number of visually impaired pupils close to each other, whereas such pupils may be many miles apart in rural areas with teachers working by themselves in isolated positions. In LEAs with small school populations this is likely to continue. The low incidence of visual handicap and the particular geographical location lead to differences in how closely advisory teachers work with each other.

Nevertheless, most services have between two and twelve teachers working in teams, although the variation in the number of teachers is not necessarily connected to the size of the visually impaired population. It may be a result of authority policy or the stage of development reached by the service. More significantly, it is difficult to say how many visually impaired pupils can be supported by one teacher, as this is determined by a variety of factors.

Although the majority of advisory teachers for the visually impaired work within a specifically designated service, a large number also operate within a team supporting all pupils with special educational needs, not only those who are visually impaired. This works particularly well in rural areas, where teachers of the visually impaired work alongside teachers of the deaf, educational psychologists and other professionals involved with special educational needs. Increasingly services for the visually impaired are being integrated with those for the deaf and hearing-impaired. There can be advantages in all these varied structures, although each one brings difficulties for the service providers. The service structure inevitably has to vary to accommodate differing geographical factors and local contexts.

Access to the educational support services for the visually impaired can be obtained in many ways. Services are available to parents, teachers and pupils. Referrals of babies and infants are usually made by health visitors, general practitioners and hospital ophthalmology departments. Nevertheless, parents who know of the service can approach it directly for advice and information, as can teachers concerned about children's vision. Frequently pupils themselves ask for advice or resources. Each LEA knows of the particular person who should be contacted when difficulties occur.

TRAINING

Teachers entering schools for the blind are required to obtain qualifications in visual impairment within three years of taking up their post. In 1988 this mandatory qualification was extended to teachers of the partially sighted, a development which recognized that the problems of partially sighted pupils are as complex as those of pupils with more severe visual disabilities. Unfortunately this applies only to teachers working within a school for children with visual disabilities and not those working in advisory services. However, the statementing procedure requires information from a qualified teacher of the visually impaired and so goes some way towards ensuring that support services employ trained teachers. Currently five universities offer a course of training recognized by the Department for Education in the education of visually impaired pupils.

A recent investigation (Stone, 1990) shows that all support services have some teachers qualified in visual impairment and that unqualified teachers recognize the need for training. Whilst national funding for the training of these teachers remains, visually impaired pupils are likely to be supported by suitably qualified teachers. Any reduction in the amount of funding available would be to the severe detriment of children's education, and should be resisted.

SERVICES OFFERED BY ADVISORY TEACHERS OF THE VISUALLY IMPAIRED

Services vary considerably in the number of personnel that they employ, making it difficult to define precisely which types of support are provided by any one service. Services with a large number of teachers are able to extend the range of expertise they offer, whereas those with only two or three teachers invariably offer only a limited type of service, despite having to support large numbers of pupils. Inevitably the range of expertise available in small services is more limited than that of larger teams.

The main services offered by advisory teachers are in the following areas:

- giving advice to mainstream teachers;
- working with parents;

- direct teaching;
- assessment;
- the special curriculum;
- resources;
- links with other professionals.

A brief review of these areas is now given.

Giving advice and information

Advisory teachers visit visually impaired pupils in mainstream schools and advise staff on adapting materials, modifying teaching approaches and obtaining resources. Usually most suggestions made by specialist teachers help the whole class and are best seen as extensions of good educational practice. However, written materials have to be modified and enlarged to make them appropriate for the low-vision child, and safety factors need to be considered in practical subjects. In general, curriculum implementation may have to emphasize the spoken rather than written word. Mainstream teachers need to be aware that concepts are often misunderstood by pupils who do not see well or at all, and teachers will need to receive guidance on how the learning environment can be adapted to make it suitable for visually impaired pupils. Mainstream staff need information about making arrangements with examining boards. Examination papers in braille or large print can be supplied, and an amanuensis arranged.

Working with parents

Working with parents is essential, particularly where services provide support for young visually impaired children. Advice usually relates to:

- appropriate educational programmes;
- the problems that typically arise for parents of children with visual impairment;
- the range of educational provision;
- establishing parent self-help groups, although parent groups may be set up by social services;
- teaching braille.

Where advisory teachers support pupils in learning braille, it is essential that parents are aware of what is involved and, ideally, also become competent in braille. In some circumstances advisory teachers may help parents to learn braille. Similarly there may be some social workers who have the skills and time to do so.

Direct teaching

Direct teaching of pupils with visual impairment takes place either in schools or the home. This is especially necessary for training children in the use of residual vision, braille and mobility. A number of issues have to be considered in relation to direct teaching. It is logistically easier to do where there are several advisory teachers in a service who have smaller caseloads. This raises concerns that pupils are not having their educational needs met in authorities where there are only two or three teachers.

Another issue is whether one-to-one, direct teaching should be done on a withdrawal basis or within the classroom setting. Obviously where pupils are being supported in specific curriculum areas, such as science, home economics or physical activities, teaching would be within the classroom. However, there are numerous teachers who prefer working in the classroom, even when teaching braille and training residual vision. This is done with the agreement of class teachers, and advisory staff find it has a number of advantages. They believe that pupils are less likely to feel different, particularly if visiting teachers teach children with a visual impairment as part of a group. It also means that mainstream teachers can still take a full part in the children's education, rather than shift the responsibility on to the specialist teachers. But there are also sound reasons for withdrawing. Braille, training residual vision and activities such as listening skills need a quiet environment, and the pastoral side of the advisory teacher's work can sometimes take place more easily on a withdrawal basis.

Assessment

Another major function of specialist teachers is giving advice to LEAs on children's educational needs as part of the statutory assessment procedure. This involves keeping well informed about existing provision in special and mainstream schools so that the advice given is appropriate. Teacher assessments consider children's general development, independence skills, tactile skills and the use of residual vision. In most cases the assessments completed by teachers of the visually handicapped are regarded as an essential element in determining whether children have special educational needs and the most appropriate provision to meet their needs.

In general, mainstream teachers look to teachers of the visually impaired to provide information on children's vision and their optimum learning environment. This is usually done in conjunction with parents and other professionals. Understandably, mainstream teachers are likely to have the most detailed day-to-day information on how pupils function. Interviews with staff and children, detailed observations and structured checklists provide a comprehensive way of obtaining the necessary information.

The special curriculum

Advisory teachers access the special curriculum for visually impaired pupils. Mobility and independent living skills have already been mentioned, but the special curriculum also includes keyboard skills, braille reading, braille writing and training in listening skills. Implementing the special curriculum raises a number of problems. When during the school day are skills going to be taught? What areas of the mainstream curriculum are going to have to be missed to allow the teaching to take place?

These questions have always caused timetabling difficulties for visually impaired pupils. Certainly it is neither appropriate nor reasonable to remove pupils regularly from art or physical education, which is often the way time-tabling pressures are resolved. Although these may be difficult areas for visually impaired children, they are essential. The issue needs careful consideration, planning and negotiation to ensure the least disturbance to the pupils' integration and all-round curriculum needs. Such concerns also have to be set alongside suggestions that specialist teaching should take place outside the normal school day. The demands of the National Curriculum ensure that pressures on time will be even greater. Regularly reviewing arrangements helps to keep the balance right.

Resources

Pupils with visual handicaps in mainstream schools rarely have the same easy access to technical aids and supports as their peers in special schools. Resources may be limited and the availability of essential aids such as an enlarging photocopier restricted. As a result, accessing brailled material from special schools for the visually impaired needs to be planned in advance. Providing the necessary pieces of technology can be expensive, not only financially, but also in terms of teacher and pupil time. Selecting, ordering and possibly collecting and delivering suitable equipment can take a tremendous amount of staff time. Maintenance and repairs also have time and financial implications, as does the training of pupils and mainstream teachers in its use. In the future, arangements for LMS may increase these difficulties.

Links with other professionals

Advisory teachers need information and support from educational professionals and others such as medical personnel and social services, especially when advice is being prepared for the statutory assessment procedure. Specialist teachers for the visually impaired frequently train other professionals, not only educational colleagues but others such as health visitors and social workers. These are often no more than very short training sessions, their purpose being to raise awareness of visual impairments and their implications. One valuable role for in-service training is preparing mainstream staff prior to a visually impaired pupil being placed within a school.

ISSUES FACING SERVICE PROVIDERS

The aim of advisory services is to prevent problems arising rather than providing remedial support. When referrals are made early in a child's life prevention is possible, as most services have staff who support the learning needs of young children. Unfortunately some pupils are identified late on in their school careers as having a visual impairment. It may then be difficult to make up the gaps in knowledge or give pupils the skills they require.

The functions undertaken by advisory services outlined in this chapter raise several questions. In particular, is it possible for teachers to have the expertise and time to fulfil all the functions expected of them? During periods of financial uncertainty, ensuring staff are adequately trained may prove difficult. Visual impairment is a specialism demanding a high level of expertise and teaching skills. Pupils, families and schools will be served appropriately only when suitably qualified teachers are available. In some instances advisory services have been asking whether some of the tasks they have undertaken in the past might more profitably be delegated to other educational advisory services.

Although advisory teachers wish to retain a sharp focus to their work, they are also looking to develop their support to young children in further education and to extend their expertise to pupils with multiple disabilities. Such children are a large proportion of the visually impaired population and, as yet, their needs are not being adequately met.

Organizing and managing a large caseload and communicating with parents and other professionals are essential parts of the advisory teacher's role and create considerable administrative demands. Teachers are often not provided with sufficient secretarial support, which restricts the amount of time that can be spent in direct contact with parents, teachers and children.

As this chapter has indicated, pupils with a visual impairment are supported in various ways. There are no clear national guidelines as to which children or which level of visual impairment should be given support. Although each advisory service could probably state its own criteria, these may vary from teacher to teacher and from authority to authority. This makes planning at both local and national levels difficult and makes comparisons between individual needs and services impossible. One consequence of this is that identifying pupils requiring support appears to be rather arbitrarily based on pragmatic factors, such as the number of staff or size of geographical area. To enable the development of national standards of provision, advisory services need to agree the criteria by which children are selected for support. Furthermore, where there are a number of teachers within a service, the range of expertise and experience that teams can offer is greater.

Advisory services also vary in status, salaries and potential for career development. As a result there is danger that suitably qualified and interested teachers are not being attracted to advisory work. It can be argued that it is crucial that advisory services are developed to the same standard in all LEAs so that the service offered does not depend on geographical location or the particular expertise of service members and that conditions of service are comparable.

A major paradox facing those making educational provision for visually impaired pupils is that problems are caused by the fact that visual impairment is uncommon. There will never be more than a few special schools for the visually impaired and many regions will be without appropriate resources or centres of expertise. As a result, many visually impaired children are effectively integrated on their own within their local schools. It is practical for advisory teachers to support groups of visually impaired pupils only in mainstream schools in large cities. However, providing support in mainstream contexts reflects the philosophy of many advisory teachers who believe that children should not have to travel out of their catchment area to receive appropriate support. Unfortunately, it is not always educational principles that determine placement or the quality of support available.

In relation to integration, although the academic side has always been a concern of teachers, services are becoming more concerned that children may not be fully integrated at a social level. It cannot be assumed that social integration will occur automatically, even though a mainstream placement is desirable on academic grounds.

Education is going through a period of immense change and it is only possible to speculate on the implications of the Education Reform Act 1988. The opportunities offered by the National Curriculum for pupils with special educational needs may well be missed because of the problems of providing equal access to the broad curriculum for the blind and visually impaired, and because of difficulties posed by the assessment procedures.

Many visually impaired children suffer from a developmental delay, not through any lack of ability but because concept formation is difficult without good vision. Where pupils' vision is poor, information received is fragmentary and sparse so some children may not be able to achieve to the same levels as sighted peers of the same age. This could lead to pupils being exempted from the National Curriculum, and there may have to be some modification to some Key Stage Standard Assessment Tasks. Where this is necessary it is important that it is done in a manner whereby the aims and nature of assessment activities are retained and that guidance is given to teachers in this area in the teachers' manual which accompanies the SATs.

CONCLUSION

There are excellent examples of good practice in advisory services in the United Kingdom. Pupils with visual impairments are flourishing in mainstream schools, reaching their academic potential, enjoying satisfying relationships with their sighted peers and being supported by qualified and committed staff. However, there are areas where this is not happening, leading to anxieties that the political and financial future will preclude development of successful services in such areas.

REFERENCES

Barraga, N. (1970) *Teacher's Guide for the Development of Visual Learning and Utilization of Low Vision.* Louisville, KY: American Printing House for the Blind.

DES (1972) *The Education of the Visually Handicapped* (The Vernon Report). London: HMSO.

DES (1978) *Special Educational Needs* (The Warnock Report). London: HMSO.

DES (1981) *Education Act.* London: HMSO.

Langdon, J.N. (1970) Parents talking. *New Beacon*, Vol. 54, No. 643: 282–8.

Lewis, C. (1981) The growth and development of peripatetic services for the visually handicapped in England. *Insight*, Vol. 2, No. 3: 51–4.

Stone, J. (1990) Educational services: a national provision. *British Journal of Visual Impairment*, Autumn 1990.

Tobin, M.J. and Chapman, E.K. (1978) *Look and Think Checklist*. London: RNIB.

FURTHER READING

Best, A.B. (1992) *Teaching Children with Visual Impairments*. Milton Keynes: Open University Press. This recent book serves not only as a general introduction to those interested in the education of children with visual impairments, but as a more advanced reader for those with experience and expertise. It discusses the theory of the developmental implications of a visual impairment and suggests suitable environmental adaptations and appropriate teaching strategies.

Chapman, E.K. and Stone, J. (1988) *The Visually Handicapped Child in Your Classroom*. London: Cassell. This book is aimed at teachers in mainstream schools with pupils who are visually impaired in their classrooms. It discusses how teachers can help these pupils to access the main curriculum, including such subjects as Physical Education and Art. It also gives teachers information about the special needs of these pupils, such as braille and help with mobility, and suggests ways in which the environment can be adapted to aid the learning process.

Corley, G., Robinson, D. and Lockett, S. (1989) *Partially Sighted Children*. Windsor: NFER-Nelson. This book discusses the problems met by pupils who are partially sighted. It then suggests many practical ways in which these problems can be overcome.

Fitt, R. and Mason, H. (1986) *Sensory Handicaps in Children*. Stratford-upon-Avon: National Council for Special Education. This is one of a series of NCSE booklets that give a brief overview of the problems for pupils with visual and hearing impairments. It also gives some practical suggestions as to ways in which these pupils can be helped.

Name Index

SUBJECT INDEX

UNIVERSITY OF WOLVERHAMPTON
LEARNING RESOURCES